Luke G. Williams

# THE
# NATURAL

The Story of
## PATSY HOULIHAN
the Greatest Snooker Player
You Never Saw

Foreword by
Jimmy White MBE

First published by Pitch Publishing, 2023

Pitch Publishing
9 Donnington Park,
85 Birdham Road,
Chichester,
West Sussex,
PO20 7AJ
www.pitchpublishing.co.uk
info@pitchpublishing.co.uk

ISBN 978 1 80150 429 4

Typesetting and origination by Pitch Publishing
Printed and bound in Great Britain by TJ Books, Padstow

# THE NATURAL

# Contents

For my daughters, with love,
and for all the Houlihan family

'The true paradises are the paradises that
we have lost.' – Marcel Proust

'He coulda been a king.' –
Bernard Malamud

# Foreword

I WAS a big fan of Alex Higgins, but if anyone asks me who was the greatest snooker player I've ever seen I always say Patsy Houlihan because, well, he was the greatest snooker player I've ever seen.

I'll never forget when I first met Patsy. I was about 12 and one day he came to Zan's snooker hall in Tooting and played a guy called Charlie Poole for a tenner a frame. Charlie was a great player too and I later wrote a book called *Jimmy White's Snooker Masterclass* with him. Anyway, I think Patsy and Charlie played 16 frames in about three hours. It was just incredible snooker.

Above all, Patsy was a phenomenal ball striker. He hit the centre of the ball so beautifully. He had everything, Houlihan, you could see that. He was so quick, so attacking. Total dynamite. Everyone wanted to watch him and no one wanted to play him because he could make you look stupid.

We spent a lot of time together from when I was a young boy to an older teenager because he was the resident professional at the Pot Black snooker club in Vardens Road in Battersea. They were exciting times at Battersea. Steve Davis would come down on a Tuesday to practise, not to play, and would watch Houlihan.

I loved being around Patsy every day. Those were great days. I was about 15 and my mate Tony Meo was 17 and not only would we play Patsy but he'd also tell us these amazing stories, he'd do these brilliant tricks, and every day we'd get bellyache from laughing so much. They were great times.

Unfortunately for Patsy, he never got the recognition that he deserved. That hustling way of life and involvement in the gambling side of snooker stopped him from becoming a professional earlier in his career, when he was at his peak in the 1950s and '60s, and in turn that probably stopped him from winning a few world titles. He just missed out by a whisker by being at his best before snooker became really big. It was such a shame.

Patsy was a hustler, but he was also a survivor. He could do tricks with coins and was just unbelievable at playing snooker. He was magical to watch, really. He was on a different level. He made snooker look so simple it was like he'd invented the game.

That's how I'll remember him.

**Jimmy White MBE**

# The trophy on the bedside table

EVERY NIGHT before she goes to bed, Patsy Girl tenderly kisses one of her dad's trophies.

'Good night, Dad, love ya.'

It's a small, slightly strange trophy. The pedestal is no more than five or six inches long and maybe half an inch tall, and three structures sit on top – a shield with a snooker cue across it, a small star emblem and an old-fashioned cup. The inscription reads, 'G.D.P.L. SINGLES WINNER 92/93 P. HOULIHAN – Harp Of Erin.'

'You heard of Flash Harry?' Patsy Girl asks me, drawing deeply on a cigarette as we sit in her flat, one of those modern but compact apartments in the new glass blocks that have incongruously sprung up just a stone's throw from the old Deptford High Street. 'Harry Haward he was called. Used to run the Harp of Erin pub. Well loved and respected man. He had that made for Dad. He loved my dad as it happened.'

She gazes at the trophy, lovingly and proudly, but also with a hint of sadness. 'I don't even like to polish it, to be honest. Prefer to keep it as it is.'

A trophy for winning a pub pool league may not be the most memorable honour that Patrick 'Patsy' Houlihan won in his astonishing but largely forgotten cue sports career, but it's one of only two that the daughter of Britain's greatest ever hustler still has in her possession. To Patsy Girl, that trophy means the world. She keeps it in her bedroom, close to her, so she stays close to the father she still loves.

At one point Houlihan's parents' sideboard used to proudly strain under the weight of more than 20 trophies their son had won with his sensational potting and silky-smooth break building. Patsy's brother Billy would lovingly polish them every Sunday afternoon after a roast beef lunch, while whistling and singing old Bing Crosby numbers.

No one quite knows when or where or how, but most of the trophies disappeared. The English Amateur Championship, six of Patsy's astonishing seven London titles and the ITV Trophy he won in that glorious and almost unbeaten season of 1965 when he toppled future world professional champions Ray Reardon and John Spencer, as well as all the other crack amateurs who played the game in those days – the days when snooker was a working man's pursuit, played out in darkened, smoke-filled halls and washed down with a pint or half a dozen after long shifts in the docks or down in the coal mines. Patsy's old mate Terry Dempsey recalls that Patsy once cashed in one of his trophies at a local pawnbrokers. It spent seven years behind the counter until the snooker official who had awarded it to him died, at which point it was, apparently, melted down. Or maybe it disappeared when the pawnbroker died. With Houlihan stories, you can never quite be sure where the myth ends and the truth begins.

A bit like Deptford, the solidly working-class area of south-east London where Patsy lived, which has been redeveloped beyond recognition in places – modern high-rises standing alongside crumbling Victorian brick remnants – some physical artefacts from Houlihan's life and career have survived.

Patsy Girl has made sure of that.

After Houlihan died, she packed away the remaining items that defined his life and career and stored them in a black box which she labelled 'Dad'. His London amateur trophy from 1962/63 is in there. Old issues of *Snooker Scene*, *Pot Gold* and *Cue World* magazine too, with Patsy's name and photos marked out with a yellow highlighter. There are files of brittle newspaper clippings and piles of photocopied articles from *The Billiard Player* magazine, many of which I posted to Patsy myself in 2005.

I sit with Patsy Girl as she looks through the box for the first time in several years. 'I decided to wait until you came to visit to look through it,' she tells me, her eyes narrowing with a mixture of pain and happiness. 'I've not looked at any of it for years.'

We leaf through a book of condolence from Patsy's funeral. There's an envelope filled with the small cards from the bouquets that were sent to the church. 'There were untold flowers,' Patsy Girl says, laughing her throaty laugh. 'On one of them someone wrote, "This was one snooker you couldn't get out of Hooley."'

There's a postcard Patsy sent Patsy Girl when he was on holiday in the Isle of Wight. Some old family photos, one of which shows Patsy's mother sharing a drink and a laugh with football legend Brian Clough. Another shows Patsy acting as best man at a wedding. A third is of the snooker table birthday cake that Patsy Girl made for her dad's 60th.

We burrow on.

'I even kept his glasses,' Patsy Girl says with a smile, slipping a pair of spectacles out of a dark case. 'These were his snooker glasses; look, they've got the swivel arms on them. Who was the other bloke that used to have special snooker glasses? Dennis Taylor, that was him. Good glasses these, Dad had them specially made. Must have cost a bob or two. He always had problems when he tried to wear contact lenses.'

We find an old watch and Patsy Girl creases up with more laughter as she screws up her eyes to study the inscription on the back. It isn't her dad's name on it. 'He probably bought it to sell on. He was always ducking and diving to make a few quid. That's what you had to do back then – you know, to survive.' She adds, with a deep chuckle, 'D'you know what else he did? When he got his first bus pass after he turned 65 he sold it.'

Sure enough, we find an old plastic wallet – Patsy's London Transport photocard is inside, but the bus pass itself is nowhere to be seen. Patsy Girl dissolves into a fit of the giggles. 'Told you, didn't I? Ain't that funny.'

I study the photocard for a few seconds and then I pick up Patsy's wristwatch and something unusual but strangely comforting happens. For about five seconds the second hand begins moving. Patsy Girl isn't as surprised as me. 'He's still there, looking over me,' she says with assurance, then she looks up and calls out, casually, confidently, 'That you, Dad?'

She takes another drag on her cigarette and tells me, 'I took his glasses to a clairvoyant once. She passed on a message from him. He said not to worry about everything that had happened. A lot of what that clairvoyant said she couldn't possibly have known. Personal stuff.'

Next, Patsy Girl brings an old audio cassette tape out of the box. 'This was his favourite tape,' she says, passing it to me. 'He used to love that tape. Ann Breen. "Pal of my Cradle Days". That's my favourite song too. Whenever I hear that song it really guts me. I used to sing it on the karaoke for my dad down the White Horse.'

Soon the evening draws to a close, the defiant summer sun finally disappearing behind the jagged skyline of the Deptford streets where Patsy Houlihan lived, worked and died.

It's time to pack away.

Patsy Girl and I do so with care as I make a few final notes, and take a few photos to help me remember.

'People loved my dad,' Patsy Girl says, her eyes slightly moist. 'No one ever had a bad word to say about him.'

It's true. Throughout the 17-year journey it has taken me to trace Patsy Houlihan's life and snooker career, everyone who has spoken about him has done so lovingly, admiringly. Cliff Thorburn broke off from a family dinner in Canada to tell me what a great guy Patsy was. Steve Davis waxed lyrical about the man he called snooker's 'folklore hero'. Patsy's great friend Jimmy White told me Patsy was the greatest snooker player he'd ever seen and 'like no one else on Earth'. Tony Meo – long retired from the baize and now in the watch trade – rang me up one afternoon to inform me that he doesn't do interviews or talk about snooker anymore, but he was making an exception for Patsy because, 'What can I say? We loved him.'

'My dad had nothing growing up,' Patsy Girl tells me. 'Same as Jimmy and Tony. That's why they all got on. They were from the same sort of background. Same sort of families.'

I remember Jimmy speaking about the times he used to enjoy with Houlihan and Meo, playing snooker, drinking and 'getting bellyache' from listening to Patsy's stories.

And – I think – that's the key to Patsy Houlihan.

The dates, the details, the facts, the trophies and other items of biographical minutiae don't really tell his story. As moving and magical as they are to look at and to touch, neither do the lovingly curated items in Patsy Girl's old black box.

No, what really tells the story of Patsy Houlihan's life are the memories. Memories of how he made people smile, how he made people laugh. And how he made people feel.

When I get home I type 'Ann Breen, Pal of My Cradle Days' into Google. I click on the first result and listen. It's an old-fashioned ballad, the kind they don't write any more. With its gentle strings and sentimental, nostalgic lyrics it evokes a world that no longer exists. A world of the wireless, of men smoking on street corners while wearing hats and ties. A world of narrow, cobbled market streets filled with fruit and veg stalls. A world where the bustling south-east London docks chimed with cockney voices as the ships arrived and departed in a constant cycle that seemed like it would never end, but ultimately did.

That world has gone forever, but the love the song evokes is still real. It's a love that will last forever. The love of a daughter for her mother or – in this case – father.

# Chapter 1

# It's time

WHERE DO obsessions begin?

For me it was in 1998. The source? A single sentence in Jimmy White's newly released autobiography *Behind the White Ball* in which my beloved 'Whirlwind' declared, 'I rate Charlie Poole, Patsy Houlihan and Alex Higgins as the three greatest snooker players I've ever seen.'

I was intrigued. Alex Higgins – of course – I knew. But Charlie Poole? Patsy Houlihan? As a child of the 1980s I'd spent hundreds, if not thousands, of hours watching snooker on television – most of them Jimmy White matches – and I'd never heard of either of these players. The Internet was somewhat primitive and limited back then and searches for 'Patsy Houlihan' and 'Charlie Poole' returned scant information. I did manage to get hold of a second-hand copy of a snooker coaching book that Jimmy had written with Charlie Poole though. Truth be told, it was informative but a bit dry. If his prose was a reflection of Poole then he wasn't for me. (Later I'd discover Charlie was a great character in his own right, but that's a story for another day.)

My sporting affections have always tended towards creative and maverick talents – one reason among many why Jimmy was my hero. From the romantic, Celtic undertones of his name, Patsy Houlihan sounded to me like he would be just such a maverick too, and probably a hard-living one at that. Patsy's unknown visage soon inhabited my subconscious. When I played snooker at Jono's in Camberwell Green or in the Archway snooker centre he was a frequent fantasy opponent on those days when I played alone, idling away sleepy weekends or lonely week nights, stumbling home half drunk, lungs burning as the sunlight began to pierce the horizon, illuminating the early morning detritus of the inner city.

Of the real Houlihan, however, I could find no information, no trace. Perhaps, I pondered, he didn't even exist. Perhaps, like Keyser Soze, he was more myth than man. Or maybe his existence was a wheeze, a practical joke inserted into his book by Jimmy – like the story of him making a century with a walking stick. Nevertheless, I filed the name of 'Patsy Houlihan' away for further use and reference – perhaps in some future pub quiz I attended there might be a question about which three snooker players Jimmy White rated as the best ever. Granted, it would be quite an obscure question, but you never know with pub quizzes.

Four years later – on Sunday 5, May 2002 to be exact – cigarette hanging from my mouth and morning coffee steaming on my desk, I was idly browsing through the day's papers when I came across an article by one of my favourite writers, Jonathan Rendall, in the much-missed *Observer Sports Monthly*. 'The Great Unknown' it was titled. With a gasp of recognition, I realised it was a whole feature about Patsy Houlihan. Or maybe it was spelt 'Hoolihan'? That's how Rendall and *The Observer* spelt it anyway.

Rendall had been told about Houlihan/Hoolihan by Jimmy White and had tracked him down to a pub in Deptford. Deptford! Just down the road from Camberwell where I had lived all my life! This was momentous news. Maybe I'd sat on the same bus as Houlihan, or even played him without knowing it on one of my youthful forays to the New Cross Inn to play pool. Wasn't there an old geezer there that night when I was in untouchable form and won ten matches on the spin? The night when my mate Row announced to the pub that I was from King's Lynn and I was nicknamed 'The Norfolk Hustler' (I've never been to King's Lynn in my life, of course)? The night I'd staggered home feeling invincible, thinking that maybe I could make my living as a pool hustler?

Houlihan and his life story – as recounted in Rendall's spare but romantic prose – did not disappoint. Here was a maverick par excellence, just my type. A brilliant amateur in the 1950s and '60s, Houlihan had won every honour going in the unpaid ranks, while working in the Deptford docks by day. However, he'd been blocked from turning pro by the tyrannical Joe Davis, the 15-time world snooker champion who controlled professional snooker for decades.

So – to make ends meet – Houlihan became a hustler. The fastest cue man in the north, east, south or west, capable of knocking in a century in less than four minutes. He'd travelled up and down the country playing for money, leaving a trail of bewildered punters in his wake when he departed, pound notes stuffed into his pockets. His name was spoken of in hushed whispers at bars, pubs and snooker halls across the land and his exploits recounted with awe. He'd also picked up a criminal record at some point, which hadn't done his chances of being accepted in the puritanical world of professional snooker much good. By the time he was finally admitted to the pros in the 1970s he was past his best and plagued with eyesight problems.

By a quirk of fate, reading Rendall's article coincided with me starting to write a snooker book with my friend Paul Gadsby. Entitled *Masters of the Baize*, it was a series of potted biographies of former snooker world champions. As part of my research, I began frequenting the British Newspaper Library in Colindale and when I should have been searching for newspaper clippings about Terry Griffiths or Walter Donaldson I instead found myself scouring back issues of *The Billiard Player* for mentions of Patsy Houlihan. I found reports of his sensational dominance of the London section of the English Amateur Championship in the 1950s and '60s. I found details of his wins against future world champions Ray Reardon and John Spencer en route to winning the national amateur title in 1965. I even found photos of Patsy, who turned out to be a slim, almost diminutive figure with matinee idol looks, immaculately groomed hair and a wry, cheeky smile.

After *Masters of the Baize* was published my plan was to write a social history of the south London snooker scene. Such a book would enable me to write about Jimmy White and Patsy, you see. So I made it my mission to track both men down. Jimmy was a straightforward find. I grabbed a few words with him at a media event on the Haymarket where he was playing an exhibition frame against Paul Hunter. I asked him about Houlihan as he sat playing cards after his media duties were complete.

For a moment, Jimmy stopped rifling through his hearts, diamonds, clubs and spades and – with a look of utter sincerity on his face – looked me dead in the eyes.

'Patsy Houlihan,' he intoned, 'was the greatest snooker player I've ever seen in my life.'

Next I tried to find Houlihan himself. Rendall had great trouble tracking him down – relying on a shadowy trail over several weeks gleaned from chatting to contacts in various Deptford boozers. For me it proved somewhat easier. I opened the local phone book and found there was just one 'P. Houlihan' listed living in Deptford. (Maybe Rendall never looked in the phone book? Perhaps that was too prosaic a route for such a romantic.)

I rang the number and held my breath. To my surprise, a pleasant female voice, earthy in its south London tones, answered.

'Hello?' the voice said.

Sensing a dead end, I recited my pre-prepared patter. 'My name's Luke Williams. I'm a local writer and I'm trying to trace a Mr Patrick Houlihan who was a snooker player. This might not be the right number …'

'Oh, it is, this is his number,' the voice replied, matter-of-fact, but still polite.

'Great. Well, I was hoping it might be possible to arrange a meeting with Mr Houlihan. I'm writing a book you see and …'

'Well, the thing is he's in bed, you see. Has been for over a year.'

'Ah.'

'I'll see what he says though. He's got a phone in there. Hang on.'

A pause of a few seconds. Then another voice, equally earthy.

'How can I help you?'

'My name's Luke Williams and I'm a local writer. I've been researching your career for a book I'm writing about snooker in south London. I wondered if you might like to meet me to talk about your career?'

'Well, I'd love to, mate, but the thing is I'm laid up in bed.'

'I understand,' I replied. Then, feeling shamefully intrusive and pushy, I persevered. 'Maybe if I wrote to you and sent you some questions?'

'Yeah, all right drop me a line, that'll be grand.'

Patsy dictated his address. I had it already from the phone book but I recorded it carefully in my notebook anyway.

'Thanks very much, Mr Houlihan. You might be interested to know that I spoke to Jimmy White last year and he told me you were the greatest snooker player he's ever seen.'

There was a pause.

'My old friend Jimmy,' Patsy said, seeming to clear a lump from his throat. 'He's a good lad.'

'Thanks again for speaking to me Mr Houlihan. Goodbye.'

'Ta-da.'

I photocopied the pile of clippings I'd found about Patsy's career in Colindale. I posted them to him, along with a letter and list of questions I wanted to ask him.

Nothing came back.

A few weeks later I decided to call on Patsy at home. Say hello. See if he had received the clippings. I rang the doorbell of his flat on the ground floor of a small four-storey block of flats made of sandy brickwork in Deptford. I had the impression that someone was at home. But no one answered.

I trudged home, disappointed.

A few weeks later I heard the news.

On 8 November 2006, the day after his 77th birthday, Patsy Houlihan had died.

\* \* \*

I didn't get to meet Patsy Houlihan, but I couldn't let his death go unnoticed. I called Jimmy White who talked to me about his memories of Patsy. And then, through Patsy's phone number, I got hold of his daughter, Patricia, known to all and sundry as Patsy Girl. She agreed to meet me in a pub she ran in Charlton called the White Horse.

Full of life, colour and character and no gastrogrub in sight, the White Horse was what my old man would have called a 'proper pub'.

Patsy Girl and I sat and we talked. Initially I sensed she was a bit suspicious. I was a journalist after all and the family had been stung by an article by Ian Wooldridge in the *Daily Mail* about Patsy's death which claimed he was once imprisoned for house-breaking. He'd never have done that. It's against the old south-east London code.

Her brother Patsy Boy also joined us. He was initially wary too, but we all warmed up after a few drinks and a few stories, and in between sips of vodka and drags on my roll-ups I spoke animatedly and – OK, yes – a bit drunkenly about how amazing Patsy's life story was, how he deserved more recognition. How we couldn't let his death pass without trying to make a bit of a fuss.

In the next few weeks *The Guardian* ran a short obituary I'd written of Patsy and Clive Everton published an appreciation I'd written in *Snooker Scene* magazine. Mission accomplished? Not really. Two articles – one barely 300 words long – to mark Patsy's life seemed all too scant considering the things he achieved, the scrapes he was involved in, the stories everyone has to tell about him and the esteem so many held him in.

One day, I told myself, I'll write a whole book about Patsy Houlihan. And then everyone will know how special he was.

\* \* \*

Fourteen years pass. I move from Camberwell in the inner city to where the south London suburbs meet rural Surrey. One day I'm unpacking some old boxes. Out of one of them my Patsy Houlihan file comes tumbling out, along with a whole host of memories of days long gone.

I'm now 44. No longer a young man entranced by the whispers and myths surrounding a snooker legend, but a middle-aged man aware of his own mortality and the rapidly diminishing sands of time.

It's time, I tell myself.

I track down Patsy Girl via Facebook. We talk like old friends. Another writer has been sniffing around, she admits, so it's fortunate that I got in touch when I did.

'Go with me and I'll do your dad justice,' I promise her.

'My heart is telling me to go with you,' she tells me.

I wouldn't do it without her blessing, you see, and once she gives it, I sit down and start writing.

And I vow I won't stop until the story of Patsy Houlihan – the greatest snooker player most people never saw – is written in full.

# Chapter 2

# Houlihan nights

A CERTAIN degree of infamy has attached itself to the name of Patrick Houlihan since Victorian times. Back in the 1890s – so the story goes – a teenager of that name, a part-time bouncer in a pub on Borough High Street in Southwark, south London, was convicted of the murder of a local policeman. Houlihan was a member of a local family of Irish extraction whose name, etymologists have theorised, gave rise to the term 'hooligan'.

The Houlihan murder case, coupled with concern about the drinking and public order habits of the working class, caused widespread alarm, leading to a stampede of self-righteous journalists documenting and condemning working-class London's 'hooligan problem'; Clarence Hook's 1899 *The Hooligan Nights*, serialised in the *Daily Chronicle* to widespread shock and alarm, was the most notable example of this 19th-century outbreak of 'moral panic'. Anti-Irish sentiment, which would become further ingrained within the English psyche throughout the 20th century, certainly did not help.

Over 50 years later, the name of Patrick Houlihan, this time attached to a lad of Lewisham rather than Southwark stock, would also spread unease, now amid the staid and conservative governing forces that nurtured post-war professional snooker so protectively from the perceived threat of 'undesirable' influences that they ended up nearly destroying the sport into the bargain.

Throughout the 1950s and '60s Houlihan's snooker career progressed conventionally, in the white heat of fierce amateur competitions that made the professional game look tame by comparison. At the same time, he also built a parallel reputation on the club circuit as a formidable hustler and 'money match' specialist. It was for this reason that Houlihan, despite his prodigious talents and commercial appeal, came to be viewed by many within the snooker establishment – principally 15-time world champion Joe Davis, who ruled admission to the sport's tiny professional ranks with an iron fist – as an undesirable maverick.

To play for money, or to 'hustle', was seen as uncouth and disreputable. The disapproval of Davis and his refusal to countenance the idea of Houlihan becoming a professional meant that in the mainstream the south-east Londoner remained an unknown and he was never able to challenge for the professional world title while at his wondrous peak. However, within the nation's sporting subculture, amid the smoke and sweat of darkened snooker halls across the country, Houlihan became a legend. A 'folklore hero' as the six-time world champion Steve Davis would later describe him, 'An underground hero of the amateur snooker scene.'

A glance at the bald statistics of Houlihan's professional career provides few clues as to why he is so revered amid certain snooker circles; he never won a professional tournament, his appearances in the World Championship never stretched beyond the last 16 and he certainly never appeared on *Pot Black*. By the time of his retirement in 1993, his win-loss record in professional snooker – according to the website Cue Tracker – stood at an unremarkable 50 victories and 98 defeats.

What is it then about Houlihan that so consumes the imagination and won the adoration of Jimmy White among many others? Well, for starters, he adhered to a crowd-pleasing philosophy of attacking snooker, playing and potting at a breakneck speed. It's hard to prove it beyond doubt, but Houlihan is commonly accepted to have been the first snooker player to compile a century break in under four minutes. None of Houlihan's amateur or professional career has been preserved on videotape, but everyone who saw him play remarked on his incredible speed and fluency around the table. Tony Drago, himself one of the swiftest players of all time, reckoned Houlihan was 'probably faster than me' and he only saw Patsy in the latter days of his career.

By the time he died, Houlihan was said to have compiled more than 2,000 or even 3,000 centuries, although proving this is impossible, of course, with many of these having come in money matches or practice sessions. Speedy break building has become commonplace in modern snooker, but in Houlihan's day it was almost unheard of. Snooker, after all, began life as an essentially conservative game played by billiards specialists who were content to become embroiled in expanses of safety play in order to tease out openings from which they might manage to force their opponent into an error and then rack up points in small clusters. As Houlihan himself once put it, players would 'score 20s and 30s and then run safe'.

So it was that snooker – like billiards – came to be seen as a game of self-control and delicacy in which striking the ball hard was regarded as the height of uncouthness. This approach was very much a hangover from the days of the British Empire, and rested on the notions of fair play and gentlemanly restraint that Britain was believed to have bequeathed to the world. Cue sports were only respectable if played delicately in a drawing room after dinner by upper-class aesthetes sipping brandy and puffing cigars – not over a pint of ale and a rolled cigarette in a tavern by the unwashed working classes.

But times were changing. Post-World War II, the British Empire was crumbling to dust and the working classes were no longer content to be kept in their place. Freed from the strictures and fears of wartime and rationing, an insatiable appetite for public entertainment, and new forms of more modern, creative expression – from rock'n'roll to teen-based movies – built inexorably throughout the 1950s and '60s. Billiards – with its stately, somnolent pace – was soon consigned to the dustbin of history and the masses began to embrace snooker instead.

And when watching snooker, what was better than watching a player who potted at speed while utilising the thrilling arts of screw, side and stun to the maximum? Hence the working-class love for Alex Higgins, Jimmy White and Ronnie O'Sullivan, upon whom the magical title of 'People's Champion' was successively conferred.

Houlihan – applying similar attacking instincts in a far earlier era – was the spiritual godfather of this trio of thrilling talents.

When Houlihan did belatedly turn pro, he was already in his 40s, beset with eyesight problems and his best days were behind him. However, although his professional record is unremarkable, it must be emphasised that he enjoyed a glittering – albeit rarely documented – amateur career, including a stunning unbeaten run across most of the 1964/65 season, which built his reputation and solidified his legend. Furthermore, from the 1950s until the early '90s he also enjoyed a rollercoaster sideline as arguably the greatest snooker hustler and money match player of all time. Away from the increasingly sanitised environment of professional snooker, in matches, conversations and escapades in snooker halls and working men's clubs up and down the land, Houlihan was an icon, as well as a valued friend to a new generation of professional players, among them Jimmy White, Tony Meo and Tony Drago, all of whom still speak effusively not only of his abilities on the baize, but also of his consistent tendency to kindness and encouragement away from it.

* * *

Patrick William Houlihan was born on 7 November 1929 at 31 Hawkins House on New King Street, Deptford, a narrow Victorian alleyway within spitting distance of the Thames. He died 77 years and one day later less than half a mile away in a ground-floor flat on Abinger Grove, having spent almost his entire existence living within a two- or three-mile radius of the place of his birth.

Deptford, a resolutely and proudly working-class area of south-east London, was not just where Houlihan came from, it was an essential part of his existence. It would be fair to say that during his lifetime he was as much a part of the local topography as any of the area's buildings or landmarks. Deptford was a part of Patsy, and Patsy a part of Deptford. 'You know the old saying,' is the view of his daughter Patricia, aka Patsy Girl. 'You can take the man out of Deptford, but you can't take Deptford out of the man. Deptford was everything to him.'

Houlihan's mother Rosina Annie Houlihan (maiden name Edghill) and father William Houlihan were also Deptford-born –

a family of solid, south-east London working-class stock. On his father's side, Houlihan was around two or three generations removed from his Irish roots, but he always insisted, 'I'm not [Irish] – I'm bred and born in Deptford.' The Houlihan family were Catholic, and although Patsy was not a churchgoer, he did have a sense of faith in God which he maintained throughout his life. William and Rosina married in October 1925; it was a union that would last 53 years until Rosina's death in 1978 and would produce four children. In and around Deptford, William was known to all and sundry by his nickname of 'Happy'. Patsy was the middle of two brothers: William junior (known as Billy) was born in 1926, while Terence (Terry) was born in 1934. A further Houlihan brother named Daniel (Danny) died, either stillborn or in early infancy. Patsy would later name one of his own sons in honour of the brother he never knew.

Eldest brother Billy was keen on the idea of a career in the army but instead, against his will, was conscripted as a coal miner by the 'Bevin Boy' scheme which was run from 1943 until 1948, an experience which appeared to damage him psychologically. 'They sent him down the mines but he didn't want to do that,' Patsy's good friend of several decades Terry Dempsey explained. 'Later, Billy spent most of his life in the house. He didn't go out for years. He was a ringer for Patsy as it goes.'

Younger brother Terry was more outgoing, despite suffering an accident when he was 12 or 13 which left him without an eye. Accounts vary concerning how this happened. 'He was hit by a bit of metal from an umbrella that came down from a block of flats behind the Osborne Arms pub,' was Dempsey's recollection. William Garrett, a friend of Terry's, had a different theory, 'In those days we all went around with catapults made out of two old washing pegs which we fixed together with an elastic band. For ammunition we'd use metal staples made of iron. I think Terry got caught by one of those in his eye.'

The Houlihans were the type of white working-class family whose traditions and way of life have largely been wiped out of the social fabric of south-east London during the last couple of decades. 'There was definitely a feeling of community in Deptford in those days,' Garrett explained. 'Everyone knew each other and all the families seemed to be related to each other in a vague sort of way. But Deptford was also very rough. A deadly place in many respects. It really was. You didn't have to look far for trouble. Terry and Patsy could definitely handle themselves though.'

Paul Moriarty, a Deptford docker ten years Houlihan's junior who knew him and his brother Terry well and later found fame as an actor under the name P.H. Moriarty, recalled, 'Like other areas of south London, Peckham, Camberwell, Brixton and so on, Deptford was its own small town. And if anyone came into Deptford you knew they wouldn't come out somewhere else.'

Another of Patsy's friends from the old days, John Butler, gave further insight into what it was like to live in Deptford. 'It was a very hard place,' he said. 'I remember once being in Wales up in the mountains and a bloke said to me, "What part of London do you come from?" I said, "Deptford." He turned to me and said, "That's the place where policemen don't walk about on their own." No one from Peckham, Bermondsey, Rotherhithe or wherever ever ventured into Deptford.'

Dempsey added, 'People from Deptford would fight among their own, but if anyone came in from outside to have a row then everyone joined together. That's how it was. It was a hard place but also a lovely place to live. I'd give my right arm to go back. They were wonderful times. It was a magical life.'

Life and work in Deptford revolved around the bustling high street, which possessed multiple pubs, and the local docks. Drinking and socialising after a long day's toil were central to the working-class community. 'I think there were about ten pubs on Deptford High Street alone,' Garrett said. 'At the bottom of the street there was the Noah's Ark. Then there was a tobacconist. Then there was Goddard's pie and eel shop. Then there were some garages, a printers and terraced houses and a hell of a lot of pubs. The Mechanics Arms was the Irish pub. There was the Brown Bear, the Centurion and several more. And everywhere you went there were horse and carts.'

Many locals worked in the nearby docks as stevedores or as barrow boys in the market, while rag and boning was also a common occupation. 'I think some of the Houlihans used to go out rag and boning,' recalled Garrett. 'Terry used to for sure because he used to knock around with my cousin Mikey Hanson.' William Houlihan was a dock worker, while at one point Rosina worked as a metal solderer, an unusual occupation for a woman of her generation that speaks to her willingness to graft.

The young Patsy had a spell in the army doing national service, including a period billeted to Reading. In the forces he proved himself a tough and accomplished boxer, even winning an amateur tournament. After leaving the army, Houlihan followed his father into the Surrey Docks in 1951. Later he would also work sporadically on a fruit and veg stall in Deptford market too. At this point, the docks were enjoying something of a post-World War II boom. Only later would irreversible decline set in. 'It was the biggest dock in Europe,' recalled Moriarty, who also worked there as a young man. 'The Surrey Docks were massive.'

During the early 1950s the streets of Deptford, Bermondsey and Rotherhithe often reverberated to the merry poetry of the dockers' unique slang, as well as the sight of rows and rows of working men with hats specifically designed to aid the carrying of softwood timber from the Baltic and Scandinavia. Life in the docks was unremittingly tough, but the dockers were a close-knit and congenial community. Shifts were eight hours long and in Houlihan's estimation a 'sugar job' was the toughest of all, involving as it did the shifting of bags weighing two to three hundred pounds each, while a 'wood job' shifting timber was 'not so tough'.

Exactly how long Patsy was in the docks for is unknown. 'How long did Patsy work there?' said Dempsey with a chuckle. 'About a day! I said to him, "Why didn't you stay any longer?" He said, "I'll tell you why, Tel. I went to work one day and they gave me something to do. I went back the next day and they gave me something else to do and I thought, 'Fuck that!' When I'd done my work I thought it would be over but all I kept getting was more work!"'

Patsy's brother Terry also worked at the docks, becoming good friends with Dempsey's father. 'They lost their ticket the same day,' Dempsey explained. 'You had to be there on time to bomp on. If you missed your bomping on you never got paid. Half a quid you got paid per day. My father lost his ticket because he threw his book at the bloke down there. He and Terry got thrown off for that.'

Patsy working at the docks for just one day is an exaggeration, of course, but it's doubtless the case that he soon found life as a stevedore dull by comparison with the magical lure of the snooker hall. At different times in later life he claimed to have been either 13 or 15 when he first picked up a cue, but what is known for sure is that his father – no mean player himself by all accounts – introduced him to the game at the Lucania Temperance Billiard Hall, then located at 133 Deptford High Street, opposite the Mechanics Arms pub. An example of early 1850s architecture, the building had originally housed the Deptford Mechanics' and Literary Institute, before becoming a cinema and then being converted into a billiards and snooker hall in 1921.

By the time Houlihan started playing snooker, cue sports had been an integral part of London's sporting culture for many decades. Billiards, which gave birth to snooker, was a staple of 19th-century English taverns and public houses. Indeed, in 1900 the *Licensed Victualler* had declared, 'One can scarcely imagine any properly furnished hotel or modern public house without its billiard room.' The inextricable connection between billiards, alcohol and gambling was perhaps one of the reasons for the derivation of the popular aphorism that an aptitude for the sport was indicative of a 'misspent youth' (a saying often attributed to philosopher Herbert Spencer, but which he probably repeated from another source).

At the beginning of the 20th century, London possessed a mere handful of dedicated billiard halls but, by 1936, the London Post Office directory listed over 130 – around half of them in the south of the capital. 'There were snooker tables and clubs all around in those days,' recalled Moriarty. 'Everyone played.' Soon the predominant and most popular game was not billiards, but snooker. Devised in 1875 by British soldiers in India, it was initially dismissed as coarse and unsubtle. However, by the 1940s, billiards was passé. The best professionals were simply too good and were boring spectators with breaks that lasted for hours. Snooker, with its faster pace and wider variety of attractively coloured balls, took over. Although Houlihan played billiards as well as snooker, it was the 22-ball game that absorbed most of his attention from the moment he first picked up a cue. By his own admission he 'came on quick' and 'was what you'd call a natural'. To begin with he would act as a marker for older players at the Lucania, being paid a few shillings to keep score and remove the balls from the pockets. These cash-in-hand earnings would then be put to use to pay for his own table time.

Houlihan's merits as a cueman were manifest: he played and potted fast, with a smooth and technically perfect cue action, and his white ball control was uncanny. His ability to manipulate heavy balls on tables that were poor quality and unresponsive compared to the modern day was also breathtaking. Moriarty recalled watching the young Houlihan at the snooker table with awe, 'He was a wizard quite frankly. To give you an example, he could spin a ball from the back of the table and get it to stop right on the blue spot.'

Soon, the teenage Houlihan was beating all the adults in the Lucania and was so absorbed in his snooker that he would look to practise for around two to three hours per day. It wasn't always easy balancing snooker with stevedoring though; indeed, Houlihan admitted that the physical exertions of working a shift in the docks meant it often took him a whole day to 'get played back' into decent form on returning to the snooker hall. Nevertheless, unlike most cueists who 'couldn't care less' about fresh air, Houlihan admitted he enjoyed being out in the open air as a much-needed antidote to the enclosed and sometimes claustrophobic environment of the snooker hall. He would invariably walk to work or the Lucania and back again rather than take public transport – a habit he maintained for the rest of his life, never bothering to learn to drive.

As well as benefiting from his father's tutelage, Houlihan was soon receiving a snooker education from Sidney Peache, captain of the Lewisham Temperance Billiards Hall team, where he also began playing in 1949. 'Houlihan gives Mr Peache generous credit for implanting in him an invaluable grounding in the principles of snooker,' noted *The Billiard Player* – the cue sports journal of record of its day – in 1954.

Both the Deptford and Lewisham halls were 'temperance' establishments and therefore completely alcohol-free. Cue sports and the temperance movement might be seen as unusual bedfellows, but in the residential suburbs of London such halls were common. The establishment of Temperance Billiard Halls Ltd in 1906 was an attempt to assert the notion that alcohol-free leisure facilities could be popular, part of the wider and growing temperance movement seeking to combat the issue of increasing rates of alcohol dependency, particularly among the working classes. The company built around 17 billiard halls over the next five years, including five in London. By 1935 temperance halls were booming, with over 1.5 million games of billiards and snooker played annually in such establishments across Britain, and by 1939 the number of temperance halls in London had swelled to over 50. In look and style, these halls deliberately aped the architectural features of pubs by, for example, utilising decorative tiled facades and stained glass. As well as billiard and snooker tables, temperance halls also provided a place for people to meet, eat and play other indoor sports, such as darts and chess.

For all their fleeting success, however, it was not a movement that would last. 'The temperance halls were opposed to the reality of the game,' recalled John Archer, a south Londoner who frequented many snooker halls in his youth in the 1950s and '60s. 'They began to die out after the war. More people wanted to have a drink with a game of snooker than not.' The Lucania chain of temperance halls abandoned the principle of abstinence sometime in the 1960s and by the '70s the temperance snooker hall movement had faded away completely. However, it was not until the snooker boom of the 1980s that many snooker halls were fully licensed to serve alcohol; beforehand the sole refreshment found in most halls was a cup of tea and, if you were lucky, a ham and cheese roll.

Despite playing in the temperance halls in his youth, Houlihan certainly didn't abstain from alcohol. 'I'm a drinker,' he would happily confirm throughout his life, although his drinking mostly came before or after playing snooker, not during a match, at one or more of the pubs along and around Deptford High Street. 'You always ended up in the pub [afterwards],' Houlihan once reflected. 'You'd play snooker in the afternoon and then have a nice drink in the evening.' Houlihan's tipple of choice was light ale. 'We all drank pints and Patsy drank halves,' Terry Dempsey observed. 'He'd ask for two halves of light ale and then he'd keep one by the side of his glass. And he'd never drink it until someone bought him another light ale. We'd say, "Hooley you gonna go and buy a drink?" And he'd say, "No, I'm all right I've got one here!"'

Houlihan could certainly hold his drink, despite rarely eating during the day after his usual breakfast of bacon and tomatoes, either made at home or bought at the local cafe. 'Only time I ever remember seeing him eat anything was when we had some scallops one time in a Chinese restaurant,' Dempsey said. 'He was very slim. He never ate anything and he could drink all day long. I swear to God, Mick in the Osborne Arms [one of Patsy's many locals] used to tell me Patsy drank a crate of light ale every day. Easy. And he held it – he was never drunk.'

It was in the Lewisham Temperance Hall, in 1952, that Houlihan made his first major impact as an amateur cueman. Just days after his 23rd birthday – on either 11 or 14 November; accounts vary – he compiled breaks of 100 and 122 on the same night. The impressive feat earned his first mentions in the local and national press. 'Balkline' – the *Manchester Evening News* snooker correspondent – pegged him as a talent to watch, while *The Billiard Player* ran news of the double centuries on page 14 of its December 1952 issue. The run of 122 also earned Houlihan the Billiards Association and Control Council (BA&CC) National Breaks Competition award, a prize given by the cue sports governing body to recognise the highest certified amateur break of the year, an honour that was announced in the February 1953 issue of *The Billiard Player*.

It was just the breakthrough and confidence boost that Houlihan required. With encouragement from mentor Peache and his family he duly submitted his entry form for the 1953/54 English Amateur Snooker Championship. Established in 1916 – predating the World Professional Snooker Championship by 11 years – the English Amateur was arguably the most prestigious and certainly the most keenly contested snooker competition in the country. Still in operation today – Ben Hancorn having won its 100th staging in 2020 – it is now the longest-running snooker tournament in the world, although its lustre has faded significantly since the professional game's expansion from the 1970s onwards.

In the 1950s it was a different story though – back then professional snooker was close to stagnant, possessing a stale and all too finite cast of rotating and ageing characters. For example, the 1954 World Professional Match-Play Championship – the World Championship in all but name, most professionals having broken away from the governing body the BA&CC – featured just 16 entrants, not including Joe Davis, who was still probably the best player in the business but had retired from competing in the championship, thus fatally undermining it. By 1957 a miserable staging of the championship in Jersey attracted just 16 spectators across its first two sessions and the tournament fell into dormancy until 1964.

In contrast, the amateur game was in rude health in the 1950s. There were around three million regular players at clubs and halls nationwide, and each year around 200 or so of these enthusiasts formed the body of excited and largely accomplished entrants for the English Amateur Championship. Divided into separate local tournaments, the winners of these area titles then advanced to the 'championship proper', held at Burroughes and Watts Limited's prestigious Soho Square match room in central London, popularly known as Burroughes Hall. With its plush table, covered in West of England woollen green cloth and fitted with Burwat steel vacuum cushions, the only venue that could really compete with Burroughes Hall was Leicester Square Hall, which was seen as the 'home' of the professional game until its closure in 1955. But while Leicester Square Hall hosted interminable professional matches that often lasted several days, or tiresome handicap contests where the leading players such as Joe Davis conceded a certain number of points start to those deemed their inferiors, Burroughes Hall saw knockout amateur matches played out over shorter periods on level terms. In short, the professional game was a bore – the amateurs were where it was at.

In 1953/54, 220 players paid the £1 1s entrance fee for the English Amateur Championship in the hope of being crowned the 'unpaid' snooker king of the UK. Among them were a host of thrusting young talents, including future world professional champion Ray Reardon,

Cliff Wilson, Jack Karnehm, Ron Gross, Markham Wildman and, of course, Patsy Houlihan. The London section of the championship – in which Houlihan had to compete – was also usually hosted at Burroughes Hall and was an ultra-competitive and much sought-after title in its own right. 'Great interest will attach to Houlihan's debut, for he is said to be exceptional,' was the assessment of *The Billiard Player* in its eve-of-tournament preview.

As Houlihan prepared for his championship debut in November 1953, the richly talented Deptford lad had no reason to fear anyone. Indeed, his debut season in competitive snooker would prove nothing short of a sensation.

Chapter 3

# The big breakthrough

BURROUGHES HALL was not a venue for the faint-hearted. Markham Wildman – later to become one of Patsy Houlihan's greatest amateur rivals – vividly described how intimidating it was to walk out into the historic arena for a championship match,

'[Referee] Mr [Frank] Collins waited for the players to enter through the double doors and climb the stairs to the match room. The genial Jack Rainbow, boss of Burroughes at the time, would welcome you as you came in from the square. On the ground floor level there were three demonstration billiard rooms set up to reflect and simulate several styles of billiard room designs. Various professional players were engaged to teach in the rooms and encourage turnover for the company in any way that they could. Sidney Lee was an almost ever present. The rooms were furnished in Edwardian, Regency and Georgian styles; each had a billiard table in a similar style as the centrepiece of the display.

'Upstairs and adjacent to the match room John Roberts looked down on three sides from pictures framed and imposing and on an ornate pedestal stood the great John Roberts World Championship Billiards trophy. Awaiting your entrance into the 125-seat arena was an experience ... the silence was, even with a full house, quite terrifying, Collins would stand expressionless, [and] it seemed as though the great Roberts, now long dead, was questioning your right to be there in the inner sanctum of billiards and later, of course, snooker.'

If Houlihan was intimidated by the long history of Burroughes Hall, or the forbidding atmosphere of the match room, he didn't show it when his competitive amateur snooker career began on 16 December 1953. He was aided by the fact that he had played at the venue before, having helped the Lee Green branch of the British Legion win the Metropolitan Area team billiards championship the previous April.

In his snooker bow, Houlihan played so fast and so fearlessly that it was as though he was back at the Lewisham Lucania with his mates from the docks. He took barely an hour to mete out a 3-0 thrashing to J.W. Hall thus advancing to round two of the London section – a win that included a fluent run of 62, made at the sort of breakneck speed that would have made those old billiards greats whose portraits looked down on him splutter while sipping a glass of after-dinner port.

In round two, despite playing without his own cue (for reasons undocumented), Houlihan fell 2-1 behind against Ronald Hoare who, according to *The Billiard Player*, was 'playing so well … that Houlihan's exit appeared probable'. However, Houlihan edged a tight fourth frame 79-48 to level matters and 'his great gift of break making manifested itself' in the decider with a wondrous effort of 74 on just his second visit to the table. The break was just four short of Jim Longden's amateur championship record mark of 78, set in 1950. More importantly it secured Houlihan's progress 3-2.

Sidney Hyams and A. Armstrong were next to fall, both by scores of 3-1. C. Barnett was then whitewashed 3-0 and Houlihan – suddenly – was in the London final against Jim Chapman. It was to prove – in the words of *The Billiard Player* – 'a one-man performance', Houlihan extending his run of successive frame victories across three matches to ten en route to a thumping 5-0 victory, scoring quickfire breaks of 41, 44 and 71 along the way. The four dead frames of the best-of-nine encounter were played out as well, Houlihan winning them 3-1, notching an impressive 56 break. It was, by any measure, a sensational performance and one hailed by the magazine's editor Richard Holt as 'a revelation'.

Houlihan's capture of the 1953/54 London title was a portent of things to come; over the next decade the area championship would become his personal fiefdom. So sensational were his performances that *The Billiard Player*'s February 1954 issue was effectively a Houlihan special – two images of him adorned the cover and the best part of four of the issue's 18 pages were devoted to exhaustive, detailed and occasionally breathless accounts of his achievement. Richard Holt – at the time the foremost writer on the sport, praised by Wildman for his 'writing skills and wit of the very highest calibre' – was so impressed with Houlihan's performances in the winter of 1953 that he was moved to declare, 'I am inclined to believe Houlihan may turn out to be the finest amateur snooker player in snooker history.'

'I cannot remember anything so fine in amateur snooker, as the exhibition given by Patrick Houlihan, of Deptford, in the final of the London section,' Holt purred. 'We knew he was well above average, as he had won the National Breaks Competition last year … but hundred breaks had been made by amateurs in various parts of the country, and one assumed that Houlihan was a really good player, but that when it came to the Amateur Championship, and playing at Burroughes Hall, where the atmosphere is vastly different from that in clubs and halls, he might, though probably giving a good account of himself, soon vanish from the scene as a result of meeting experienced players, doubtless superior to himself. However, he duly made his debut and soon startled good judges, not by winning or even making a 62 break, but by the advanced technique he showed, and the beautiful style in which he made the break.'

The admiring Holt provided the most detailed eyewitness analysis of Houlihan's strengths and virtues as a cueman ever committed to print; a valuable assessment given that no video footage of Houlihan in action – bar a few seconds – still exists:

'His potting is masterly. He will pot the blue [on its spot], far from straight, into a bottom pocket, and screw back to get on a red at the top, without turning a hair. His play at the top is brilliant in its ease and fluency, and he pots the black at any particular angle with effortless accuracy, and also gets on to a particular red afterwards, amongst a cluster of them, when pinpoint accuracy is necessary, with conspicuous precision. His play on the blue, particularly in sharp angle screw-pots, is admirable. In the all-important phase of positional play, he excels – the series of fine breaks he has made form full proof – and when delicacy is needed, he is not found wanting. His defensive shots to "baulk" are finely gauged and often subtle in the use of side. In the break-making areas, black and pink, he is deadly.'

Holt went so far as to call Houlihan 'a real artist and natural genius of snooker', commenting, 'A remarkable feature of his play is its speed and easy rhythm; it is all done without the slightest hesitancy, and the seemingly intuitive way he grasps the positional potentialities of a complicated set-up is also striking. His admirable stance and cue delivery, of course, are the basis of his command, and a quiet, confident demeanour, completes his equipment.'

Holt also sought to justify his assessment of Houlihan as potentially the greatest amateur in snooker history,

'I am not ... taking the winning of games as a criterion, in appraising Houlihan's status as a snooker player. He may go out in the first round in the Competition Proper, but it won't change my opinion at all – I am basing my judgement on the quality and technique of his play. Let it [also] not be thought that I forget our other amateur stars, all of whom have at one time or another given outstanding exhibitions in the Championship, and are capable of beating Houlihan in a day's play. Houlihan may not be this year's champion, he may not be next year's, but that he will be champion at no distant date is, I think, certain. Independently of that, what I do make bold to declare is that the quality of snooker he has so far displayed surpasses in sheer artistry, accuracy, quick-minded grasp of essentials, and speedy fluency, anything I have yet seen in the amateur sphere.'

Holt's judgement was backed up by referee Frank Collins, who officiated the London final against Chapman. The moustachioed Collins was a diminutive but distinctive figure, with his formal Edwardian dress and high wing collar. Nearly 80 years of age, he was something of an institution at Burroughes Hall and spoke with great authority, having known billiards greats such as John Roberts senior and junior, Walter Lindrum and W.J. Peall. Collins was not a man easily impressed or given to unnecessary hyperbole, yet his reaction after seeing Houlihan's demolition of Chapman was unequivocal, 'I consider Houlihan the best amateur snooker player I have ever seen.'

Despite the plaudits, Holt also drew attention to some of Houlihan's weaknesses. 'His game is not yet flawless,' he admitted. 'He leaves openings frequently, but he has not had time to devise his tactics in Championship play, and brilliance is not invulnerable!' Nevertheless, Holt felt Houlihan had the edge on another great natural talent of the era, Wales's Cliff Wilson. 'Wilson is, perhaps, the fastest-ever snooker player of real ability,' he noted, 'But, as yet, he lacks defence, and also, Houlihan has by far the more craft and greater control of the cue ball … Win or lose, Patrick Houlihan has inimitable magic in his cue, not to mention a style all his own. And so I venture to call him the "Frank Edwards" of snooker.' The reference to Edwards, a billiards player of great class and aesthetic excellence who won the English Amateur Billiards title on several occasions, was telling, and indicative of the esteem in which Holt held Houlihan.

Although Houlihan's London title triumph ignited excitement in the snooker world, it made only small ripples in the national press – an indication of what Clive Everton later termed snooker's 'folk sport' status at the time. *The Billiard Player* in its February 1954 editorial bemoaned the failure of Houlihan's success to be granted any significant press attention, pointing out what it saw as the disproportionate attention granted to 'girl and women, boy and youth' snooker players in the national press.

'Where is the sense of proportion, or even the sense?' the journal complained. 'Patrick Houlihan makes breaks in the London final, of 41, 44, 31, 71, 27 and 56, wins by eight frames to one, and silence greets the feat … Yet a young lady who played in male attire recently, and to whom Houlihan … could give at least ten blacks, was greeted with reams of precious space. Must Houlihan … play in feminine garments to hit the headlines? Achievements on the table, it would appear, are small beer when it comes to "news value" … Do we exaggerate? If anyone thinks so, let him show us a report, even a bare mention, of Houlihan's recent brilliant performance.'

Houlihan might not have been garnering national newspaper coverage, but in Deptford his exploits had seen him begin to acquire a loyal following. Around 30 supporters were present for several of his matches en route to the London title and as his campaign progressed against other regional title holders in the final stages of the English Amateur Championship this army of fans would grow spectacularly. Previewing the 'championship proper', ahead of its commencement on Monday, 8 March at Burroughes Hall, *The Billiard Player* was confident Houlihan would be among the leading contenders, declaring, 'Given the necessary assistance from the snooker gods – everyone needs it to win a knock-out event – Houlihan will not be far off at the end. That he is good enough to win the title goes without saying, for his snooker is superlative.'

Thirty-two cueists from across the country were still standing but Houlihan had no reason to fear any of them.

Chapter 4

# Sensation in Soho Square

PORTSMOUTH CHAMPION Alf Hobbs was the man handed the unenviable task of trying to halt a rampant Patsy Houlihan in the last 32 of the English Amateur Championship at Burroughes Hall on Wednesday, 10 March 1954.

A quickfire and brilliant break of 40 saw Houlihan march away with the first frame in double-quick time and it was soon clear that Hobbs was not in the London champion's class. 'The end result was never in doubt,' noted *The Billiard Player*, '[although] Hobbs, a quiet and accomplished player, gave him a lot of trouble, depriving him of chances to pot.' Despite Hobbs's efforts, and the fact that the Deptford man 'often went out for pots he would not have tried against the best players', Houlihan won 5-0 – extending his run of consecutive competitive frames won to a remarkable 15. The world beyond the snooker press was now finally beginning to take note of Houlihan's talents with the *Birmingham Daily Post* remarking that it was a 'brilliant debut'.

Next up was Manchester champion James Heaton, a colliery worker from Bolton. It was to prove a sensational last-16 encounter in front of full houses for both sessions of play at Burroughes Hall. 'No finer amateur game can have taken place,' declared *The Billiard Player*. Heaton started fast, reeling off the first two frames in the afternoon with breaks of 37 and 47. 'Houlihan was a spectator,' *The Billiard Player* noted. '[He] got few chances, but some characteristically careless and reckless shots helped his opponent.' As for Heaton he was running hot with 'ball after ball ... disappearing into the pockets like scared rabbits into their burrows'. Houlihan edged a tight third frame, however, slotting a difficult pink from baulk and getting in position to sink the black along the top cushion to narrow the deficit to 2-1.

A series of careless fouls by Houlihan in frame four enabled Heaton to nick it 54-51, courtesy of a brilliant screw-back on the pink and a delicately cut black to lead 3-1. Houlihan won the fifth, but the Manchester champion took the sixth to lead 4-2 at which point 'a Heaton win appeared certain'. Displaying steely nerves, however, Houlihan – combining 'magnificent potting' and 'clever snookering' – won three frames in succession to close out a 5-4 victory, including the final frame by a convincing margin of 79-1. 'A remarkable recovery, against a remarkable player,' intoned *The Billiard Player*, while the *Daily Herald* – unusually for a national newspaper – also carried a short report of Houlihan's sensational comeback, headlining its story 'Snooker recovery'.

The Heaton match was dramatic, but Houlihan's quarter-final against Home Counties champion Norman Buck, from Romford, Essex, on Wednesday, 24 March would create a hullabaloo in Soho Square such as amateur snooker had never previously seen. The four-frame afternoon session began late after Buck forgot his glasses and ended with honours even at two frames apiece. Houlihan was a touch fortunate not to be behind, snatching the final frame of the session after laying a 'peach of a snooker' on the pink – forcing Buck to miss – before potting it himself from a tight angle. Buck made the highest break of the afternoon – 54 – and 'had held the whip hand', but Houlihan's 'brilliance ... and opportunism' had kept him in the match.

Ahead of the evening session there were scenes of pandemonium in Soho Square as a crowd of hundreds – most of them Houlihan fans from Deptford without tickets – converged on Burroughes Hall hoping to see the eagerly awaited conclusion to the match. 'A pint-sized audience tried to get into a quart-sized hall,' was how *The Billiard Player* reported the incident, which left those with tickets unable to gain entrance to the hall for around 30 minutes, such was the crush and confusion. In the end the police had to be called to assist in dispersing the crowds, clearing a path to enable the officials and players to get inside. The incident made considerable waves in the local and national press, with the *Daily Herald* declaring that 'hundreds of people besieged' the hall under the headline 'Hundreds rush Snooker match'.

Twenty-eight years later – speaking to author Jean Rafferty – Houlihan vividly recalled the night he caused such a stir in Soho that coppers had to be called in to keep order. 'I was the draw in them days,' he said proudly. 'They had to have two police cars to control the crowds. I couldn't even get myself in. I had to force my way through.' Houlihan was clearly a box-office attraction; according to the *Yorkshire Evening Post*, attendance figures for the tournament were running 60 per cent in excess of the previous year, which themselves had been record breaking.

However, once the chaos had subsided and the police had restored order it was Buck who edged ahead 3-2, Houlihan's opening stroke proving loose. 'When will this gifted player learn that the opening strokes in serious snooker are vital?' despaired Holt. Houlihan drew level at 3-3 courtesy of some brilliant pots, but Buck dominated the next frame to go one up with two to play. Buck led 57-48 in the next with just three colours remaining. A 'long defensive bout ensued' before a Buck error enabled Houlihan to clear blue, pink and black to snatch the frame and set up a decider.

The final frame was a nervy affair, with both men squandering opportunities. Buck led narrowly with just pink and black left and when Houlihan snaffled six points from a 'superb snooker' he looked favourite to prevail, but he left the pink on and Buck duly snaffled it, earning a 'great cheer' from his fans as he took the frame 62-41 and secured a place in the semi-finals. 'Buck, by his admirably clean and accurate potting and striking position play, [was] deserving of the victory,' was the verdict of *The Billiard Player*, before adding, 'Houlihan did not produce his best form, and was many times erratic, which gave Buck chances he should never have had.'

Houlihan may have lost, but the impact he had made in his debut season of amateur competition had been seismic. A couple of weeks later, he was back at Burroughes Hall for something of an encore, helping the Lee Green British Legion branch secure a notable double by winning the Metropolitan Area snooker and billiards team shields on the same night.

In a further indication of the booming status of amateur snooker, the build-up to the following season's amateur championship saw a prestigious invitation event held at Burroughes Hall from 3–14 October 1954. The six-man field for this enticing event was packed with exciting and accomplished amateur talents. There was 1952/53 national champion Tommy Gordon; the man he defeated to win the title, George Humphries; 1953/54 runner-up Cliff Wilson; rising Londoner Ron Gross; Buck, who had knocked Houlihan out in the championship quarter-finals a few months earlier, and Houlihan himself.

Played on a league basis, with all six players facing each other once in five-frame encounters, the tournament was dominated by Wilson, Houlihan and Buck, who each won four matches against a single defeat. Wilson took the title on 'frame average' from Houlihan, who took the runners-up slot just ahead of Buck. '[All three] played at times brilliant snooker' was the assessment of *The Billiard Player*. 'We say "at times" for they also had some bad patches. Nevertheless, their best play was top quality, and savoured of professional technique.'

Houlihan really should have won the whole tournament; his sole reverse was a 3-2 defeat against Buck in a match he somehow lost after leading 2-0. 'It is hard to say why [he lost this game],' pondered *The Billiard Player*. 'At his best, there is no finer or dazzlingly skilful amateur, as we stated before. Like Wilson, he is, in his way, unique, and like him, his play spells personality. Both are out on their own for spontaneity and quickness of perception. His trouble, we believe, is the carelessness born of wiping up inferior players over a long period.'

Buoyed by his performance in the invitation event, Houlihan swaggered into the 1954/55 championship as one of the favourites to lift the title. However, his cavalier attitude towards safety play came back to haunt him on Monday, 29 November, when his defence of his London title shockingly faltered at the very first hurdle as he fell to a surprise 3-1 defeat to Brixton's Doug Melchior. Given his large following among Deptford locals and London snooker enthusiasts,

Houlihan's defeat was, *The Billiard Player* concluded, 'A real disaster for London spectators.'

'What happened was that Houlihan won the first frame of this match 83-19, and seemed set for a "walk-over",' ran the journal's shell-shocked post-mortem. 'Missing an easy pink in frame two, Houlihan met with a surprise, for Melchior who had looked mediocre suddenly made a fine 42 break. It must have shaken Houlihan somewhat, for, although afterwards he played pretty well, chances seemed to elude him, and Melchior, who showed a flair for snookering, and potted reliably, somehow maintained the initiative to the end. In a long bout of snookering in the fourth frame, Houlihan suffered some bad luck, and he could never get the chances for those rapid and dazzling breaks which win him his matches. So the better player lost, but all praise to his opponent for a fine achievement.'

Later in the year, *The Billiard Player* reflected further on Houlihan's defeat, noting, 'One fears that he [Houlihan] has by incessant playing here, there and everywhere, so to speak, developed a rather careless style. We hope, however, to see this gifted player, a "natural" if ever there was one, next season and, given a due degree of discretion, he can be relied on to go far.' The reference to 'here, there and everywhere' was a coy admission that Houlihan's focus was not solely on amateur competition but also on the myriad money-making opportunities that he was discovering were available in snooker halls up and down the country.

Unfortunately, amateur snooker offered no financial and material inducements bar the odd reward voucher and silver cups and trophies, which looked good on the mantelpiece but did nothing to put food on the table – as Houlihan once so pithily put it, 'You can't eat trophies.'

With this in mind, Houlihan discerned that if he was to make some decent money out of his considerable skills on the green baize he would need to take a detour into an altogether shadier world than the polished and refined environment of Burroughes Hall.

It was time to turn hustler.

# Chapter 5

# 'Pound notes tell stories'

THE WORD 'hustler' probably originates from the Dutch terms 'hutselen' and 'husseln', meaning to shake or to toss. The term came to be associated with a gambling activity known as 'hustle cap' – a game in which players had to guess which way coins shaken (or 'hustled') in a hat would fall when thrown on the floor. Given Patsy Houlihan's incredible facility for coin tricks and games, as well as his prowess as a snooker hustler, it's an incredibly apt piece of etymology. Peasants playing 'hustle cap' are depicted in Flemish art of the 17th century and there is clear evidence that the game also became popular among the working class in the UK too; for example, newspaper *The Star* observed on 4 October 1813 that a group of 'disorderly persons' had been arrested and hauled before the magistrates for playing 'unlawful games' including 'hustle cap'.

Exactly when the term 'hustler' became associated with cue sports is unclear, but as well as its gambling origins it also seems to have been a term employed in the UK to signify speed, both on the green baize and in everyday life. Certainly, the epithet of 'hustler' was applied with this meaning to Charlie Simpson, a Sheffield cueman, club owner and promoter born in 1895 who was once described by Joe Davis as 'the fastest player I ever saw'. The *Sheffield Star Green 'Un* of 9 February 1935 wrote of Simpson, '[He] is Sheffield's champion billiards "hustler"! Seconds are extremely valuable to him, and many people watching him for the first time are amazed at the speed at which he plays. He's round the table waiting for the balls to stop rolling before you can say "Jack Robinson".' This usage appears to have endured over several decades; Houlihan himself was affixed with the adjective 'hustling' in a 1955 newspaper report that focused – awestruck – on the speed of his play in a match against Doug Melchior.

In North America, meanwhile, by the early 19th century, the term 'hustler' had acquired nefarious shades of meaning in keeping with the disreputable status of 'hustle cap', being used to refer to a thief, particularly one who roughed up their victims. Later it also metamorphosed into a term meaning to be energetic in work or business. By the mid-20th century it is likely it was in informal usage on both sides of the Atlantic with regards snooker, billiards or pool players who competed for money, often disguising the excellence of their play to lure their opponents into unwise wagers. However, it was Walter Tevis's 1959 novel *The Hustler* and its iconic 1961 film adaptation starring Paul Newman as 'Fast' Eddie Felson that firmly established the connection between cue sports and the term 'hustler' in the public imagination.

Four years before Tevis's novel hit bookshelves, Houlihan came to the realisation that if he was to make money from his uncanny facility to manipulate snooker balls with his cue, he would need to get creative. The imperative for him to earn was – he later admitted – a reaction to his marriage, in October 1955, to a local Deptford woman, Brenda Chapman. Faced with the demands and added expenses of married life, rather than living rent-free with his parents, Houlihan soon realised that his propensity to gamble his earnings from the docks on the horses or the greyhounds would not be conducive to a settled or happy marriage. 'I was a gambler – horses, dogs – and I'd done my money,' Houlihan later admitted. Gambling was an integral part of the culture of working-class Deptford, and the Houlihan family. In 1952, Patsy's father William had even been fined £15 by the police for 'loitering to bet' in New Cross Road (until the 1960 Betting and Gaming Act, 'off-course' gambling and betting was illegal in the UK).

Explaining why he took up serious hustling, Houlihan later said, '[After getting married] we had to have new this, new that, everything new. So I said [to my wife], "Don't worry, I've got to go away for a week." And the next day I was back indoors before she got up. I put the money on the bed and said, "Pay your debts, love.'"

Houlihan had to work hard to provide financial support for his soon expanding family. He and Brenda's first child, named Patrick after his father but known as Patsy Boy, was born in 1956. Further sons with Brenda were Daniel – aka Danny Boy – and Lee. After Patsy's relationship with Brenda came to an end he had his beloved and only daughter Patricia – aka Patsy Girl – with his new partner Julie Arnold, who he was with for 18 years. He also brought up Jean and Janet, Julie's children from a previous relationship, as though they were his own, in time also acting as grandfather to their children Julie, Victoria, Michael and Sam.

It was the desire to provide for family that led Houlihan to increase his efforts as a hustler. He had always made some money from snooker, but soon his earnings and the stakes he would gamble were in a new financial league. 'I first started at the age of 13,' he told Janet Street-Porter in an interview broadcast on *The London Weekend Show* in 1977. '[I] started in them days playing for a sixpence, then a shilling. And then, I thought it was easy money, started to improve me play and eventually was going all around the country, playing for hundreds eventually.'

Houlihan's routine was that of the classic hustler. 'What I used to do was walk in, go up to the counter and say, "Cup of tea, please, and I'll have a roll,"' he told Jean Rafferty. 'And then all I'd do was pull out a few quid, and all of a sudden you've got people coming up to you going, "All right mate? Fancy a game?" I'd say, "Nah," and I'd sit down and have my tea and then some fella would say, "Anybody else?" and I'd say, "Oh, all right, then." I'd let them win for not a lot of money and then they're thinking, "This is all right," and then I'd start coming back. Once a fella said to me, "Want two quid on it? I'll give you a 16-point start." I ended up getting £140 off him, which was a lot of money in those days. I went all around the country, Manchester, Leeds, down to the coast.'

If Burroughes Hall, with its veneer of sophistication, represented snooker's desire to project an image of public respectability, then it was the snooker halls on ordinary high streets or in more disreputable back alleys or otherwise anonymous industrial districts that represented the gritty reality of cue sports' working-class roots and deep connection to gambling.

In the 1950s, John Archer lived on Old Kent Road – not far from Houlihan's Deptford. Like many working-class Londoners of his generation, he frequented the snooker halls of the city throughout the mid-to-late 1950s. 'It was a colourful scene, full of colourful people,' reflected Archer, who worked as a runaround boy for a newspaper before being apprenticed to a printer. 'There were clubs all over London in the '50s. Snooker had really taken over from billiards by now. There was a snooker hall on the corner of Tottenham Court Road, backing on to the Astoria. It was downstairs and there was quite a large gallery where people used to watch or wait to play. There was always gambling going on.

'There was a club on Oxford Street where all sorts of money matches would go on. All the spectators would be betting. There'd be house players at certain clubs and there were a lot of very good amateurs in those days. They'd be able to earn a living from money matches. Joe Davis called the shots in the pros and he made a lot of money. Clubs like the ones in the West End were the other side of the coin – they were dominated by people scrapping for a living.'

In one such West End venue in the winter of 1954, Houlihan and another rising talent, Mark Wildman – later to become World Billiards Champion – faced off and exchanged a series of massive breaks, delighting the packed crowd as they reeled off shot after spectacular shot. Houlihan fired in a 136 (Wildman not even paying a visit to the table in this frame), as well as breaks of 91, 83, 65 and 56 while Wildman rattled off runs of 104, 97, 91, 89, 84, 64 and 57. 'That West End club,' Houlihan would recall fondly in later years with a rueful shake of his head. 'All the tearaways, all the lads came down there. The Krays even had a snooker club, a place down the east end … I played in there lots of times. You knew what they were and what they weren't. They didn't take any liberties as long as people just played snooker and paid for their tables.'

The reference to the Krays raises the issue of the darker side of the snooker hall scene which was – paradoxically – part of the reason for the game's transgressive glamour and appeal; the fact that some of the seedier elements of city life flocked to the darkened and largely private halls to plot activities involving various forms of criminal enterprise merely added to the colour. 'It was all a bit shady really,' Archer admitted. 'There were a lot of seedy activities going on in the clubs. All sorts of people on the fringes of criminality would show up. All sorts of plans would be made in the snooker halls – for robberies and what have you. People would show up if they needed a getaway driver or whatever. Something was always going on under the surface. But a lot of people were there just because they loved the game. Hardworking people. Regular people.'

Wielding his cue like a magic wand, Houlihan's reputation for conjuring supernatural snooker grew in this twilight world to mythic proportions via word of mouth, tales of his exploits spreading across the country. Harry Pearson was a local Deptford lad who frequented Lewisham Temperance Hall in the 1950s and witnessed Houlihan in action. 'He was just amazing,' Pearson recalled. 'Especially playing the mugs who thought they could beat him. The hall was a real den of iniquity. All the villains from Deptford and Lewisham would go there for a game or bet on people playing each other. Some people would spend all day there, doing deals and dreaming up schemes to make some money.'

Archer added, 'Everyone in the clubs knew who Patsy Houlihan was. He was a great player. He had quite the reputation. Everyone talked about him.' A man who knew Houlihan particularly well during this period was Mike Goodchild, a talented cueist who also built a strong reputation on the money-match circuit. 'Houlihan was the best snooker hall player, the best money player in England,' Goodchild argued. 'I knew him for 50 years, going back to the 1950s. The first time I met him was at the Richmond Temperance Hall. I can still remember it. The balls were much heavier then, of course. Patsy just walked up, potted a red at a hundred miles an hour, spread the pack all over the place and cleared the lot of them.

'He was the greatest potter I'd ever seen. Cliff Wilson was a great potter but I think Patsy used to pot better than Cliff. Patsy and I got on. He was a real nice fella. Easy-going and exceptionally talented. I really liked him and always enjoyed watching him play. His potting ability was absolutely unbelievable.'

Goodchild had a spell as resident player at the RAC Club on Pall Mall. Due to the strictures of the amateur game this meant he couldn't participate in official unpaid competitions. 'The only way to earn money was in the halls,' he explained. 'There were hundreds of people up and down the country playing for money, trying to make a living. Patsy was the best at playing for dough. Although we knew each other we didn't play – that would have been a case of us bashing our heads together.' Goodchild also provided an insight into the skills required to succeed as a hustler, pointing out, 'You have to be able to turn your form on like a tap and Patsy could do that.'

Houlihan himself once expanded on the importance to a hustler of disguising your own cuing stance and studying your opponent's stance; of how – in the words of Paul Newman's Eddie Felson in *The Color of Money* – 'You got to be a student of human moves.'

'It's your stance,' Houlihan asserted. 'You can stand different and people look at you and think "he's a right mug", or whatever the case may be. If you've got a chap who plays snooker and as he's going to the table, he's got his head right up … you can rest assured that he's not a good player. You can always tell.'

Disguising his formidable talent was a key component in Houlihan's ability to lure an opponent into a false sense of security before taking them for as much money as possible. 'If you're playing a man who's – how can I put it? – much worse than yourself, you play as much as you can to the way he's playing,' Houlihan explained. 'Then, if needs be that you've got to get down more, then you get down more. You disguise your play. And then if you have got to bring it up, then you've got to bring it up, because pound notes tell stories.'

Houlihan took his dedication to hustling to such heights that he would even practise missing shots in as convincing a manner as possible. Frank Gumbrell, a snooker coach who knew Houlihan in the 1980s, revealed, 'Patsy told me he used to practise wobbling balls, jawing them in the pocket, to draw the punters in.' Houlihan would also rarely play at the full capacity of his powers. 'He would never absolutely murder people,' Terry Dempsey said. 'He'd always keep it just close enough to keep people keen.'

Holding back your true form and ability was common on the hustling circuit. Charlie Poole, a money-match fixture in the 1970s who was known as 'Checkside Charlie', explained, 'It was all about gambling so people were reluctant to show how good they were a lot of the times. There was a lot of holding back of your best form.'

It was certainly an occupational hazard with hustling that the better you were at it, the more your face became known and therefore the harder it became to hustle. Soon that was the problem facing Houlihan. His son Patsy-Boy recalled, 'Once he went all the way up north and walked into a hall looking to hustle. Straight away someone recognised him and that was it – he had to come all the way back home again!' Houlihan himself recounted a similar experience of a trip to the Channel Islands, 'Once someone suggested going to Jersey but when I got there I was known. There wasn't nothing for me in Jersey … After a while they got to know you. It was just a matter of time. So then, they started putting the local champion on to you. When I got well known I just used to go in and ask for the best player.'

At other times, if his face had been spotted and the best local player wasn't available, Houlihan would improvise, finding innovative ways to establish wagers that would be sufficiently tempting for even those who knew how good a player he was to accept. Roy Bacon, a fine money player from Essex, faced off against Houlihan several times in the 1970s, and recalled, 'Patsy would beat most people easily, that's why he had to give handicaps – because everyone knew who Patsy Houlihan was! He was known for giving ridiculous handicaps – he might play a frame and only be allowed to pot the yellow and no other colours. Another thing he'd do is only be allowed to play with the very long cues. Sometimes when doing that he'd have to open a window down the side of the table to play certain shots as there wasn't space for the cue!'

John Butler added, 'Something Patsy used to do when he challenged people is say that they could play with a cue and he'd have to play with a broom handle. That's the truth.' Houlihan himself once outlined some of the lengths he would go to in luring opponents into his hustling web. 'I played left-handed and right-handed, one-handed, everything,' he said. 'I played a fella for money years ago with the bottom of my cue.'

Mere mortals stood no chance against Houlihan. A call-out made by the author via Facebook and other social media channels for memories of Houlihan elicited several responses during the research of this book. 'I played Patsy in the Regal Billiard and Snooker Club in Rye Lane, Peckham,' recalled Malcolm Dale. 'He gave me 60 [points] start and still beat me every game.' David Cook had a similar story to tell. 'I played Patsy at Peckham snooker hall back in the day. I broke off and he proceeded to pot every single ball apart from the pink and black.' Another who sent his memories of Patsy was Terry McCarthy who declared, 'Patsy was a gentleman. I met him many times [in the snooker club] above Burton's in Lewisham. He was a great player and a nice guy.'

William Garrett knew Houlihan, and his skills on the baize well, and lived to regret cockily taking him on one afternoon. 'My brief moment of glory was losing money to Patsy,' he chuckled. 'It was around 1954, so I would have been 22 years old. I lost £20 to him, which was a lot of money in those days.'

Losing the money put Garrett in a sour mood. 'I was with my cousin Mike, who I was sure had set me up to play Patsy. We came out of the hall below Burton's in Lewisham and there were no trams for me to get home. So we went to wait in the terminus caff. I was sitting there brooding over the fact I'd lost all this money to Houlihan. As I was sitting there someone came past and bashed me in the back. I was on a swivel chair, so I swung round and I was so angry having lost this money that I jobbed this bloke, really put him away. He was on the floor. Mike had to stop me taking it any further.

'Turned out the bloke I knocked to the floor was Marty Wilde [later a famous singer]. He was known back then as Smithy [Wilde's birth name was Reginald Leonard Smith]. He lived on Christchurch Street. Later I remember when he got married in the local church and I couldn't get through because of the women that had gathered. So I jobbed Marty Wilde because Houlihan took me for £20. And this is definitely true – I'm not giving you any old jazz here!'

In Bacon's estimation, 'Patsy was a hustler. A lovable rogue – that's how I thought of him. But he was totally trustworthy – there was no question he would pay you if you won.' If a game was on the level, Houlihan rarely lost. However, with so much cash in hand betting going on, not all matches in the behind closed doors snooker scene were on the level. Fixed matches and betting coups were commonplace and part of the accepted culture of the snooker hall. They were part of the hustle and the fun, and as such there was no moral judgement attached to them. After all, these weren't official sporting fixtures that established bookmakers were laying odds on, they were private matches within a subterranean world where the only rule was 'anything goes'.

'At times you never knew if Patsy was going to win or lose,' John Butler said. 'Patsy knew, but you never knew! I remember he said to me one day, "When I was younger I used to go up the West End and play a lot of snooker in a nightclub up there. One night I would have earned £20 if I won and £30 if I lost. So what was I going to do?"'

Dempsey added, 'With Patsy you always wondered if there was an ulterior motive to what he was doing or what he was saying, but that's what made him so brilliant. You might say to him, "Pats, are you going to beat that geezer you're playing?" He might say yes but you never knew whether it was true or not. He was slippery as an eel. It was impossible to get to the bottom of what he was doing. But that's why he lasted so long in that hustling world. That's what he had to do. And it worked because he'd win money off people like you wouldn't believe. If you played him you'd go home potless – guaranteed. He'd be losing, losing, losing, then suddenly he'd turn it on – bang, bang, bang! And if you wanted to play him you'd have to pay for the privilege. If he lost he'd pay up, but he knew that money would be coming back to him sooner or later. It was an impossibility to go home with his money. We saw it time and time again.'

Dempsey recalled a series of games that Houlihan had against a man named Joe Collier, 'Collier was a millionaire who had a scrap metal business. His father had left the business to him. Everyone would gamble on their games. The guy who took all the money in before the matches would have a fag in his mouth – if you were in the know, then you knew that when the fag was on the right side of his mouth Patsy would win, the left side then Joe would win. And when the fag was in the middle of his mouth he didn't know who was going to win. That's how they used to do it.'

Such was Houlihan's fearless confidence in his own abilities that he would take on anyone, anytime, any place, anywhere, and up the stakes as high as he could. Clive Everton, writing in *World Snooker* magazine in 1971, recalled a famous money match victory that Houlihan enjoyed:

'He was once challenged to a match by the then-current English Amateur champion. The conversation ran something like this:

'Pat, "How many frames do we play?"

'Challenger, "Eleven."

'Pat, "Where shall we play?"

'Challenger, "On my table."

'Pat, what shall we play for?"

'Challenger, "£200."

'Pat, "So you want to play 11 frames on your table for £200?"

'Challenger, "Yes."

'Pat, "I'll tell you what."

'Challenger, "What?"

'Pat, "Let's play for £300."

'Houlihan won the match.'

In a similar vein, Bill King, the father of snooker pro Mark King, recalls Houlihan becoming the first player to defeat formidable Romford cueist Norman Buck on his home table. 'Norman had never been beaten on his table,' King said. 'And then Houlihan played him and wiped the floor with him. He was a good player, Norman, but nothing like Houlihan.'

Many snooker aficionados and followers who saw Houlihan in action during the 1950s and '60s agree that he had all the tools required to have reached the very top of professional snooker. It's a conviction many of them in turn passed down to their children and grandchildren. Thus, although no extended film or video exists of Houlihan at the snooker table, the magic he wove on the baize has become a shared folk memory that still lingers in the collective consciousness of many south Londoners. 'My father Cyril "Nick"

Carter played against Patsy in Deptford and Lewisham,' reflected David Carter. 'He agreed he could have been world champion. He said he was a wonderful player.'

It's a conviction echoed by the ever-decreasing numbers of those still alive from the 1950s and '60s who saw Houlihan play during what were the peak years of his preternatural powers. The aforementioned Bill King, who has seen every leading snooker player in action during seven decades on and around the snooker circuit, is unequivocal in his assessment of Houlihan's greatness.

'He was one of the best snooker players I've ever seen, probably the greatest I've seen for all-round ability,' King said. 'He made everybody else look silly, honestly. Marcus Owen was a great player but he couldn't live with Houlihan at his best – Houlihan was too good. Steve Davis was a calculating player, a good tactician, but I don't think Davis would have beaten Houlihan at his best. One of the best potters I've seen is the kid now, Judd Trump. He's got to be one of the greatest I've ever seen at potting long balls. I think Trump is maybe the next best to Houlihan. Maybe Trump would beat Houlihan. Or [Stephen] Hendry. But Houlihan had it all and could play billiards an' all.

'I first saw Houlihan play back in the '50s. The shots he pulled off were unbelievable and that was on the old tables with tighter pockets and heavier balls. The pockets now are wider. They were squarer back then and there was more of the table in the pocket so it was hard to make big breaks, but that didn't seem to bother Houlihan.

'He's the only bloke I've ever seen who could put the black on the spot, the white in the D and guaranteed could screw the white back into the D. It was a joke! I've never seen anyone pot a ball like him. He was a very loveable character too and a great hustler. He had plenty of banter and all that. What a great player!'

Chapter 6

# 'An excess of daring'

PATSY HOULIHAN'S late-night hustling lifestyle, often rolling back home in the small hours after days on the road, migrating from one smoky snooker hall to another in search of a quick buck, was far from ideal preparation for the sort of tough matchplay snooker he faced at Burroughes Hall in the English Amateur Championship. For one, there was a world of difference between the erratic style of play required to succeed as a hustler, and the solid tactics that succeeded in the white heat of competitive matchplay.

In the lead-up to the 1955/56 championship. *The Billiard Player* pointed out that Houlihan's policy of uncompromising and incessant attacking snooker while playing in clubs and halls was poor preparation for the tactical rigours of tournament play, noting that he should scale back his commitment to 'matches that don't matter' (Houlihan might have disagreed with that sentiment, seeing as these matches paid his bills!). The journal also noted, correctly if somewhat po-facedly, 'The "all-out" style of play … eliminating as it does the tactical and defensive side of the game, engenders in brilliant break-makers like Houlihan and others, a lack of prudence which causes them to "come unstuck" in championship play against players much inferior who cannot match them in penetrative power.'

Despite the imperfect nature of his preparation, Houlihan entered the championship utterly determined to regain his status as London's top amateur, and banish memories of his shock first-round exit the previous winter. He also entered the tournament in fine break-building form – in the space of eight days from 31 October to 7 November he smashed in five centuries in various snooker halls, scoring 126, 109, 112, 103 and 105. This hot streak continued during his first three matches once the London section commenced in November, as he secured three successive 3-0 victories against R.C. Witt, A.H. Hunter and A.S. Foster to set up a semi-final meeting against Doug Melchior – his surprise conqueror of the previous season. On this occasion there was to be no upset. Truth be told, the match was even something of an anticlimax, Houlihan winning 4-1 while barely breaking sweat as the five frames took just 71 minutes to complete. 'Melchior is a good player, and by no means easy to dispose of – he played a really good game when he beat Houlihan last season,' *The Billiard Player* observed. 'In this game he [Melchior] was by no means out of the hunt up to frame four, but it was obvious that, barring accidents, Houlihan's class would tell.'

In the London final in the first week of December, Houlihan met Eric Stickler, a talented Southgate cueist who had reached the same stage the previous season, only to be denied the title by George Humphries. Earlier in the tournament Stickler had overcome a remarkable challenge from George Orrell, one of the more unusual players of the day. A one-armed newspaper vendor with a pitch – appropriately enough – just around the corner from Burroughes Hall, Orrell won his first two matches in the London section and was only edged out 3-2 by Stickler in a match which went to the final brown after a tough struggle of two hours and 25 minutes. 'Orrell labours under the handicap of an artificial arm,' explained *The Billiard Player*. 'In the majority of strokes he either forms his bridge by laying it on the table as support, or lets it hang down if a table bridge (support in his case) is not practicable.'

Having found the one arm of Orrell a challenge, it was little surprise that the doughty Stickler found the two arms of a confident and cocky Houlihan an insurmountable obstacle. The difference in the two men's stylistic approaches was aptly summarised by *The Billiard Player*, 'Stickler is an outstanding player … but he cannot be said ever to shape like one brimful of confidence, and the tempo of his play is not a quick one, so that, whereas a break by Houlihan flows like a rapid stream, one by Stickler takes time, and also due toll of the player's concentration, etc. Houlihan's quick-thinking spontaneity, rapid delivery and instinctive sensing of the positional possibilities, on the other hand, exact little in such respect.'

Stickler edged ahead in the first frame, but a swift Houlihan break of 29 saw him snatch it 67-41 before an excellent run of 53 by Stickler in the second tied things up at 1-1. However, Houlihan won the next two frames with runs of 33, 32, 32 and 33 to head into the interval 3-1 up. When the match reconvened in the evening Houlihan reeled off the two frames he needed to win with few alarms, a 'lovely break' of 41 clinching frame, match and a second London title. It was a measure of Houlihan's growing popularity and profile that the *Daily Mirror* – then enjoying a massive circulation of around 4.5 million – reported on the victory, albeit just with score details. *The Billiard Player* paid tribute to both cueists in its report, noting, 'On paper it looks like an easy win but Stickler played very well and up to frame four always threatened to be a menace. It is disconcerting, however, to meet such a player as Houlihan, who (like [Cliff] Wilson) rattles up a 30 or 40 break inside two minutes as soon as a real opening occurs.'

Houlihan's dominance of the London section had been total – 18 frames won against the loss of just two. Such form augured well for an assault on the 'championship proper'. 'Houlihan's play dominated the event,' reflected *The Billiard Player*. 'He played dazzling snooker, and of a type that surely can never have been surpassed in amateur or in professional play for sheer brilliance and dexterity … If all goes well, that is, unless he has an off-day, he will not be far off at the finish if not actually champion.'

Editor Richard Holt was transparent about what he saw as the dream final; namely, a showdown between Houlihan and the only other man on the circuit who could come close to matching him for speed around the table and natural fluency – Wales's Cliff Wilson. 'I certainly think a week's battle between the two would provide as exciting and spectacular a contest as was ever seen,' Holt noted. 'Maybe we will see these two magnetic protagonists in opposition this season. A final between them would indeed form a tasty dish.' If the duo were to meet, Holt felt that Houlihan would have the slight edge. 'Houlihan's play, in comparison to Wilson's, just merits a higher ranking, I think,' he explained, 'by virtue of its approximating more closely to what one might term classical snooker. There is precious little in it, I think, but a certain rash element in Wilson's make-up, which, against the best opponents tends perhaps to leave more openings to the opposition, tilts the scales, I think, in Houlihan's favour.'

Holt, however, also sounded a cautionary note concerning Houlihan's sometimes loose style, 'He is unsurpassed at the top end, and executes a black and red sequence with astonishing fluency and facility ... In his earlier games [in the London section] he certainly left a lot on after missing, but I have the impression that he had taken the measure of the opposition. Nevertheless, he must not do this against first-class players who do not chance their arm without a strong motive. In such frames I noted that out of 12 visits he left something on ten times and that partially accounted for his quick exit last year.'

Dennis Hushley of Cosham, Hampshire, was Houlihan's first-round opponent in the 'championship proper' on 28 February 1956 and the Deptford dynamo – in the words of the *Birmingham Daily Post* – had 'little difficulty' clinching a 5-2 win. Alan Barnett of Wolverhampton lay in wait in round two and was a tougher proposition; the Midlander would go on to reach the final of the English Amateur in 1959 and win it in 1961. However, Houlihan edged a tense, nip-and-tuck affair 5-4 to take his place in the quarter-finals against Jack Seffers, a public transport worker from Sheffield and no mean player. At the interval the duo were tied 2-2 but Houlihan pulled away 5-2 to advance to the last four.

Suddenly, the aesthete's dream final between Houlihan and Wilson – the two purest and most attacking players in the amateur sphere – was a real possibility. In the semi-finals the Welshman was due to face 1949 and 1953 champion Tommy Gordon while Houlihan was scheduled to square up to fast-rising Ray Reardon in the other half of the draw. A Reardon-Wilson final – you could argue – would have been almost as attractive a proposition as a Houlihan-Wilson duel given that both men hailed from Tredegar in Wales, where they had enjoyed a fierce rivalry, head-to-heads between the duo having been known to attract hundreds of spectators. Clive Everton would later describe these Reardon-Wilson showdowns as 'modern snooker's nearest equivalent to a bare-knuckle prize fight'.

In the event, however, neither 'dream final' came to pass. On 16 March, Wilson found the astute tactics and hardened matchplay of Gordon too much to handle, frequently gifting the heating engineer from London gilt-edged opportunities en route to losing 6-3. 'Santa Claus has nothing on him for generous gifts,' *The Billiard Player* observed archly of Wilson's tendency to profligacy. Houlihan was an interested spectator at the match; in the interval he even popped into a nearby snooker hall, knocking in a total clearance of 134 to the wide-eyed amazement of the punters in attendance.

Although the dream scenarios of a Wilson-Houlihan or Wilson-Reardon final had evaporated, a potential all-London showdown between the dashing Houlihan and the steady-as-you-like Gordon was still an attractive proposition, offering as it did a fascinating contrast in styles. First, though, Houlihan had to try and overcome Reardon – which was no easy task. The Welshman's genial exterior masked an iron will and he would in time become one of the most revered cuemen of them all.

Born in 1932 in Tredegar, a coal mining town in Monmouthshire, Reardon played billiards and then snooker from an early age at the local working men's club. Aged 14 he had forsaken the opportunity to go to grammar school in favour of following his father into the mines. In a concession to his snooker playing, however, he wore white gloves while working to protect his hands. 'I got my leg pulled quite a bit as a result of wearing those gloves,' he later admitted. By the time of his showdown with Houlihan, pit closures had forced Reardon – six times Welsh amateur champion already – to move to Stoke-on-Trent, where he found work initially in a local mine, before later moving into the police force.

Reardon approached his semi-final against Houlihan in fine form, having comprehensively thrashed Charlie Downey, an Irishman living in Welshpool, 5-1. The best-of-11 Reardon-Houlihan match on Saturday, 17 March 1956 – the first of two epic English Amateur Championship encounters between the men spread almost a decade apart – would enter amateur snooker folklore.

Reardon took the opener after Houlihan, on a break of 27, was unfortunate enough to snooker himself. However a wondrous Houlihan break of 50 in the second frame made 'at speed' followed by a run of 46 in frame three saw him surge 2-1 ahead before a 'foolish smash' in frame four gave Reardon the chance to dominate and level matters. In the fifth Houlihan took the initiative, snaring Reardon with a clever snooker, but with the frame at his mercy he made a crucial error, missing a green from an angle that 'he would get nine times out of ten'. Reardon pounced and took the frame 53-39 to lead 3-2 at the end of the afternoon session.

Houlihan drew first blood in the evening, winning the sixth frame 64-37. However, Reardon's precise safety play to baulk in frame seven enabled him to put together a run of small but crucial breaks to take the frame 96-14 and edge ahead. In the eighth, a fatal miscue by Reardon when well set enabled Houlihan to level at 4-4. With three frames still to play it was either man's match, but Houlihan's unwillingness to eschew a policy of all-out attack cost him dear. In the ninth he played a rash shot, dislodging a red from the cushion rather than cutting it and returning to baulk, handing Reardon the initiative. '[Houlihan] might still have taken the frame,' intoned *The Billiard Player*, 'but [he] tried to pot the last red slowly instead of snookering and that was that!' In the tenth frame Reardon took an early lead, only for Houlihan to cleverly manoeuvre him into giving away 16 points in penalties. With the colours, and seemingly the frame, at his mercy though, Houlihan fatefully missed his second pottable green of the match and Reardon edged through 6-4.

It was a dramatic match that left *The Billiard Player* drooling. '[Reardon] seems to possess everything,' the report concluded. 'He pots superbly, gets position with striking precision, and is a fine tactician, his astute returns to "baulk" invariably giving his opponent plenty to think about. Yet had Houlihan resisted his propensity to go for risky reds at a distance, and put more thought into his return strokes to the bottom area, I think he might have won … Reardon deserved victory because he never, like Houlihan, took unnecessary risks, and he gave nothing away. Nevertheless, at least, a 6-5 margin would have done Houlihan greater justice. A great game, and great snooker.'

Post-match, Reardon paid tribute to Houlihan's 'fine knowledge of the craft of the game' but the Welshman's sportsmanship was scant consolation to the Londoner. Reardon would go on to surprisingly lose the final 11-9 to Gordon having led 7-3 at the end of the first day, his hopes stymied after his cue tip broke off during morning practice and he had to play the next five frames with a borrowed cue. Reardon and Houlihan wouldn't cross paths again for nine long years, with the Welshman taking a breather from the championship for a few years to work on his game.

It wasn't in Houlihan's psychological make-up to pause for breath, either in life or at the snooker table, so after a philosophical shrug of the shoulders he dusted himself off, went back on the hustle and was back in the championship again the following season – 1956/57 – aiming for a third London title in four years. He began his campaign in sensational form against P. Garnett of Kensington. Although he dropped the first frame due to 'slapdash methods' – giving away 22 points in penalties – a break of 49 in the second frame and a wondrous 63 in frame four, which might well have provided the championship with its first century were it not for a narrowly missed red, saw him wrap up a 3-1 win. Ernest Ball of Haringey was repelled 3-0 in the next round (Houlihan notching a 67 break) and S. Hall of Fulham fell 3-1 in the quarter-finals. Stanley Walklett provided only fleeting resistance in the semi-final as Houlihan ran out a 4-1 winner.

For the second year in a row, Houlihan faced the luckless Eric Stickler in the London final, the match taking place on 5 December 1956. Unlike the previous year, Stickler provided a stern challenge. Houlihan won the opening two frames but the Southgate man hit back with three on the bounce to move 3-2 up with four to play. Once again, Houlihan's tendency to go for risky pots was proving his undoing, *The Billiard Player* noting, 'Houlihan … can run away with a frame, but his rare break-making capacity, which rests on brilliant, speedy potting, and remarkable cue ball control, coupled with audacity, often lead to danger.' The journal also argued that Houlihan was risking defeat by his self-declared attempts to better the tournament record break of 78 set by Jim Longden in 1950, a landmark that had thus far narrowly eluded him on several occasions, claiming, 'He is clearly bent on beating the break record, which can prove a will-o'-the-wisp, for break making, strictly speaking, must always be tempered by other considerations in serious snooker.'

Nevertheless, having thrown away a 2-0 lead, Houlihan steeled himself, winning a scrappy sixth frame to level at 3-3. 'Some very interesting strategic exchanges' characterised the seventh frame, which Houlihan took 61-40 to move within one of victory. A 'capital 45 break' in the next frame, including several 'pots the length of the table away', saw Houlihan strut imperiously over the finish line in frame eight, the 5-3 margin of victory securing his third London title in four years.

While expressing admiration for his breathtaking abilities, *The Billiard Player* also saw fit to once again fret about Houlihan's prospects against the 'deadly tacticians' gathering in the 'championship proper':

'In this section, he [Houlihan] has given many hostages to fortune, so to speak, and taken many risks. It may be that he was suiting his game and tactics to the opposition, but personally, I consider one should play the same type of game against any opposition, weak or strong. Taking undue liberties in some games promotes carelessness in others. The fact remains, however, that he has won the Section three times, and got into the semi-final of the Championship during his short championship career of three years and a bit.

'Now that he has reached the "best of nine" stage, provided he adopts consistently the right championship tactics, that is, does not put break-making before winning, in other words, seek to prolong the break when it is odds against the pot – an effective snooker then brings the dividends! – and provided he eliminates a certain carelessness born of his exceptional facility in potting, I think he has it in him to win the title. I would not suggest, for a moment, that he forsook his attacking policy but it must be tightened up by discretion.'

In his first match in the 'championship proper', Houlihan knuckled down, grinding out a tough win against doughty Alfred Burdett of Nottingham, a fluked pink helping him win 5-3 after trailing 3-2. It had taken all the self-control Houlihan could muster to play a more disciplined game, *The Billiard Player* noted, commenting, 'Houlihan, naturally, in keeping with his temperament, was always, so to speak, "straining at the leash" to get in, but Burdett saw to it that he didn't, and he had to perforce play the latter's tune.'

In the next round, against an even tougher opponent in Birmingham's Jack Fitzmaurice, Houlihan's adoption of a measured game was more successful. Although he trailed 3-2 once again, he produced crucial shots when it mattered, including two beautifully cut pots in frame six to level matters at 3-3, before winning the last two frames to progress to the quarter-finals. It was a performance that seemed to herald a new style of more restrained matchplay snooker on Houlihan's part, with *The Billiard Player* observing, 'For his win [Houlihan] must thank his timely success in tempering what in previous seasons has been an excess of daring and a want of discretion.'

However, in the last eight against the wily Home Counties champion Ronald Gross, Houlihan came unstuck, falling to a surprisingly wide 5-2 defeat. Gross would go on to win the title, defeating Stan Haslam in the final – the first of three English Amateur title successes he would enjoy between 1957 and 1962. One of many remarkable talents of the 1950s and '60s who eventually turned professional when past their best, Gross also overcame the severe handicap of a childhood accident which had hospitalised him for 11 months and required him to wear a metal brace to support his leg for the rest of his life.

Speaking after the final, Gross provided some insight into the tactical approach and self control needed to triumph in the English Amateur Championship – qualities that at this stage the ultra-attacking Houlihan seemed unable or unwilling to provide. 'I felt convinced that potting, however good, wouldn't win the title,' Gross reflected. 'I had to try and make myself a "killer", as a friend of mine who has seen most of my games, advised me, so I made myself into a "poker face" type and also did no talking in between but concentrated on the game as much when I wasn't at the table as when I was. In my game against Pat Houlihan, I tried to keep him from getting the chances he usually takes advantage of to make those brilliant breaks of his, and I think I succeeded.

'I had noticed some time ago that the winners of the Amateur Championship were nearly always the good tacticians, and not the great potters ... This made me decide to do likewise and concentrate on defensive tactics whenever I thought the balls did not favour trying to continue with the break. I saw no sense in making breaks and then giving my opponent a chance to hit back ... I waited for the breaks but didn't mind if they didn't come so long as I was building up a winning lead. Breaks to me came second.'

For now, at least, adopting greater caution and a more conservative approach was a lesson Houlihan refused to heed. To slow down, to turn down the risky pots that it gave him such a buzz to sink, would be to compromise the philosophy that defined his very existence.

Patsy Houlihan was determined to be his own man and to live life on his own terms.

## Chapter 7

# The doubters gather

THE HOULIHAN family supported Patsy's snooker career from the beginning. As he progressed to play at the top amateur level, they would huddle together around the radio on the nights that he was competing in the English Amateur Championship to listen to the scores being read out during the BBC sports bulletin.

The three Houlihan brothers were a close-knit trio. The eldest, Billy, was so proud of Patsy's achievements that he would polish the ever-growing collection of snooker silverware that adorned his parents' mantelpiece every Sunday.

Patsy's younger brother Terry, meanwhile, played a crucial role in securing that silverware. A handy cueist himself, Terry often played with Patsy in practice, patch over one eye, helping sharpen up his sibling's game for his big amateur matches. 'Terry was a very good snooker player,' was Paul Moriarty's assessment. 'He could have been a pro himself, seriously. He was a bit behind Patsy obviously but he was very good.'

Terry regularly played alongside Patsy in team competitions for Lewisham Temperance Hall. In 1956/57, the Lewisham team – including both Terry and Patsy – swept all before them in the popular Temperance Billiard Halls London Inter-Hall Snooker League, being crowned champions after picking up 13 wins out of 18 matches played. For good measure, Patsy also won the highest break award for the season after a superb run of exactly 100 – an incredible scoring feat in an age when centuries in competitive matches, amateur or pro, were rare.

On 24 April 1957, the annual league winners versus 'The Rest' match ended in another triumph for Lewisham as they emerged 12-6 victors against a team composed of the best players from the other nine teams in the league. Patsy gained a measure of revenge against Ron Gross, his conqueror in the English Amateur Championship, by edging him out 2-1 in the most eagerly anticipated of the six showdowns, while Terry won his match against G. Bruce 3-0. Mr A.M. Stalker, the manager of the Temperance Halls Company, was delighted with the showpiece event, noting that there was 'a large and appreciative audience, as it is seldom that so many local stars are on view at the same time'.

The following season, with Patsy promoted to team captain but Terry absent, Lewisham won the league title for a second year in succession. Patsy sat out the match against 'The Rest' on this occasion, but did face off against the great Australian snooker professional Horace Lindrum in a showpiece exhibition afterwards, besting the 1952 world champion 110-38 in the first frame but being edged out 72-58 in the second.

Frustratingly, however, Houlihan's quest to be crowned individual amateur champion was meeting with varied obstacles. In 1957/58 he was stymied by poor organisation after his entry form for the championship 'was received too late' to be accepted. 'We hope he will enter in good time for next season's event,' *The Billiard Player* sadly concluded. In Houlihan's absence Marcus Owen, another flamboyant talent, won both the London and English titles. Although Houlihan played Owen on numerous occasions in money matches, the duo – much like Houlihan and Cliff Wilson – were fated never to meet in the championship, but Houlihan did go on to face Marcus's brother Gary in a mighty showdown in 1964/65. Marcus and Patsy did frequently meet in money matches, however, with Patsy usually having the edge. 'There was one time when he and Marcus Owen both went up to Nottingham,' recalled Bill King. 'Owen started playing matches on one side of the county and Houlihan the other. They both cleaned up then met in the middle for a big money match.'

There were no entry form mix-ups for the 1958/59 championship and Houlihan celebrated his return by racing away with the London title for the fourth time in six years – an unprecedented period of dominance. On his way to the title, he notched victories against Alex Hyams (3-1), T. Wright (3-0, accumulating 309 points to just 22 by his opponent), Noel Miller Cheevers (3-2) and Ron Millard (4-1). In the 4 December final Houlihan met Irishman George Gibson, who had moved to London after sweeping all before him in amateur competitions in the Emerald Isle. Houlihan won 5-3, despite not being at his best. 'Houlihan's besetting sin was carelessness, or over-confidence, whichever you like to call it,' *The Billiard Player* noted. 'This landed him in plenty of trouble … He showed a lack of consistency, promising decisive progress and then missing unexpectedly.'

At 4-3 up, however, Houlihan's ever-present spirit of derring-do eventually proved decisive. 'Completely disregarding the fact that many venturesome pots at long range had failed to come off and landed him in difficulties, [Houlihan] went out for one which few players would have looked at and got it, a real beauty, and out of it he had a 30 break in his inimitably flowing style,' *The Billiard Player* explained. 'This enabled him to win the frame and the match. Erratic though he was at times, [Houlihan] was, on the whole, a worthy winner, if only for his periodic brilliance.' *The Billiard Player* also saw fit to praise the 'subtlety' of Houlihan's safety play, while dryly noting, 'Needless to say, Houlihan took to snookering only under compulsion!'

When it came to the 'championship proper', Houlihan played with even more cavalier abandon than usual in his first-round match, demolishing Burroughes Hall debutant Ken Newsham from Lancaster 5-0 with some 'whiz bang stuff', knocking off the first four frames in just over an hour. *The Billiard Player* editor Richard Holt, usually a staunch Houlihan advocate, was not impressed with this approach. 'Houlihan at his best is a stylist,' he wrote, 'and I have never seen a more naturally gifted player, but I think that even when an easy win is certain one should still, if a stylist, maintain one's style and this taking of pot-shots, so to speak, at terrific speed, presumably to make an effect, does not appeal to the connoisseur.'

In the next round, Houlihan surprisingly came unstuck, losing 5-4 to Alan Barnett of Wolverhampton in a rematch of their 1956 quarter-final struggle. Having trailed 4-2, Houlihan hauled himself back to 4-4, partly courtesy of a break of 53 which contained several brilliant pots, but he committed several fouls in the decider and was edged out.

It was a reverse that presaged a comparatively lean period for Houlihan in the championship. In 1959/60 he began the tournament at a canter, demolishing Noel Miller Cheevers 3-0, a victory which included a 59 break that *The Billiard Player* argued 'no player could have beaten … for brilliant potting and control, not to mention speed'. However, after beating Geoff Foulds (father of future top pro Neal) 4-1 in round two, Houlihan was toppled 4-3 in a tense semi-final of the London section by Mark Wildman, a match that saw spectators turned away from Soho Square such was the demand for seats.

Even worse was to follow in 1960/61, when Houlihan fell to a shock 3-0 first-round defeat against Ken Price. 'Houlihan gave many chances,' wrote *Billiards and Snooker* (*The Billiard Player* having been renamed in January 1961 to reflect snooker's continuing rise), 'but Price's display was well-nigh faultless.' In 1961/62, alongside Cliff Wilson and Marcus Owen, Houlihan didn't even enter the tournament. Exactly why is something of a mystery.

Houlihan was back in 1962/63, however, the same season that the tournament received a somewhat unnecessary and convoluted structural revamp. The competition was divided into northern and southern sections, with 32 entrants participating in each of these regional tournaments before the winners of each section faced off for the title. With 64 cueists now competing in the expanded 'championship proper', the various area titles, which previously players had needed to win to reach the final stages at Burroughes Hall, were somewhat devalued. This created several absurdities; for example, of London's 31 entrants, 11 were guaranteed a place in the southern section. Furthermore, of these 31, 13 were granted byes and therefore had to win only one match to qualify while the other 18 only needed to win two matches. Houlihan – who did not receive a bye (presumably a random draw decided who did and didn't) – duly qualified by beating Michael Lieberman and C.F. Key 3-0 apiece, barely getting out of first gear but still 'dispatching the balls in a way to marvel at' to take his place in the last 32 of the southern section.

Instantly, the sudden-death drama surrounding who would reach the championship by lifting the London title was removed, even more so as the remainder of the London section matches weren't scheduled until after the completion of a new combined London and Home Counties tournament, the presence of which added to the general sense of organisational overload. The results of this combined tournament, like the latter stages of the London Area championship, had no bearing on qualification for the championship. In the combined event, Houlihan beat Christopher Marks 3-1, the dangerous Geoff Thompson 3-0 and Bill Smith 4-0 to take his place in the final against Wildman, the London area winner of the past two seasons. A 'barnstorming affair' between 'two of the fastest and most dashing players in the country' was anticipated, but in the event it proved a slow-paced tactical encounter. A frustrated Houlihan never found top form, and suffered several 'in-offs' causing him to joke to the packed crowd, 'I'm playing billiards not snooker!' Wildman ran out a surprisingly easy 6-1 victor.

Houlihan determinedly made amends in the remaining matches for the London title, however, sweeping aside L.A. Poole (4-0), Ron Millard (4-1) and George Marioni (4-1) before duly clinching his fifth championship with a 6-3 victory against George Humphries – conqueror of holder Wildman – in the final. It was not a particularly memorable match, but Houlihan had clearly re-asserted himself as cock of the London snooker walk – no mean feat given the staggering level of competition at the time in the capital. 'Humphries played with a mixture of the "brilliant" and the "mediocre",' ran the unnamed referee's report. 'He was up against a "potting machine" which functioned periodically.'

In the newly formed southern section of the 'championship proper' a characteristically cavalier Houlihan beat A. Powell 4-1 and then Ronald Foxley 4-3, earning an admonishment from Richard Holt after the Foxley scare that he would need to 'tighten up' if he was to win the title. Sure enough, Geoff Thompson outfoxed the 'surprisingly erratic' Houlihan 4-1 in the next round and that was that for another year.

A few weeks later, Houlihan and Thompson met again, this time in aid of a good cause. Keith Jeffs, a promising young snooker player and member of the Alfred Herberts snooker club in Cross Road, Coventry, had tragically passed away aged just 21 of leukaemia, leaving a bereft widow and baby son. Rallying to the cause of raising money to help the struggling Jeffs family, Houlihan and Thompson joined forces with Ron Gross to take part in a three-man charity tournament which took place on Friday 5 April. It was a typical act of kindness on Houlihan's part – on the snooker table he was a steely competitor and ruthless hustler, but away from the table he had a sentimental and compassionate streak, particularly where families and children were concerned. The plight of the Jeffs family moved him and he was determined to do what he could to help.

The following season – 1963/64 – the pattern of the previous year recurred, with Houlihan sweeping all before him in the London championship, but again falling short in the 'championship proper'. In the London section, Houlihan defeated Ron Millard, A.M. Gantert, George Marioni and Ken Price comfortably enough (by scores of 4-0, 4-1, 4-1 and 4-1 respectively) but had a major scare in the semi-finals, trailing debutant Anthony Hodge of Streatham in the decider before conjuring a 'pukka Houlihan' break of 45 and thus averting disaster.

The London final was a high-quality affair, pitting Houlihan against Wildman for the title for the first time. Houlihan trailed 3-2 in the best of seven encounter, but a 'superb 44' in frame six levelled matters and he won the final frame by a comfortable 38-point margin. In the estimation of *Billiards and Snooker* it was 'an engrossing and … extraordinary game' in which 'cautious tactics were the order of the day … Houlihan, it seemed, was rather more ready to mix it then Wildman. [He] certainly surprised with his unfamiliar accent on defence. The match was a great attraction, not a seat vacant.'

After winning two successive deciders to lift an unprecedented sixth London title, Houlihan entered the southern section of the 'championship proper' on a high. However, after squeezing past Albert Ford 4-3 he then suffered one of the most devastating losses of his career, against the wily George Humphries. Houlihan ran into an early 3-1 lead and needed just one of the remaining three frames to secure an enticing last-16 showdown with reigning champion Gary Owen (older brother of the prodigiously talented Marcus).

However the wheels then fell off Houlihan's campaign in spectacular fashion. Firstly, Humphries took a tight fifth frame 62-48 to close the gap to 3-2. Then, in the sixth, Houlihan led by two points with just the black remaining and the white perfectly placed. 'All seemed over,' *Billiards and Snooker* admitted, before explaining what happened next, 'To the amazement of all [Houlihan] missed, and Humphries did the needful!'

Humphries duly took the seventh and final frame with ease against a shell-shocked Houlihan to progress to the last 16. It was, the journal argued, 'a great recovery [by Humphries] but hard lines for a player who has yet to win the title, his inclination to put scoring before timely tactics doubtless the explanation'. For a player of Houlihan's ability and class to miss a straightforward black was devastating; the sort of miss, in fact, that could have ended up defining and ruining his career in much the same way that Willie Thorne was forever haunted by a missed blue against Steve Davis in the 1985 UK Championship Final and Mike Hallett never shook off the trauma of a fluffed pink against Stephen Hendry in the 1991 Masters Final.

Certainly, many observers felt that this loss indicated that Houlihan – ten years on from his memorable competition debut – was now a busted flush, his tactical approach blunted by the constant showmanship of hustling. Significant question marks now hung over him: was he simply unable to consistently win at the highest level of amateur snooker, where tactics and caution invariably seemed to prevail? And what psychological damage had that missed black against Humphries wrought? Harold Phillips, the chairman of the sport's governing body the BA&CC, as well as a clerk at the Admiralty, seemed to high-handedly sum up the prevailing opinion, 'Houlihan will never succeed in winning the title.'

It was time for Patsy Houlihan to make fools of the doubters.

## Chapter 8

# Patsy's near-perfect year

PERFECTION IN sports performance is an illusion, as it is in any creative art form. It's an aesthetic ideal for which the most ambitious constantly strive, while subconsciously acknowledging the reality that such a utopia can never be definitively reached. Da Vinci's *Mona Lisa*, a Roger Federer forehand or a Mozart symphony are things of beauty, but for all their brilliance they could never be objectively classified as perfect. Statistically, it's a slightly different matter. A team or individual in any sport can, and indeed have in the past, performed certain feats of statistical perfection both on a small scale – whether it be a 147 break in snooker, or a nine-dart finish in darts – or on a broader canvas, such as the unbeaten league football seasons achieved by Preston North End in 1888/89 and Arsenal in 2003/04.

During a near one-year period from the summer of 1964 to April 1965, Patsy Houlihan produced such a feat of statistical perfection with one of the greatest runs of winning form in snooker history, winning 17 successive competitive matches to be crowned London, southern section and English Amateur champion, while also picking up the BA&CC ITV Trophy and the Muswell Hill Green Man title trophy too. '1965 was my best year,' Houlihan would happily recollect in later life. 'In '65 I won the lot. Five major tournaments in all.'

Houlihan's recollection is not quite accurate. True, he won five trophies, and at the end of the 1964/65 season he even extended his unbeaten run to 20 matches in the next tournament he played, winning three times in the Finsbury Park Conservative Club invitational tournament before he was toppled by Ron Gross in the final.

Despite the Gross blemish, Houlihan's winning run was – by any metric – a formidable achievement, coming as it did during a period when amateur snooker was probably in its strongest ever state. Among the remarkably high quality opponents he faced and defeated in these 20 matches were a veritable who's who of the amateur game from the 1950s and '60s, including future six-time world professional champion Ray Reardon, future three-time champ John Spencer (who Houlihan beat twice during the season), former English and reigning world amateur champion Gary Owen, former three-time English Amateur champion Gross, former champion Geoff Thompson and former runners-up George Humphries and John Price. Houlihan's unbeaten run deserves to be regarded as one of the greatest winning streaks in snooker history, alongside other such notable feats as Joe Davis's perfect 100 per cent record in his 34 world professional snooker championship matches, Ronnie O'Sullivan's 38 consecutive victories in ranking event qualifiers in 1992/93 and Stephen Hendry's 36 consecutive wins in ranking events during 1990 and into 1991.

Houlihan's assault on snooker immortality began in the summer of 1964, when he defeated Ron Gross in the quarter-finals and then Ken Price in the semi-finals of the Muswell Hill Green Man tournament. On 17 July he lifted the title by edging out Mark Wildman 4-3 in the final. After a break in competitive action for the rest of the summer and early autumn, Houlihan returned to action in November, racing through the London section of the English Amateur Championship, which he won for an unprecedented seventh time. After receiving a bye in round one, he demolished W.H. Bedworth and George Marioni 4-0 apiece in rounds two and three and then repelled R. Pacitti 4-2 in the quarter-finals, thus notching his 50th career victory in the tournament.

Lying in wait in the semi-finals was the 1954 champion Geoff Thompson. It was to prove a classic encounter, with Houlihan prevailing 4-3 after what journalist Richard Holt called 'one of the finest [matches] I have ever seen'. Houlihan lost the first two frames before snatching the third 'out of the fire' and also taking the fourth to draw level at 2-2. Thompson hit back to lead 3-2 only for Houlihan to again fight back to 3-3. In the decider Thompson took an early lead, but ultimately blinked first, an unexpected miss giving Houlihan a chance to fight his way back and seal the match on the final black. 'The quality of the snooker was superb,' Holt reflected in *Billiards and Snooker*.

'Thompson's positional play and Houlihan's colourful potting in particular taking the eye. Neither player displayed the least lapse from his best, Thompson showing the form which makes him a leading amateur exponent of the professional style and Houlihan introducing into his play an element of control and discipline that I for one had not seen him exhibit before, or, at least, but rarely if at all … I would like to emphasise the skill and sparkle of the play and the fine sportsmanship shown by both.'

Another dangerman in the form of 1953 English Amateur finalist George Humphries opposed Houlihan in the final. Humphries, of course, had knocked Patsy out of the championship's southern section the previous season. There was no repeat, however, as a rampant and imperious Houlihan slaughtered him 4-0 to clinch his seventh London title in ten entries spread over 12 seasons – a staggering return given the high standard of players in the capital at the time.

As well as the 'championship proper' to look forward to, there was the added bonus for Houlihan and seven of his fellow amateurs of participation in one of snooker's earliest television tournaments, the ITV Trophy. Televised in black and white by the commercial broadcasters on Saturday afternoons, the trophy had first been contested in 1962/63 as a pro-am invitational. By virtue of having not reached the semi-finals of the English Amateur Championship that season Houlihan did not receive an invitation, but the four amateurs who did (Ron Gross, John Price, Geoff Thompson and Jonathan Barron) all defeated their professional opponents (Fred Davis, Jackie Rea, Rex Williams and Kingsley Kennerley) with various degrees of ease. The pros had conceded starts ranging from seven to 21 points but it was still a humiliating outcome which offered further evidence that amateur snooker at the time was far more competitive and, arguably, of an equal, if not superior, standard to the stale professional game.

For the 1964/65 staging of the ITV Trophy the pros were dropped and Houlihan received an invite, as did John Spencer, Dennis Robertson, Mario Berni, Maurice Chapman, Mark Wildman, Eric Stickler and Ron Gross. Spencer, who hailed from Radcliffe, Greater Manchester, had caused a sensation the previous season by reaching the English Amateur Championship final at his first attempt, before losing 11-8 to Ray Reardon. A talented long potter with a powerful cue action, as well as a solid tactician, Spencer was drawn against Houlihan in the first round and their rivalry would end up dominating and defining the season.

The Spencer-Houlihan TV tussle – the first television appearance for both men – was a best-of-seven encounter at the National Liberal Club in London and took place on 5 December 1964. Spencer won the first frame but Houlihan edged a close second and also snatched the third and fourth, the former courtesy of a fluent run of 44. Spencer hit back spectacularly in frame five, breaks of 39 and 60 securing a comprehensive 122-6 victory, but Houlihan's steady nerves and a break of 38 saw him over the line 4-2. 'Excellent snooker' was the verdict of referee Ken Blackwell. 'This match could be replayed tomorrow with a different result.'

Houlihan's son Patsy Boy later recalled watching the match – and the others in the tournament – on television. The tension he felt watching his father in action was acute. 'We watched them all,' he said. 'It was always very tense but also I remember how excited I was. It was a big thing in those days to be on the TV, because snooker hardly ever was. And no one we knew was ever on TV, except the Royal family!' Sadly, despite the fact all the matches in the tournament were screened live on ITV, none of the footage has survived in the network's archive.

While Houlihan awaited his ITV Trophy semi-final, he began his English Amateur southern section campaign on 21 January 1965, being given a significant scare by Stan Bate and only emerging a 4-3 winner after a tough battle. However, in the last 16 a week later he hit his stride, demolishing John Bawden 4-0 in just an hour and ten minutes. 'All Houlihan, with dazzling spells of potting,' read the referee's report card.

It was just as well that Houlihan had found his best form, for lying in wait in the quarter-finals was Gary Owen, the reigning world amateur champion as well as the 1963 English Amateur champion. There was a case to be made that Owen was the best player in the world at the time. After all, the world professional championship had only been revived in April 1964 after a seven-year hiatus with a challenge match between John Pulman and Fred Davis. The duo's rustiness and lack of match sharpness was striking and, truth be told, somewhat embarrassing in comparison to the ultra-competitive amateur scene at the time. Owen had also roared into the quarter-finals in dazzling form, thrashing Chris Ross 4-0, and thus entered his 1 February showdown with Houlihan as the hot favourite.

It proved a tense encounter played amid a packed crowd teeming with atmosphere. Owen won the opener before Houlihan reeled off the next two frames. Owen levelled at 2-2 and the next two frames were extremely tight, Houlihan snatching both on the black, thus definitively banishing the demons of his miss against Humphries the previous year, to round off a memorable 4-2 victory. 'An extremely good and close match,' was the verdict of referee Blackwell in his report card, while *Billiards and Snooker* assessed, 'Owen played with all his admirable finesse and all-round virtuosity. Houlihan's newly found discipline much in evidence. The level character of the play is shown by the aggregates: Houlihan 316; Owen 320. The rivalry was too keen for big breaks though all those made were models of top-class snooker. Houlihan's invulnerability to nerves served him well and all told it was a match of great equals.'

In the semi-finals of the southern section, Houlihan faced John Price, an experienced and hardened competitor who had finished runner-up to Ron Gross in the 1960 championship. Hailing from the Welsh town of Tredegar – the snooker hotbed that had also bred Cliff Wilson and Ray Reardon – Price was no pushover. Houlihan was never behind, however, as he wrapped up a 5-3 win. 'Houlihan had no easy passage,' reflected *Billiards and Snooker*. 'Price's potting was always a menace ... Houlihan, although he led 3-1 and, later, 4-2, could never afford to ease up and take liberties ... In the end Houlihan's greater consistency and flair for the odds-against pot won the battle.'

In the southern area final on Friday, 5 February, Houlihan faced the toughest of all possible foes, reigning champion Ray Reardon, in a rematch of their memorable 1956 encounter, which the Welshman had won 6-4. In later years, whenever he spoke of the match and his career, Houlihan would always maintain it was the toughest challenge he ever faced. 'You know my hardest match? It was against Ray Reardon,' he told Jean Rafferty in 1982.

Previewing the match, *Billiards and Snooker* put matters into context with perfect and eloquent concision,

'Reardon, at his best, has no superior when it comes to artistry and the beautifully graded delicacy of his touch and strength, the pinpoint certitude of his potting and the intuitive choice of stroke are such as to enthral the connoisseurs of the game. Pat Houlihan, in his turn, possesses rare gifts, the most outstanding perhaps being his deadly potting irrespective of distance, angle or position. I think, however, his daring and optimistic temperament has always led him to take unjustifiable risks in big games with the result that players, well inferior, have profits by his leaves which often negate his own breaks. Notwithstanding, he has made his mark in the game and earned a well-deserved reputation as a master of potting and attacking play which is so colourful that no player excels him as a crowd-drawer. In a word, he's unique!'

In the early stages, Houlihan looked nervous and out of sorts while Reardon was relaxed. 'It seemed as though a gulf in class separated the players,' reflected *Billiards and Snooker* of the opening frame, which Reardon won 59-24. Houlihan took the second and raced into a 44-0 lead in the third, but Reardon rallied with a 'superb 53 break, made in that deceptively easy-going style that seems to denote complete confidence', and after two fouls by Houlihan the Welshman sunk blue and pink to move 2-1 ahead. The final two frames of the afternoon session were tight, but Reardon took them both, to go into the evening with a commanding 4-1 advantage.

'The outcome now appeared black for Houlihan,' surmised *Billiards and Snooker*. Even more so when Reardon clinched the first frame of the evening to move into a 5-1 advantage, needing just one of the remaining five frames to prevail. For a player of Reardon's class and experience to lose from such a dominant position seemed unthinkable. Sure enough, the Welshman struck first in frame seven, a run of 25 moving him closer to the finish line and appearing to hammer 'the final nail in Houlihan's coffin'.

However, at the moment he needed it most, Houlihan found inspiration, conjuring a magnificent break of 67, the highest in the championship that season. It was made under the utmost pressure and characterised by 'inimitable speed and bull's eye precision'. The dumbfounded Burroughes Hall crowd responded with 'resounding applause' but the feeling remained that although Houlihan 'had saved something from the wreck', Reardon 'would not be long in delivering the knockout blow'.

Somehow, however, defying all logic, Houlihan continued to reel Reardon in. He cut the deficit to 5-3 with a 68-35 victory in frame eight and the change in atmosphere among the capacity crowd was marked. 'It was now that one began to scent the possibility of a "miracle",' Richard Holt claimed, 'though immediately reality seemed to step in, for two conclusions obtruded themselves: one, could Houlihan possibly keep it up? And was it credible that Reardon could lose the remaining three frames which would make it five off the reel?'

The ninth frame was a lengthy, tense, tactical affair. Houlihan snared Reardon in several canny snookers, but the Welshman escaped each time without forfeiture of points or a calamitous positional outcome. There were no significant breaks but Houlihan edged the frame 63-43 to send his voluble supporters into a paroxysm of excitement. From 5-1 down the deficit was now just one frame and suddenly the usually ice-cool Reardon looked uncertain. He barely seemed able to pot a ball and also produced three nervy and unaccountable misses in frame ten, which Houlihan ran away with, 69-23.

An expectant hush fell over the crowd as the 11th and decisive frame began. All the momentum was now with Houlihan, but Reardon, such a hardy matchplayer, could surely not be discounted. Houlihan struck first with a 38 but then fouled. End of break. Reardon hit back and with just the colours remaining he had edged into the lead. When he then snaffled the yellow and green, all that stood between the Welshman and the final was a straightforward brown on its spot, at which point Houlihan benefited from the good fortune that his career – before and after – often lacked. Reardon elected to play the pot slowly, trying to bring the cue ball off the side cushion to roll into position on the blue. But he hit it too softly, and the brown drifted across the nap of the cloth, ending up in the jaws of the pocket but not dropping. In later years the memory of the miss would still haunt Reardon, and on more than one occasion he would refer to it as the one shot from his career that he would like the opportunity to play again.

Houlihan showed no such nerves. He took the brown, followed by blue and pink as well to trail 58-61, but, infuriatingly, ran out of position on the final and now decisive black. A safety exchange ensued until, finally, Reardon left a ghost of a chance, the black lingering around three feet from the top right-hand pocket while the cue ball was close to baulk. 'A 50-50 chance,' assessed Holt. Houlihan – ever the gambler – backed himself and took on the pot rather than playing safe. Everyone in the crowd knew he would. Insouciant, cocky almost, Houlihan strode to the table and – in the words of his great advocate Holt, who had marked him out as a future champion over a decade earlier – 'a grand shot ended this Homeric struggle'.

The genteel Burroughes Hall, with its Georgian, Edwardian and Victorian trappings, had never seen anything like it. Houlihan's army of south-east London supporters clambered joyfully out of their seats, rushing past the referee and a still shell-shocked Reardon in order to mob their man. It was only after several minutes of 'hefty thumpings and huggings' that Houlihan finally emerged from the scrum of spectators, a little dazed, his usually immaculately combed hair slightly ruffled, but his face exultant and wide-eyed with the delight of having reached the final of the championship that for so long it seemed would elude him.

Reardon, to his credit, found time for a characteristically witty quip. 'As we shook hands, Ray said I ought to be locked up,' Houlihan later recalled. 'As he was a policeman then, I thought that was rather good.'

## Chapter 9

# Slaughter at the Circus

SINCE OPENING in 1894, in response to the insatiable growth in the Victorian public's appetite for leisure and tourism, the Blackpool Tower Circus has been a magnet for those seeking extravagant entertainment. The oldest permanent circus facility in the world, the legendary 110ft by 110ft arena, which rests between the four giant legs at the base of the 518ft 9in tall steel and cast-iron Blackpool Tower, has played host to acrobats and clowns, trapeze artists and ringmasters, wild animals and knife throwers. It has witnessed laughter, tears, thrills, spills and even tragic deaths.

But in March 1965, it was a magician wielding a snooker cue who was the main attraction at the Tower Circus.

Patsy Houlihan was 35 years old as he waited off-stage just before 3pm on the afternoon of Thursday, 18 March for the first session of his English Amateur Championship final against John Spencer. As he strode out in front of a packed house of 1,750 spectators, Houlihan had no idea that what would unfold over the next two days would represent the peak of his sporting career for, frustratingly, what came after Blackpool for Houlihan would – predominantly – be anti-climax.

But at this moment in time none of that mattered, because it was all in the future and Houlihan was a man who lived defiantly for the moment, for the thrill of whatever game or gamble he was engaged in today, rather than what might unfold or unfurl tomorrow. Houlihan's engagement in the present moment, on the 22 balls on the pristine green baize in the centre of the arena, was absolute and he began the match with a sublime stroke, snookering Spencer with a perfectly weighted break-off shot that returned the white to the comforting safety of baulk.

The symbolism was apt – Houlihan was in Blackpool not just to win, but to dominate.

\* \* \*

The Houlihan-Spencer duel was eagerly awaited and widely reported in the British media. The *Daily Mirror*, for example, previewed the match in Mike Grade's popular 'Sportslight' column. 'QUESTION,' Grade wrote. 'What will a London barrow boy and a Bolton costing clerk be doing for the next two days in the ring of the Blackpool Tower circus? ANSWER: Playing snooker! John Spencer, the clerk, and Pat Houlihan, who sells fruit in Deptford market, are the finalists in the English Amateur Championship.' Truth be told, Houlihan rarely sold fruit in the market, but it made for a good media angle. Grade then quoted BA&CC chairman Harold Phillips's declaration, 'They are both great players.'

*Billiards and Snooker* also gave extensive coverage to the match, as you would expect. Editor Richard Holt, who had long championed Houlihan's merits, was clearly delighted to see the Deptford wonder in the final, writing,

'Houlihan must be very much on top of the world at the moment. At the Tower, he will "enter the ring" with a grand chance of winning the title for the first time after some years of trying. His two victories over the world champion, Gary Owen, by four frames to two, and Ray Reardon, the 1964 title holder, by six to five, after being 5-1 down, appear to confirm the impression that we had formed this season, which is that he is paying serious attention to the strategic side of the game, that is, he has realised that all-out attack in championship play cannot succeed when it comes to meeting top players who employ discretion in tactics and who batten on gratuitous leaves, such as Houlihan has often left in previous seasons as a result of his proneness to misplaced audacity. This season he has shown that he can vie with anyone in tactical play ... If he rounds off his capture of the southern title, which honour he cannot, of course, be robbed of, by winning at

Blackpool we think every lover of the game will consider the feat an outstanding illustration of the proof of the old adage try, try, try again.'

Houlihan-Spencer was not the first snooker match of significance to be held at the Tower Circus; Fred Davis and Walter Donaldson had met there in the World Championship finals of 1950 and 1951 as well as in the world matchplay final in 1952, while Davis and John Pulman had clashed there for the world matchplay title in 1955 and 1956. Gary Owen and Ron Gross also duelled there in the 1963 English Amateur Championship Final, after the BA&CC had broken with tradition and moved the amateur showpiece away from its usual Burroughes Hall home (Reardon's triumph against Spencer in the following year's final was staged in the Central Hall, Birmingham).

Although Joe Davis never played a World Championship match at the Tower Circus, he rated it 'the finest venue for snooker in the world', perhaps because its impressive size dramatically distinguished it from the venues that usually hosted major snooker matches. When it first opened in the late 19th century, newspapers reported that its capacity was 5,000. By the 1960s, however, the greater regard that existed for public safety and comfort meant this had been reduced to 1,750 – still more than ten times the number that could fit into the Burroughes Hall match room. Although not as intimate as Burroughes, none of the seats in the Tower Circus – even those high in the gods – were more than 80ft from the action, creating something of a pressure cooker atmosphere for big-match snooker.

The best-of-21-frames Houlihan-Spencer match was scheduled for four sessions across Thursday, 18 and Friday, 19 March, with afternoon play commencing at 3pm and the evening frames from 7pm. 'Ringside seats' cost five shillings in the afternoon and seven shillings at night, while stalls seating was available at four and five shillings respectively. If you decided to sit high up in the balcony then admission was just one shilling in the afternoon and two shillings in the evening. The organisers stressed there was an 'uninterrupted view from any seat', and once the Tower Circus was full or close to capacity, as it was for the entirety of the Houlihan-Spencer match, it was an electrifying venue. 'The atmosphere was terrific,' Houlihan would later recall. 'It was like going out to a bullfight.'

The trappings of the venue for the Houlihan-Spencer match were also steeped in symbolic totems from snooker history. The board used to display the scores throughout the match, for example, was the same one that had been used at Thurston's Hall in London's Leicester Square in 'the old days'. Thurston's had been a major snooker venue between 1901 and 16 October 1940, when it was destroyed during the Blitz by a German parachute bomb. Rebuilt and reopened as Leicester Square Hall in October 1947, the original Thurston's scoreboard was later bought by Blackpool businessman Bill Cartmell, owner of a billiards works in the town, a prominent Freemason and later the chairman of Blackpool FC. Cartmell also supplied and erected the snooker table used for the Houlihan-Spencer final, which was the same one used for the World Championship and World Matchplay finals previously hosted in the Tower Circus.

By virtue of his greater competitive experience over a longer period of time, Houlihan was slight favourite to prevail. Spencer, however, was also a formidable cueist. Almost six years younger than Houlihan, he had been born in Radcliffe, Greater Manchester, in 1935. He first picked up a snooker cue aged 15 and soon made his first century. However, after turning 18, Spencer lost interest in the game and stopped playing for ten years. He only returned by chance in 1963 and immediately made a huge impact, reaching the final of the 1964 English Amateur Championship – the very first time he had entered the competition – although he was beaten 11-8 by Reardon. 'From complete obscurity, he has hit the headlines in astonishing fashion,' remarked one admiring reader's letter in *Billiards and Snooker*.

So unaccustomed was Spencer to the spotlight that when he was asked by the magazine to supply a photo he sent them one of him stood with his brother and mother on holiday wearing only a pair of dark swimming trunks. Comically, the holiday snap duly ended up on the front cover of the May 1964 edition of the magazine, alongside a more conventional shot of Reardon smiling with the English Amateur trophy. Spencer may have been naive about dealing with the media, but on the table he played with a maturity that belied his relative inexperience. A formidable tactician and an accomplished break builder, he possessed an unusually long backswing, and was a powerful striker of the ball. He was also one of the few players who could almost match Houlihan for deep screw shots from distance.

Spencer's home of Radcliffe was only 42 miles south-east from Blackpool, so he was very much the hometown favourite. A young John Virgo was among those in the audience cheering on his fellow Lancastrian. An unknown 19-year-old amateur at the time, Virgo would later recall, 'The only things I knew about Houlihan, I'd read from reports in the snooker magazines. He had a number of backers with him from London who clearly fancied his chances.' Not only had many of Houlihan's Deptford-based devotees made the journey north to cheer on their man but, as Virgo suggests, many of them staked a lot of cash on him to win. Houlihan also placed myriad side bets on himself to triumph – it might have been an amateur match, but the opportunity to clean up and snaffle some cold, hard cash as well as the English Amateur trophy was too tempting to pass up.

Houlihan's performance in the final would, unexpectedly, prove to be a masterclass of controlled, tactical snooker. Although he would take on many outrageous pots at the beginning of a break, once he had accumulated enough points to forge a lead in a frame he would run safe, rather than risk leaving Spencer an inviting opportunity to make a large break himself. It was a pragmatic performance, and one that proved Houlihan had many more facets to his game than he is usually given credit for. The highest break Houlihan made in the final was 39, which seems ridiculously low by modern standards. However it is worth emphasising how different playing conditions were in the 1960s compared to today. Pockets in those days were no smaller, but they were far less generously cut than in the modern game, so balls had to travel further into the pocket if they were to drop, thus rendering, for example, pots along the cushion far more difficult. The crystalate balls used as standard in the 1960s were also far heavier than the balls used today and the cloths much slower. As a consequence, the cue ball was much more difficult to manoeuvre around the table and it was almost impossible to widely split the whole pack of reds in order to build big breaks. Instead, players would have to nibble away at the pack gradually, dislodging reds in ones and twos rather than as a collective mass.

This led to a prevailing culture of tactical restraint and a bigger focus on safety play than today. Houlihan frequently attempted to challenge this orthodoxy and with heavier balls was capable of shots that few others could perform. Roy Bacon, for example, said, 'I remember chatting to Patsy in a club in the 1970s where there were one or two up-and-comers about, and he said to me, "The trouble is now with these new balls, is that all these players can now play the shots that only one or two of us used to be able to play." With the old balls, you see, from the baulk line Patsy could screw back off the black to the baulk cushion without touching a cushion. That's a shot that some players with new balls could probably do today, but they'd have no chance with the old balls.'

By 1965, Houlihan had come to the realisation that if he was to secure the English title some form of compromise from his usual all-out attacking style would be necessary. His new approach was not only clear from the opening shot of the final – which snookered Spencer straight from the break – but also from the more measured approach he took throughout the match. It was also, perhaps, an approach partly formed by the shape of the action in the first frame. After Spencer left an opening in the early exchanges, Houlihan secured a beautifully constructed break of 39, the run only ending when he unfortunately and inadvertently potted a red while potting a black that would have taken him to the verge of a half century. In looking to extend his break, rather than consolidate his position with a safety, Houlihan had made a potentially costly error. It was not a mistake he would repeat. Fortunately, Spencer did not take advantage and in the rest of the frame Houlihan denied him any clear-cut chances to retaliate, ultimately taking the frame 74-43.

In the second frame, Houlihan's new-found caution was evident as he secured runs of 25 and 24 before tying Spencer up each time when the break had run its natural course and easing to an 80-20 win. Frame three proved the longest and most unusual frame in the match, a stalemate situation emerging which ultimately required a re-rack. At the time this was a sufficiently unusual occurrence to find its way into *The Times* under the headline 'Snooker Frame Abandoned'. 'There was a remarkable incident during the first period yesterday,' the newspaper reported. 'With Houlihan leading Spencer 2-0, the third frame had to be abandoned and the balls set up again. Spencer was in front 25-14 when the black was left on the brink of a pocket with the remaining 11 reds massed in front of it. For 25 minutes the players brushed the pack, which eventually became immovable. The players consulted the referee who decided that the deadlock could only be ended by starting the frame again.' The *Newcastle Journal* claimed the incident was 'unprecedented in the history of the competition'.

Spencer struck first in the re-racked frame, notching a useful break of 23 before snookering Houlihan, but a run of 36 edged Patsy ahead and by the time only the colours remained, Spencer was too far adrift to come back. Houlihan took the frame 76-40 and now led 3-0. He also took the fourth frame courtesy of a break of 23, at the end of which he wisely snookered Spencer behind the yellow rather than taking on a risky red. With three reds left, Houlihan led 40-27 before clearing them all with blacks and taking the yellow, green and brown to boot for a break of 33 and a 4-0 lead. With just one frame of the first session remaining Spencer was already in deep trouble. *Billiards and Snooker* noted that thus far he had 'never really seemed at ease' in the face of Houlihan's mixture of assured potting and watertight safety. Spencer did rally, however, taking frame five 80-8 thanks to 'consistent and assured potting combined with judicious defensive strokes'. Houlihan thus ended the opening session 4-1 ahead.

The early exchanges in the evening were tight and characterised by caution from both men. Spencer won two of the first three frames as the score inched to 5-3 in Houlihan's favour. However, showing the same instinct for picking his pots but then running safe when necessary which had served him so well in the afternoon, Houlihan made neat runs of 28 and 26 to take the ninth and move 6-3 ahead, with just one frame remaining on day one.

Houlihan's countenance now assumed an increasingly steely demeanour as he ruthlessly pressed his advantage. Frame ten was tight and tense. With just five colours remaining, Spencer led 47-39 and, seeking to protect this slender but potentially decisive advantage, he snookered Houlihan on the green. However, Patsy escaped brilliantly and then snaffled the green himself with a brilliant long-range pot. He then sunk the brown, blue and pink and stole the frame 57-47.

It was a demoralising end to the opening day for Spencer but far worse was to follow on day two. In the first frame of the afternoon, Spencer played safe behind the black after a break of 19, only for Houlihan to smash in a red that few would have dared take on and construct a break of 25. By the time there were just four colours left, Spencer had the advantage 52-42 but Houlihan snared the brown and tightened the noose around his opponent's neck by trapping Spencer in a fiendish snooker on the blue. The Lancashire man couldn't make contact and Houlihan rattled in a fantastic pot, adding the crucial pink as well to take the frame 62-52 and extend his lead to 8-3.

In frame 12 Spencer missed an easy brown when he looked set for a decent break and Houlihan proceeded to toy with him in almost sadistic fashion, knocking in rapid runs of 24, 23 and 22. On each occasion he conjured magical pots 'out of thin air' and then, once he had secured a useful tally, he turned down further risky pots in favour of playing safe and increasing the pressure on his embattled foe by moving 76-7 ahead with just one red remaining. Although he could no longer win the frame a shell-shocked Spencer played on in an effort to pot a few balls and rebuild his shattered confidence. Finally, though, he bowed to the inevitable, conceding the frame 76-35 and falling 9-3 behind. 'On this form Houlihan was unbeatable,' assessed Harold Phillips, the BA&CC chairman who had previously declared that Deptford man would never win the title. 'His mastery of every facet of the game was made manifest. It was Houlihan all the way, he made snooker look so easy.'

In a tight frame 13, however, Houlihan – for the first time in the match – displayed some nerves. With just the black remaining Spencer led 42-40 and Houlihan missed four chances to pot it and clinch the frame, albeit from positions which were 'far from easy'. Fortunately for Houlihan the white ran safe on each occasion. Then came perhaps the most memorable moment of the match as, with the sort of insouciant flair and showmanship that had endeared him to so many since his emergence just over a decade earlier, Houlihan played a 'cleanly executed' and superlative double, rocketing the black into the centre pocket. For a moment, his poker face cracked and he allowed himself a wry grin as the crowd exploded and stood to salute him.

Houlihan now only needed to win one of the two remaining frames in the afternoon to be crowned English Amateur champion with a whole six-frame evening session to spare. Barring an unprecedented collapse, the match was over. Spencer began the 14th frame with a spirited rally, making a 37 break but then – inexplicably – missed a black off its spot. Houlihan responded immediately with a run of 38 before pointedly running safe. With just the colours left, Houlihan led 48-38 and soon potted yellow, green, brown and blue to secure the frame and match by the absurdly one-sided score of 11-3. Spencer had barely had a sniff.

The relief for Houlihan was palpable. Eleven years after he had first entered the tournament in a blaze of break-making brilliance, snooker's most natural talent had finally won the amateur game's most coveted prize. The plaudits poured in. One experienced watcher in the audience – who remained anonymous, no doubt lest he offend the prickly Joe Davis – breathlessly declared, 'This fellow [Houlihan] is the best potter in the world, Joe Davis or no Joe Davis.' Davis had, in fact, finally retired from all competitive play the previous year, although he remained the game's most recognisable face.

To his credit, Phillips, the BA&CC chairman who had written off Houlihan's chances of ever becoming champion, graciously ate his words, congratulating him warmly. Phillips explained that the reason he believed Houlihan would never accede to the status of English champion was that although he possessed 'outstanding mastery of every phase of the game, the hurried injudicious shot he is, or rather, was so prone to make consistently proved his downfall'. Phillips argued – correctly, to be fair – that the 1965 version of Houlihan wore a 'new look' and 'now eschews the ten-to-one shot which, when missed, cost him many a frame'. In *Billiards and Snooker*, Richard Holt added praise of his own for Houlihan, including a fulsome tribute to his 'fine sportsmanship and model behaviour'.

Houlihan's victory also won attention outside the specialist snooker press, with many newspapers across the country reporting on his triumph, notably the *Daily Mirror* which screamed excitedly, 'PAT IS

CHAMPION'. Pointedly, Houlihan's victory and the progress of the final had been given priority in many newspapers ahead of the World Professional Championship match that had been unfolding at the same time between John Pulman and Fred Davis at Burroughes Hall. Pulman won that six-day contest 37-36 in a final-frame decider, but the contrast between an amateur championship contested between hundreds of players across multiple regions and multiple rounds and a professional championship contested as a one-off between just two entitled and cosseted players was stark. Long governed by self-interest and operating as a closed shop for the few rather than seeking to potentially benefit the many, the winds of change would soon blow through professional snooker, but – for a variety of reasons – it would be too late to benefit Patsy Houlihan.

# Chapter 10

# Chaos and Karachi

IN AUGUST 1947, Governor-General Louis Mountbatten oversaw the division of the British Indian Empire into the separate nations of India and Pakistan. A particular point of contention during the process of partition was what to do with the state of Kashmir, whose population was predominantly Muslim. Connected to India via the Punjab, but also sharing a substantial border with Pakistan, both newly created 'dominion states' made competing claims to the Himalayan territory. The preference of Kashmir's Hindu ruler – Maharaja Hari Singh – was for Kashmir to remain independent. However, in order to gain protection from Indian soldiers to quell an uprising among some of his Muslim subjects and repel an invasion of tribal 'lashkar' militia from Pakistan, the Maharaja reluctantly agreed to accede the kingdom to Indian control. The terms of the controversial 'Instrument of Accession', signed by the Maharajah in late October 1947, would have far-reaching and long-lasting effects for relations between India and Pakistan, and ultimately lead to four wars between the two countries.

As unlikely as it might seem, the long-running Indo-Pakistani tension over Kashmir would also end up having a pivotal effect on the life and career of Patsy Houlihan.

Chaos theory was about to collide with the snooker world.

\* \* \*

In the wake of his sensational demolition of John Spencer in Blackpool in March 1965, there was not much time for Houlihan to enjoy the

96

spoils of victory, although he doubtless had a light ale or few to celebrate – after all, as he later admitted of the match, 'I won a lot on bets.' Just 15 days after lifting the English Amateur trophy at the Tower Circus he was due to face his old rival Eric Stickler in the final of the BA&CC Television Tournament. Stickler – back on the English snooker scene after a few years living in South Africa – had accounted for Mark Wildman in the semi-finals, but had never beaten Houlihan in championship play, having lost London area finals to him in 1956 and 1957.

The match was televised by ITV as part of its popular *World of Sport* offering, a Saturday afternoon programme which was compiled for the ITV network by ABC Weekend Television. ITV's riposte to the BBC's highly popular and well-established *Grandstand*, which began its near 49-year run in 1958, *World of Sport* launched in January 1965, and for six weeks was known as *Wide World of Sport* until editor John Bromley dropped the word 'wide' as he felt the show's offering was too parochial to warrant such an expansive adjective. It would run – in direct competition with *Grandstand* – until September 1985.

Following coverage of a cricket Test match between West Indies and Australia, sections of the Houlihan-Stickler showdown were televised at 1.45pm, 2.40pm and 3.10pm on Saturday, 3 April, interspersed with horseracing from Catterick. In the event there was little tension on the baize; as had been the case in Blackpool against Spencer, Houlihan secured victory while barely breaking into a sweat. Utilising the same hit-and-run tactics he employed against Spencer, in which he balanced assured potting and sure-handed safety to perfection, he won 4-1, with breaks of 21, 33, 27, 36 and 22 along the way. Staggeringly, it was Houlihan's 17th successive competitive victory. For his last defeat in tournament play you had to go way back to early 1964, when he had missed an elementary black against George Humphries in the last 32 of the southern section of the English Amateur Championship. From the wreckage of that devastating defeat, he had conjured one of the greatest winning runs in amateur snooker history.

And Houlihan wasn't done yet either. In the annual Finsbury Park Conservative Club Invitation Tournament a few weeks later he demolished Harry K. Welch 3-1 in the last 16, then K. Lewis by the same score in the quarter-finals. Chris Ross was then whitewashed 3-0 in the semi-finals, with Houlihan notching an impressive 61 break. J.F. Matthews, MC for the event and a committee member of the club, declared, 'Ross was a little out of touch. Pat seemed a bit stale but showed his class. His 61 break could easily have been a hundred.'

Houlihan's run of consecutive victories in tournament play now stood at 20, but ahead of the final it was clear he was nearing a state of exhaustion, both mental and physical. Up against the tenacious Ron Gross – three times the national amateur champion, lest we forget – Houlihan trailed just 2-1 after three frames, but then his weariness told and Gross ran out a 4-1 winner. 'Pat, having a little cue trouble, played rather spasmodically,' was the view of Matthews. *Billiards and Snooker* concurred in its report, declaring, 'Houlihan was by no means at his best, whereas Gross recalled his best displays by playing a game of remarkable accuracy and judgement ... I was disappointed with Houlihan's display in view of his great form this season but I should think he was a trifle jaded after the many critical games he has played ... The magical mastery of Houlihan at his best we saw but rarely but, with a season's record like his, criticism seems quite out of place.'

Although the scoreline of one encounter from this incredible 20-match unbeaten run has been lost to the seeds of time, in the other 19 matches Houlihan's record was remarkable – 83 frames won against the loss of just 32. Along the way he had also beaten a phalanx of top talents from the strongest era the amateur game has ever known – namely Reardon, Spencer (twice), Gross, Owen, Price, Thompson et al. It was little surprise, given such superlative form, that the BA&CC anointed him as their 'Snooker Player of the Year', declaring, 'We are sure that our readers, and also, all amateurs will agree that Pat Houlihan of Deptford fully deserves the title.'

Houlihan hoped to take his strong run of form into the next big event on his radar – the World Amateur Snooker Championship, scheduled to take place in November 1965. A global amateur championship for snooker players had first been mooted by the BA&CC as far back in 1951, when the governing body had organised the first World Amateur Billiards Championship (replacing the pre-World War II Empire Billiards Championship). In 1957, South Africa, ahead of a planned hosting that year of the global billiards event, had offered to stage a snooker world amateur championship alongside it, but the BA&CC refused 'for the time being' as they felt it would be too much of a drain on their slender financial resources.

In 1958, the BA&CC announced they would hold a world snooker event in England the following year, but it never came to pass, again for financial reasons. In the end, the first staging of the World Amateur Snooker Championship did not take place until 1963/64, when it was held over the post-Christmas and new year period in Calcutta, India. Structured as a five-man round robin tournament, the inaugural event was won by Gary Owen, who had qualified as a result of his victory in the 1963 English Amateur Championship. Intended to be a biennial event, Houlihan's status as the 1965 English amateur champion thus secured his qualification for the world event while Owen, as holder, was also invited to participate. The championship was scheduled to take place in November in Karachi, Pakistan, and Houlihan confirmed in the June 1965 issue of *Billiards and Snooker* that he would 'definitely' be participating. At this stage Owen was unsure of his involvement due to his work commitments as a fireman, although he would eventually also confirm that he would compete, using two weeks of his annual holiday allowance and also receiving a generous two weeks' paid leave.

Houlihan, who had never previously travelled abroad, was eagerly looking forward to the opportunity to be crowned world amateur champion. However, events across the spring, summer and autumn of 1965 would conspire to deny him of his opportunity to shine on the global sporting stage.

An uneasy relationship had existed between India and Pakistan since the partition in 1947. Periods of heightened tension, political wrangling and military skirmishes within Kashmir had become commonplace in the years since and, in 1965, these tensions exploded. In August, the Pakistani army launched 'Operation Gibraltar', a covert plan in which troops entered Indian-administered territory in Kashmir in an attempt to incite rebellion among the Muslim population. The operation failed and a full-scale war soon followed, which ran from 5 August through to almost the end of September, when a UN-brokered ceasefire was finally accepted by both countries.

With tensions between the two countries still running high, however, the Pakistan Billiards Association informed the BA&CC in October that a November event was impractical and impossible, suggesting February 1966 as an alternative. The BA&CC were not keen, as it would mean the world event clashing with the closing stages of the English Amateur Championship. The Australian Billiards Association offered to step in and host instead, but – according to the *Sports Argus* – this proposal was rejected by the BA&CC who felt 'with time running out, the organisation presented too many difficulties'.

As 1965 turned into 1966 the uncertainty surrounding the tournament rumbled on. In January it was tentatively announced that the championship would take place in April, and at this stage Owen and Houlihan were still the chosen representatives to take part. With air fares to India alone costing in the region of £250 per person – these were still the relatively early days of commercial aviation – the governing body had organised an appeal fund several months earlier to raise travel costs for Owen and Houlihan, as well as to cover their accommodation and other expenses. As part of this fundraising drive both players had been taking part in exhibition events, with the proceeds going towards the appeal.

Nevertheless, a sense of ill luck and foreboding seemed to be hovering over the championship and its mooted participants. Owen hurt his hand fighting a massive blazing line of railway tankers near the Nechells gasworks in Birmingham in early January. Although the injury was not serious it was a reminder that, for amateur snooker players, the harsh realities of working life were never far away. As for Houlihan, while he waited for confirmation of when the Karachi event would finally take place, his form was becoming inconsistent and he was about to become subsumed by turbulent off-the-table events.

A homecoming challenge match Houlihan played against George Humphries in Deptford was televised on Saturday, 12 February as part of *World of Sport* and he began his 1966 English Amateur Championship campaign later the same month with a 4-2 victory against Anthony Hodge, a run of 54 proving his highest break. As national champion, Houlihan had received a five-year exemption from the London section, and automatic qualification for the southern section. Truth be told, this was something of a shame as it deprived him of the chance to add to the seven London titles he had won between his debut in 1953/54 and his *annus mirabilis* of 1965. It also deprived him of some much-needed competitive match practice, as was seen when his bid to retain the English amateur title was curtailed in surprisingly premature fashion with a 4-0 loss against John Shepherd on 4 March at the last-16 stage of the southern section.

Without so much as a 20 break to his credit in the whole match, it was the most meagre performance of Houlihan's championship career thus far. 'A real sensation, and the explanation puzzling,' admitted *Billiards and Snooker*. 'Shepherd played admirably though, I think, not well enough to have won if Houlihan had shown his form of last season … On this occasion he missed many times unaccountably and, without his well-known brilliant potting, he was at a loss to keep Shepherd from profiting by the many chances he wasted.'

With the English title gone, and the World Amateur Championship still to be rescheduled, hushed whispers in the staid corridors of the BA&CC now turned to whether Houlihan should keep his place for the Karachi showpiece, or whether he should be superseded by whoever ultimately replaced him as English Amateur champion. As it happened, John Spencer, the man Houlihan had thrashed the year before, went on to lift the crown by beating Gary Owen's brother Marcus 11-5 in the March final in Huddersfield (Gary had lost 4-0 to Graham Miles in the quarter-finals). Gary Owen and Houlihan, meanwhile, met in a televised challenge match on Saturday, 26 March, Owen winning a tight encounter 3-2, while also continuing with their fundraising efforts.

The whispers that Spencer might replace Houlihan became a roar after the events of one fateful night later in the spring of 1966. Houlihan was drinking in one of his favoured Deptford pubs when he was talked into breaking into a warehouse by two of his fellow regulars, one named Brian Donovan. It was a dare more than anything, a spot of drunken high jinks, but it would cost him dear.

'I was sitting in the pub,' Houlihan told Jonathan Rendall in 2002. 'And I was with two other chaps, drink after drink, after drink. I'm not blaming them. Anyway, I done something and I ended up in the nick ... Breaking and entering. I got four months. I started off in Wandsworth and I ended up in Ford.'

Houlihan's daughter Patsy Girl has vivid memories of visiting her dad in prison. 'I was five when he went inside,' she recalls. 'I remember me and my brother being taken by me mum to see him in Ford open prison. My mum bought him a big bar of chocolate that he used to love but me and my brother ate it all without her knowing before we got there. I don't know why we did that.'

In prison, Houlihan was in something of a bind. 'I was in a unique situation,' he said in an interview in 1986. 'Walking around the prison with a letter in my pocket which confirmed my entry into the World Amateur Championship in Karachi. A trip to India [sic] with Gary Owen, who had won the world title three years before in Calcutta – that was my dream. But I was in a dilemma. Should I show my letter to the governor, or keep quiet? Anyway, I showed him, and he gave me the job I wanted – looking after the prison's billiards table. After all, I was going nowhere and John Spencer took my place.'

Houlihan's recollection creates the impression that he was in prison during the rearranged World Amateur Championship, which finally took place between 20 November and 10 December. However, this was not the case. By September he was a free man, but by then the decision had been made by the BA&CC that Spencer would go instead of him. How much this decision owed to the fact Spencer was now the amateur champion, and how much was due to the fact that Houlihan's spell in prison ruled him out of contention in the eyes of the governing body it is impossible to say. Given the minor nature of his criminal transgression, and the fact he had been tirelessly playing exhibitions to help raise money for the trip to Pakistan, it seems a harsh decision, but not altogether surprising given that the BA&CC – like most governing bodies in British sport – were somewhat puritanical and conservative in nature.

News of Houlihan's conviction did not make its way into the press, but by September it was public knowledge that Spencer and not the Londoner would be going to Karachi. With astonishing good grace and generosity, Houlihan continued to appear in fundraising exhibitions to assist Owen and Spencer, squaring off against the former on 13 September in a challenge match at Yardley Wood Social Club in Birmingham. Owen won the entertaining match 4-3, knocking in a 129 break along the way, and followed up with matches at the same location on the next two nights against Ray Reardon and Geoffrey Thompson.

In October, Houlihan was one of 12 leading amateurs invited to participate in an ambitious invitation tournament in Coventry. The players were initially divided into groups for one-frame matches against all the other players in their groups, with progress to further semi-final groups decided on aggregate scores rather than frame scores. An out of sorts Houlihan fell in the first group stage, while Owen and Spencer ultimately met in the final over nine frames, with Owen emerging the victor by 529-488, despite having trailed by 133 points heading into the final three frames. Ambitious in conception but unsatisfying in its departure from snooker norms, the tournament attracted decent crowds but it was an initiative that was not repeated.

The following month, Owen and Spencer jetted out to Pakistan for the World Amateur Championship, Houlihan remaining in England to reflect on what might have been. 'Spencer is perhaps a little lucky to be making the trip,' the *Coventry Evening Telegraph* observed with admirable honesty. 'But for the trouble between Pakistan and India which caused the championship to be postponed for several months, Pat Houlihan of London, the 1965 champion, would have gone. By the time a new date had been fixed, Houlihan had lost his title, and in the circumstances the Billiards Association and Control Council decided that as Spencer was now champion, he should represent England.'

Six men in all competed for the title in Karachi in a round robin format. Owen retained his title, winning all five of his matches, while Spencer finished second, only losing to Owen. Both men would use the publicity from the tournament as a springboard to launch professional careers. Ironically, one of the main motivations for Spencer to turn pro was a disagreement he had with the BA&CC after returning to England about the expense payments for the Karachi trip, after which he vowed never to compete as an amateur again.

In his 1973 book *Spencer on Snooker*, the future three-time world professional champion mentioned the dispute, but didn't see fit to mention how fortunate he had been to go to Karachi in Houlihan's place. Indeed, Spencer's sole mention of his London rival in the entire book was to state, rather ungraciously, that his performance against him in the 1965 English Amateur final was 'the worst I have ever played in a match'.

The jibe hurt Houlihan, whose sportsmanship before and after matches as well as at the table was always immaculate and above reproach. 'There was no call for him to do that,' he would later say of Spencer's hurtful dismissal of the most glorious day in his career. 'He played badly because he was forced to.'

Chapter 11

# Davis the dictator

PRIOR TO becoming English Amateur champion in 1965, Patsy Houlihan had – for years – longed for a crack at life in the professional snooker ranks. The problem was, as Clive Everton once put it, 'If you wanted to paint high ceilings in Michelangelo's day, it paid to know the Pope. If you wanted to be a professional snooker player just after the 1939–45 war, you needed Joe Davis's seal of approval.'

Getting Joe Davis's seal of approval was not easy. Despite – or perhaps because of – his dictatorial nature, for decades Davis's name was synonymous with snooker. Through the force of his ambition and personality, he dragged snooker from the fuzzy margins of public consciousness, from being seen as an uncouth bastard offspring of billiards, to being the dominant game in the cue sports firmament. At least that's how the well-worn story goes. The truth is somewhat more complex.

For starters, although Davis was snooker's first great player and was responsible for organising the first World Championship (then referred to as the 'professional snooker championship') in 1927 – with crucial assistance from Birmingham billiards hall owner, equipment maker and promoter Bill Camkin – it is often overlooked that Davis's attitude to the game, for years, oscillated between ambivalence and hostility. For example, writing in 1934 in the *Sporting Globe*, Davis declared, 'For eight successive years I have been snooker champion of the world. It may surprise your readers to learn that I regard snooker as a slapdash, "agricultural" game as compared with billiards, in which artistry and scientific methods are essential to the development of skill. It is deplorable that snooker has become far more popular than billiards.'

Davis suggested several ways of making billiards more popular in order to repel snooker's aggressive advance, including making the pockets larger for amateur players. Ultimately, however, billiards was doomed by its own three-ball limitations, as well as its somnolent pace and the ability of its top players to make breaks that lasted hours, sometimes even days. Davis may have deplored snooker's popularity, but once he saw that the 22-ball game provided him with greater earning potential than billiards he didn't hesitate to throw his weight behind it. Funnily enough, his talk of snooker's 'slapdash' nature also soon ceased.

That was Davis in a nutshell – an arch pragmatist whose chief priorities were his own glorification and his own bank balance, rather than the good of the game as a whole. As Everton said, 'If there was five bob to be made from snooker, Joe made it. He had it all sewn up.' A one-third shareholder in the lease on leading venue Leicester Square Hall, where he trousered a bulky 30 per cent of the gate receipts when he played (as opposed to the 15 per cent that found its way into most other players' pockets), it was also Davis who negotiated the early deals for televised snooker coverage with the BBC, who screened 17 broadcasts from the London venue between 1950 and 1955.

Nowhere was Davis's desire to protect his own reputation, whatever the negative consequences to snooker as a whole, more evident than in his unusual decision in 1946 to retire from the World Snooker Championship, but not other tournament play, after winning the title for the 15th time. The wording of Davis's announcement of this 'retirement' was an accurate reflection of his gargantuan ego. 'For many years past it has been continually said that the championship was a foregone conclusion for me,' he droned, without even an iota of false modesty. 'Now the field is more open. Last season I played better than ever, so it is not the question of decline at the age of 45.' Such pronouncements utterly undermined his rivals who went on to become his successors as world champion – namely younger brother Fred, Walter Donaldson and John Pulman – none of whom was ever truly accepted or embraced by the public as the new king of snooker. With Joe still hovering like a ghost at the feast, they didn't stand a chance.

Although Davis would never admit it, of course, many believed that the real reason for his retreat from World Championship play was that he was scared of the prospect of losing his unbeaten record in the tournament and thus damaging his reputation and earning power. He was particularly concerned – it was said – that he might lose to his younger brother Fred, who had pushed him hard in the semi-final of the 1939 championship and the final itself a year later. By opting out of the game's premier tournament just as professional snooker was becoming more competitive, with Fred and Donaldson nearing their peaks and new players like Pulman, John Barrie, Kingsley Kennerley and Rex Williams having joined the circuit between 1945 and 1951, Davis was able to rule – as Everton neatly put it – like a 'king in exile'.

In order to further preserve his reputation, the matches Davis did play after retiring from the World Championship were almost always 'handicap' contests, in which he ceded several points start per frame to his opponents. Such a practice, which had been commonplace in the billiards era, enabled Davis to have things both ways – if he won he had overcome an obstacle to do so, if he lost, well, he had conceded a start so he had a ready-made excuse. The largest professional tournament of the 1950s, the *News of the World* tournament, used a handicap system, with Davis even granting starts to whoever was the reigning world champion. So it was that Joe was able to protect his own reputation and status, thus ensuring he was in pole position to acquire as much paid exhibition work as possible, while around him the pro game gradually withered on the vine.

By the mid to late-1950s the momentum which professional snooker had possessed when Davis beat the popular Australian Horace Lindrum in the 1946 World Championship final, to widespread acclaim and packed houses of 1,200 spectators at the Royal Horticultural Hall in London, had evaporated. The amateur scene, as we have seen, was buoyant, with bumper entries for the English Amateur Championship each year, but the professional championship, with its top player absent, became stale and increasingly irrelevant. It did not help that a schism had opened up between the governing body of billiards and snooker – the BA&CC – and the Professional Billiard Players' Association (PBPA) of which Joe, inevitably, was chairman. This split had been precipitated when the vast majority of professionals split from the BA&CC, boycotting the World Championship due to a disagreement over their share of tournament receipts, forming the World Professional Match-play Championship instead, leaving just a pair of BA&CC loyalists – Lindrum and Clark McConachy – to contest a tarnished world crown in 1952.

As chairman of the PBPA, Davis effectively controlled entry into the professional game, and he eagerly wielded this power with an iron fist. As the ageing cast of professionals dwindled ever further, largely due to retirement and disaffection – Donaldson, Alec Brown and Sidney Smith all drifted away from the game in the 1950s – Davis decided to protect his own interests and those of the other existing professionals, rather than seek to reinvigorate the game with an injection of new talent. Remarkably and ridiculously, after Rex Williams's admittance to the PBPA in 1951, there would be a near 16-year gap before another new professional was anointed. It was a terrible and almost fatal error on Davis's part, and one that would have significant consequences, depriving the wider public of the chance to see many talented players enter the professional game.

During the 1950s there were a host of exciting amateur players, Houlihan, Marcus Owen and Cliff Wilson chief among them, but Davis made no attempt to persuade any of this trio – or anyone else – into the protected professional ranks, which were now effectively a closed shop. Indeed, Davis openly admitted that he discouraged overtures to turn pro from young players who had shone in the English Amateur Championship. In a 1958 article in the *Torbay Express and South Devon Echo*, which pondered why it had been such 'a long time since there was any notable addition to the professional ranks', Davis was quoted as saying, 'Snooker requires the longest sporting apprenticeship in the world. But there is not so much encouragement to turn pro these days. In the last few years, we have had one or two players who, having won the amateur championship, felt that they would like to turn professional but the prospects were not good enough.'

In other words, new pros might take a slice of Davis's carefully guarded financial pie and therefore were not to be encouraged. A more daring and selfless man than Davis might have discerned that taking a short-term financial hit in exchange for greater riches for all further down the road if snooker grew in popularity was a risk worth taking.

Certainly the view at the time was that the top amateurs could have coped more than admirably if they had been permitted or encouraged to join the existing pros. Arthur Goundrill, a well-known cue sports writer who was also famous for his billiards exhibitions despite having only one arm, examined the issue in his *Daily Herald* column of 24 March 1956. Goundrill and many others believed snooker was missing a trick by not expanding its professional pool. 'Undoubtedly the standard of play among the top amateurs is rapidly approaching that of the professionals,' he wrote. 'I feel sure that this year's [English Amateur Championship] semi-finalists, R. Reardon and C. Wilson from Wales, and the Londoners Tommy Gordon and J. (sic.) Houlihan, could put up a good show on level terms with any professional, apart from the Davis brothers, Joe and Fred. Certainly they are equally good at potting and in temperament. Indeed in temperament all four are admirably served. Where the professionals excel is in experience, but from my observations, the four amateurs already named lack little in this respect. Their "safety" moves are of the highest quality. I feel sure that the time is not too far distant when an Open championship will become a reality, if not a necessity! This would prove a great attraction, and it would not be long odds against an amateur winning.'

Goundrill returned to the same theme in a column of 23 February 1957, writing, 'My view is that ... the standard of play among amateur snooker players has so improved that [Houlihan, Ray Reardon, Cliff Wilson, Tom Gordon and Ron Gross] could be said to have a really good chance on level terms [against professionals].'

Appropriately, Goundrill voiced these sentiments in a year that arguably proved the nadir of professional snooker. The PBPA-organised World Professional Match-play Championship (regarded at the time – and still today – as the de facto World Championship of the era) was staged in Jersey from 1–13 April 1957. It was a miserable tournament consisting of a pitiful four entrants. Not only was Joe

Davis absent, but his brother Fred – winner of the past five titles – also turned down the chance to play in favour of 'a rest'. John Pulman won the hollowest of world crowns, beating Irishman Jackie Rea in the final. Attendances were poor, with only four spectators attending the first session of the opening semi-final between Rea and Kingsley Kennerley. There would be no further staging of a professional World Championship until 1964, when the energetic and ambitious Rex Williams was responsible for reviving it as a series of one-off showdowns between champion and a challenger, starting with a match between John Pulman and Fred Davis.

As for Joe Davis, his sole attempt to reinvigorate snooker during the dark days with no professional championship between 1957 and 1964 was the introduction of a new form of the game called 'Snooker Plus' in 1959. It was a desperate move, at a time when the only sane option for raising the the game's profile lay in the introduction of new players. 'Snooker Plus' transformed snooker from a 22- to a 24-ball game, with two additional coloured balls – an orange (worth eight points, positioned midway between the pink and blue) and a purple (worth ten points, positioned midway between the blue and brown). It was intended to create bigger, crowd-pleasing breaks (a maximum break of 210 was now possible, rather than a 147), but in reality the addition of two extra balls merely made the table more cluttered and, if anything, break building more difficult. Furthermore, the positioning of the purple between blue and brown, when players were used to break building around the black spot, made it virtually impossible that a maximum break could ever be made.

For a man as astute as Davis it was a surprisingly ham-fisted attempt to revitalise the game, which probably sprang more from his desire to create a further income stream than any altruistic motives about reviving professional snooker. Davis had lined up a healthy percentage cut of the sales of new 24-ball snooker sets but was left disappointed when clubs across the country almost universally snubbed the 'Snooker Plus' experiment for the shameless money grab it undoubtedly was.

Due to a Davis diktat, the 1959 *News of the World* tournament, a shrunken round-robin between just the Davis brothers and Pulman, featured the format and was an abject failure, signalling the death knell for the well-established event after ten previously successful stagings. The limited three-man field also caused resentment among those professionals not invited to compete. 'The decision of a national newspaper to sponsor a cash tournament of "Snooker Plus" ... is causing much unrest in the professional ranks,' reported Stan Bate in the *Sports Argus*. 'Both the Midlands' leading professionals, Kingsley Kennerley and Rex Williams, feel that they have once again been shut out by the big boys and are not being given a fair crack of the whip.'

\* \* \*

While Davis was experimenting with 'Snooker Plus', Houlihan was dreaming of breaking into professional snooker and revitalising it with his unique and attractive attacking game. Exactly when he first attempted to enter the professional ranks is unclear and efforts to locate the archived files of the PBPA or the BA&CC – which might shed light on such matters – were unsuccessful during the research of this book. In 2002, however, Clive Everton claimed that 'a few years before Davis last played in public in 1964 he was sounded out about Houlihan becoming a professional and squashed the idea flat'. This statement chimes with the anecdotal accounts of Houlihan and his family, which suggest he enquired about turning pro well before his 1965 English Amateur Championship triumph and his 1966 spell in prison. 'It was sewn up in them days,' Houlihan would later say regretfully. 'It was very, very hard to turn pro. Joe Davis was the kingpin. His word was bond. When he said yes or no, that was it.'

Davis was certainly aware of Houlihan's talents and from early in the Londoner's career too. In February 1954, *The Billiard Player* reported that Davis had played, and lost, a frame of snooker against Houlihan, albeit after giving him a 28-point head start. At one point Houlihan apparently even made an attempt to curry favour with Davis in an effort to potentially smooth his passage to the pros. Roy Bacon recounted to the author a fascinating anecdote about Houlihan acting as caddy for Davis during a round of golf ahead of an exhibition they played. It's a story that Houlihan told Bacon during one of their many money matches and it's a tale which reveals much about Davis, particularly his hatred of losing and his condescending attitude to those he regarded as his social inferiors. 'Patsy played Joe in an exhibition and beat him,' Bacon explained. 'Joe didn't like getting beaten, of course. Anyway, Joe gave a speech after the match and his excuse for losing was that he'd been playing golf all day. Well, that was some excuse, because, as Patsy told me, "What Joe didn't tell people is that I was carrying his bags!" Patsy had caddied for him and carried his bloody bag around all day! That story was straight from Patsy's lips, he told me that one several times.'

At other times, however, Houlihan couldn't resist playing the showman against Joe and his brother Fred. 'What ruined it for Patsy in his early days was that he was very lairy, very flash,' Terry Dempsey recalled with a chuckle. 'When he'd play Fred or Joe Davis, he'd line up his shots, turn to talk to them and pot the ball without looking at it while he was chatting to them. They hated that. It humiliated them.' Paul Moriarty recalled a match that Houlihan once played against Joe in Woolwich, in which Patsy reeled off six centuries against an embarrassed Davis. 'Joe Davis didn't like him,' Moriarty said. 'He wouldn't take him into his little gang.'

Davis also disapproved of Houlihan's penchant for hustling, which he considered too convergent with the 'misspent youth' image of snooker which he was trying to banish from the game. There was undoubtedly an element of snobbery in Davis's attitude towards Houlihan. Although Joe's father had been a humble coal miner and then a publican, Davis was the archetypal social climber, forever seeking the respectability and fiscal security of a place among the upper middle class. Watch archive footage of him being interviewed and it is striking that Davis's accent desperately strives for the perceived sophistication of 'received pronunciation'. Houlihan – a proudly working-class man who would have considered it an act of betrayal to his family and roots to alter his earthy south-east London accent – could not have been more different. With his liking for a drink, a gamble and a hustle, Houlihan represented the realities of a working-class lifestyle that the socially ambitious Davis had scrambled so earnestly to escape from. Davis's vision of snooker was in line with Victorian expectations of cue sports as an after-dinner game for gentlemen, rather than members of the working class who mixed in circles which sometimes intersected with the 'criminal classes'.

In later years, Houlihan professed admiration for Davis's abilities but he was clearly hurt by his refusal to countenance the idea of allowing him to join the pros. 'He never said it to my face,' Houlihan reflected. 'Joe Davis was a good player, but as a gentleman? No. I played [him] on five occasions and I think he won one. He just shook his head. But he was the king. For 20 years he was.'

Rex Williams, who knew Davis and Houlihan well, explained in more detail to the author some of Davis's attitudes and prejudices. 'Joe was the ultimate professional in every way,' Williams said. 'And he did everything he possibly could to promote snooker. But I will say this: Joe was very, very particular who came into the professional ranks. He looked into your background and if your background was even slightly shady there was no chance you were going to get in in those days. Pat Houlihan was a friend of mine. I liked Pat. He applied [to turn pro] and was turned down. I don't know what his background was. He came from a very poor working-class background. Full marks to him for making headway. That shouldn't have been held against him, but it may have been held against him in those days. There were one or two players who didn't get in. John Barrie came into the game and was accepted, I came in, John Pulman and Jackie Rea were all accepted. But they did look very much more carefully at a player's background then. As far as I was concerned Pat was a very nice fella. I liked Pat very, very much and he was a very good player. I think there were also one or two others who tried and failed to get in in those days.'

Charlie Poole, an extravagant talent of the late 1960s and early '70s who never turned pro, summed up succinctly the social divide that seemed to separate the professional game from the amateur game and the reality of life in the snooker halls. 'The people playing the game on TV – the Joe Davises and so on, I'd look at them and think, "Nah, that's not for me." It was all a bit stuffy and poncey with the bow ties and all that. The way I looked at it, to be a pro you had to be a bit of a cunt. I didn't want to be a part of that and wouldn't have been accepted anyway.'

Clive Everton also made a telling point, stressing that the way the professional game shrunk in the 1950s and '60s made it far more unlikely for players to be admitted, as there was barely enough money in the game to support existing pros, let alone new ones. 'The main problem is that there were several players who probably wanted to turn professional but there was no real professional game to speak of,' he said. 'The amateur game existed in a sort of subterranean culture of its own. What interest there was in snooker was at the top of the amateur game and focused on the likes of Houlihan and Marcus Owen. They were very, very good players. Joe was very scathing about people who he imagined were not the right type. Patsy didn't fit the mould Joe had in mind. And at that time you really couldn't move a hand or lift a finger without Joe's approval, certainly until well into the 1960s.'

The tragedy is that had Davis thought of the wider health of the sport, rather than merely his own self-interest, then professional snooker might never have reached the parlous position it had sunk to by 1964, when Davis finally retired for good. Legend has it that when asked about snooker's future in the wake of this announcement Joe replied, 'What future? Professional snooker has no future.'

Not for the first time, Davis would be proved wrong. With its long-time kingpin finally leaving the stage, professional snooker gradually began a period of tentative revival from 1964 onwards. A key force in this process was the aforementioned Williams, who explained to the author how he helped bring snooker back from the brink, 'I rang Fred Davis up one day in around 1963 or 1964 and I said, "Look Fred, we've got to do something. We can't let the game die." Fred said, "The interest has gone, Rex." I said, "Well, we just can't let it die." So I rang the other players – John Pulman, Jackie Rea, Kingsley Kennerley and so on. We all met in my house in Stourbridge. I said, "I'll get it organised and I think the two people who should play for the championship are Fred and John [Pulman]." John had held the title from 1957 and Fred had won it several times. So I rang Burroughes and Watts in London because they still had a hall in Soho Square where all the amateur games were being played. They said they'd be delighted to host it. There were a couple more challenge matches and then John and Fred had a tour of South Africa where they played a long series of matches. I also played John over in South Africa and we got the game going again.'

As well as helping revive the World Championship, Williams also helped to resuscitate the PBPA from the comatose state that had enveloped it since Joe Davis's departure. In 1967, three amateurs joined the pro ranks, the first new professionals since Williams himself in 1951. John Spencer was the first in February, followed by Gary Owen in August and Ray Reardon in December. All three were able to turn pro due to specific earning opportunities or contracts they were granted: Spencer received a series of paid engagements from the National Spastics Society and Pontin's holiday camp; Owen signed a £250 sponsorship contract with billiards and snooker manufacturer Riley Burwat (formed after Burroughes and Watts went bust and their assets were taken over by E.J. Riley); while Reardon received a paid invitation to tour South Africa, and duly resigned from the Stoke-on-Trent police force to take up the opportunity.

Spencer's decision to turn pro was a direct result of his fury at not having received his expenses for the World Amateur Championship trip to Karachi by the end of January 1967. Of the £903 raised to send Owen and Spencer to Pakistan, much of it due to Houlihan's efforts even after he was removed as one of the representatives, £509 had been spent on air fares. The BA&CC claimed that Spencer and Owen's cheques were 'made out' but still awaiting a co-signatory. The truth was, the association was in dire financial difficulties, having made a loss of over £600 in the previous year. Spencer announced that he was 'disgusted' by the situation and promptly withdrew from the 1967 English Amateur Championship in protest, declaring he would 'turn professional or give up snooker altogether'. Owen also pulled out of the championship, declaring that he had already taken more than enough time off work to play in the world amateurs, although the expenses farrago was likely a further factor in his decision.

Roger Coates, who had been due to meet Owen in the first round of the southern section of the championship, made the most of his good fortune in gaining a bye by eliminating Houlihan 4-2 in the southern quarter-finals. Gary's brother Marcus went on to win the tournament, but with Reardon, Gary Owen and Spencer all departing the amateur game that year the sun had firmly set on the golden era of unpaid snooker.

Houlihan had looked in good form early in the tournament, eliminating the accomplished future world professional finalist Graham Miles 4-1 in round two, but, concerningly, he had begun to suffer with eyesight issues which badly affected the consistency of his form. Not only had his eyesight gradually been deteriorating as he approached 40, but he also began to suffer with recurrent and increasingly serious bouts of conjunctivitis, which he believed he originally picked up in prison. Such issues would plague him for the rest of his career.

The following season Houlihan suffered a disappointing reverse in the English Amateur Championship, losing in the first round of the southern section, 4-2 to Harold 'Dickie' Laws, a flamboyant and crafty veteran who had found himself frozen out of the professional game in the 1950s due to his money match connections and whose career thus echoed Houlihan's. Laws, who had won the London title in Houlihan's absence, successfully and cleverly slowed the tempo of the action, ensuring that Patsy never found his rhythm. Over 400 spectators attended the match, which had to be moved to a larger room in the BA&CC's snooker centre in Great Windmill Street such was the demand for tickets.

Houlihan arguably displayed better form at billiards in 1968 than at snooker as, alongside his good friend Bill Smith (a former Home Counties snooker champion), he represented Belvedere Working Men's Club in the All England CIU Team Billiards Championship, helping his side reach the final. Houlihan showed particularly fine form in the semi-finals in Coventry against Lime Tree Park, slaughtering Joe Pitchford 452-151, notching breaks of 92 and 60 (twice) along the way.

Sportingly, Pitchford's response after the match was to utter a paean to Houlihan's excellence. 'Pat played brilliantly and it was a joy to watch him,' he said. 'Everything I tried failed. I succeeded only in sticking him up every time – and did he make me pay for it! His potting was fantastic and three times during the match he took a maximum 15 reds in succession. He had breaks of 92 and three or four in the 60s to give me a right pasting!'

In the final in Derby, Houlihan won his match against Brian Simpson, but Belvedere were defeated 954-595 by a strong Blaydon team which included Alf Nolan, a former national amateur champion at both snooker (in 1950) and billiards (in 1964).

Although he didn't play billiards often, Houlihan was a very capable player of the three-ball game. Bill King recalled, 'One time I took Patsy up to the Regal club in Romford and a few of the blokes who were good billiard players said to him, "Do you want a game?" They were playing scrub, a game where you have to make cannons and that and get to 71 to win. They said to Patsy, "You're a top snooker player, you'll have to get 101 to win." He said, "Oh, all right then." Well, by the end he was getting breaks of *601*. He was that good.'

Although Houlihan's form was far from vintage in 1967 or 1968, and it is unclear if he made moves to join the pros in either of these two years, by not moving into the paid ranks he undoubtedly missed an opportunity to position himself advantageously at the beginning of an era which would see professional snooker's revival quickly gather pace. While he still languished in an amateur game that was beginning to lose relevance, Reardon, Spencer and Owen were securing sponsorship and exhibition contracts and making a name for themselves in the pros, thus establishing a crucial commercial and sporting advantage over those amateurs who joined the circuit later. The vast majority of top amateurs from the 1950s and '60s would join the pros eventually – Houlihan, Ron Gross, Marcus Owen, Jonathan Barron, David Taylor and even Cliff Wilson, after a period away from the game – but it is striking that the pair of players from that richly talented generation to transition most successfully were two of the first three to join, namely Reardon and Spencer, who would end up winning nine world titles between them.

One difficulty that Houlihan faced was that, as a Londoner, he was at a regional disadvantage when seeking paid snooker work. There were far less snooker clubs in London per head of population at this time than in the Midlands or the north, where the majority of professionals hailed from, while south London was particularly poorly served for clubs in the late 1960s and '70s. Furthermore, despite his crowd-pleasing potential, Houlihan was unable to find sponsors to help smooth his path into the pro ranks or to help sustain him once he did eventually reach the pros. Players based in the north and the Midlands seemed to find it much easier to pick up both exhibition work and corporate sponsors.

'Everything that happens in the game seems to be in the north,' Houlihan once reflected. 'Perhaps that's why there's a predominance of northern players. We have a tremendous wealth of talent in the London area, but somehow it never seems to materialise.' Houlihan's resolutely working-class background and lack of corporate connections also didn't help his cause. Although he could always find people willing to act as a cash backer for him in behind-closed-doors money matches, such sources of income were not of the 'official' nature which would help advance his competitive snooker career, or bolster his claims to turn professional.

While Houlihan sat on the sidelines, the power structure of the new wave sweeping through snooker was beginning to establish itself. In April 1968, in the wake of encouraging attendances for John Pulman's world title defence against Eddie Charlton in Bolton, it was announced that the world professional championship would finally return to the guise of a proper knockout tournament for the 1968/69 season for the first time since the nadir of Jersey in 1957. The newly formed PBPA – under Williams's aegis now rather than Joe Davis's – consisted of eight players who would compete for what has retrospectively been recognised as the first snooker world title of the modern era. From the old guard of established pros came holder Pulman, Rex Williams, Fred Davis and Jackie Rea, while newcomers Reardon, Spencer and Owen were also joined, inexplicably, by Bernard Bennett from Southampton. Bennett had scant amateur pedigree but he was able to stump up the £100 entry fee, then a huge and somewhat prohibitive sum, and had a reputation as a good organiser of tournaments and matches, owning as he did the Castle snooker club in his hometown. A master builder, Bennett had also been helping the BA&CC with a project to construct a potential purpose-built headquarters in London.

It would have made far more competitive sense for a top amateur such as Houlihan, Owen or Gross to take up the eighth slot, but Bennett's connections sealed the deal – the fact he was a poor player who was unlikely to beat any of the old guard was probably seen by them as a welcome bonus too. Bill King was scathing about the decision to admit Bennett. 'I can't believe they let Bennett in,' King said. 'Even *I* could beat him. Seemed like to get in the pros you had to own a snooker club and be no good.' In the 1980s, somewhat ironically given that his entry to the pros had effectively blocked Houlihan, Bennett would become Patsy's doubles partner, proving once again that the south-east Londoner rarely held a grudge.

Somewhat conveniently, each quarter-final of the new-look World Championship pitted a member of the 'old guard' versus the 'new wave'. Bennett was unsurprisingly thrashed by Williams and Fred Davis edged out Reardon, but Spencer toppled reigning champion Pulman and Owen disposed of Jackie Rea. In the semi-finals, Spencer and Owen swept aside the last remnants of the old order, defeating Williams and Davis respectively. Spencer then won the title, securing a winning 37-24 lead on 22 March 1969, the last day of a marathon six-day, 73-frame final, thus pocketing a first prize of £750, plus bonuses based on gate receipts. The healthy prize fund offered by tobacco company John Player, who had sponsored the event under the aegis of their Player's No.6 brand, totalled a promising £3,500.

The 'new wave' had arrived and – having witnessed the burgeoning professional success of three men he had beaten in his barnstorming run to the 1965 amateur title – Houlihan was desperate to join them in the next staging of the World Championship, scheduled for the end of 1969 and early months of 1970 in London. Manchester's David Taylor, who in October 1968 had added the World Amateur title to the English Amateur title he won earlier the same year, had been admitted to the PBPA on returning home, while Maurice Parkin, the 1955 English Amateur champion from Sheffield, had also been allowed in a month earlier. Given his experience and pedigree, Houlihan had every reason to expect to be admitted too and duly submitted his application to join the PBPA.

To bolster his case, after a couple of below-par seasons Houlihan had made an encouraging return to form in 1969, although the climax to his season would sadly be marked by tragedy. In the 1968/69 Watney's Snooker Pairs Championship, Houlihan partnered up once again with his friend Bill Smith for Belvedere WMC, winning the Kent and Sussex Area section and then disposing of Abertillery to reach the last eight of the nationals. Once again alongside Smith, Houlihan also helped Belvedere reach the National Billiards Team semi-finals, although they lost to Mountain Ash of Glamorgan as they fell short of their achievement of reaching the final from the previous season.

In a strange twist of fate, Houlihan was then drawn to face Smith in the first round of the southern section of the English Amateur Championship. Given the men's friendship it was, unsurprisingly, a fiercely contested but friendly match. 'We were both playing for Belvedere at the time so there was a lot of interest in the match,' Houlihan later recalled. 'I'd played Bill about four times [before] and never lost so he was really determined.' According to *Billiards and Snooker*, Houlihan moved into an early 2-0 lead but was trailing 68-45 in frame three with four balls left when Smith – suddenly and without warning – collapsed into unconsciousness and was rushed to Charing Cross Hospital.

Houlihan recalled the match situation slightly differently, 'I won the first two frames and Bill needed a snooker on the brown in the third. Bill got the snooker but he was just looking at the next shot when he fell over. It was very hot in there but, in my opinion, tension was the cause of it.' Match referee Arthur Baker also gave his account of what happened to *Billiards and Snooker*, 'Bill had played six matches in the preceding seven days and this, combined with the tension of this particular match and the warm atmosphere, must have been too much for him.'

Not long afterwards, Smith passed away in hospital. The death hit Houlihan hard. In the days before his friend's death, he had visited him in hospital, as he later explained. 'When I went to see him in hospital he kept asking, "Was it a good game? Was I in with a chance?" This is what I mean when I say tension was the cause of it. His mind was so full of the match that he kept coming back to it. I felt awful when he died. It took me weeks to get over it.' Smith's death certainly seemed to take some of the wind out of Houlihan's sails. He beat A. White 4-0 and then Frank Gibbins 6-2 in the southern section semis without hitting top gear to move within one match of his second English Amateur final. In the southern final, Houlihan faced Cornwall's Jonathan Barron, a talented and experienced player. Houlihan led 3-1 early on but Barron found his form to take the final frame of the afternoon session and won the first three frames in the evening to triumph 6-3 in what would ultimately prove Houlihan's last career match in the English Amateur Championship. His overall record was a stellar one comprising 64 victories from his 77 championship matches since his debut in the winter of 1953.

Despite the loss, Houlihan's feat in having reached the final four of the English Amateur coupled with his superb record over the past decade and a half in the tournament meant that he surely had a strong case to be admitted to the PBPA when his application was considered in a meeting held on Friday, 30 May 1969. However, the PBPA summarily rejected his application, as well as that of his old rival Ron Gross. On what grounds Houlihan and Gross were denied entry has never been made clear, although it might have been the case that they did not possess any offers of sponsorship or any sort of contracts for exhibition matches. Certainly, the PBPA liked to see some proof of forthcoming snooker-related income from its applicants.

'The rules of the PBPA state that members must be earning their living from the game,' commented Michael Green in remarks reported in the *Birmingham Daily Post*, in reference to an application for PBPA membership from Graham Miles that was also rejected in 1969. Green was a soft drinks manufacturer and snooker fan who had somehow ended up as PBPA secretary, a sign that the days of well-meaning but often ineffective amateurs pulling the strings of sporting governing bodies were still in operation.

A further possible reason for Gross and Houlihan's exclusion was because they both had 'form' for involvement in gambling and money matches and this had been held against them. Yet another possibility is that their applications were not proposed or seconded by fellow PBPA members, as the rules stated was a prerequisite for acceptance. Those who had been admitted already to the pro ranks were hardly likely to be keen to let in a dangerous crowd pleaser such as Houlihan, who might take away some of the lucrative endorsement deals offered by snooker table and equipment manufacturers that they were in the process of hoovering up; Gary Owen and John Spencer had deals with Riley Burwat, E.A. Clare and Son signed Rex Williams and Fred Davis and Riley's had deals with Ray Reardon and David Taylor.

There was little time for Houlihan to mourn his exclusion from the professional ranks. A few days after the PBPA meeting he was in Wales at a major event – the inaugural official amateur snooker international, between England and Wales, mounted at the Afan Lido in Port Talbot on 7 June as part of the nationwide celebrations to mark the upcoming investiture of Prince Charles as the Prince of Wales. Houlihan was part of an extremely strong England team, lining up alongside Ray Edmonds, Jonathan Barron, Sidney Hood, Geoff Thompson and Chris Ross. In front of a bumper crowd of over 1,000 spectators England won the contest 10-8.

The victory was scant consolation to Houlihan for being blocked from the pro game. Regardless of the reasons for the PBPA's decision, it was undoubtedly a 'sliding doors' moment in his career, depriving him as it did of the opportunity to compete in the 1970 World Professional Snooker Championship, which began in October 1969 and did not conclude until April of 1970, when Reardon beat former champion Pulman in the final to win his first world crown, having disposed of holder Spencer in the semis. Houlihan's prospects of making it to the pros while they remained a relatively level playing field were receding as fast as one of his fabled clearances. As he reflected on his rejection by the professional snooker establishment, turbulent times lay ahead.

Chapter 12

# The promised land turns sour

EXACTLY WHEN Patsy Houlihan was finally accepted into snooker's professional ranks is a little unclear. Most sources state that he turned pro in early 1971, but there is strong evidence that it may actually have happened in mid-1970. Certainly, Houlihan did not enter that season's English Amateur Championship and in July 1970 he participated in a tournament organised by the Chester and District League which was advertised and described as a 'professional invitation tournament'. Houlihan lost 5-2 to John Spencer on 13 July in the semi-finals, having led 2-0, in what might well have been his first professional match. Spencer went on to lose 4-3 in the final to Jackie Rea, who had beaten John Dunning in the other semi. It is possible that Houlihan finally turned pro under his own steam, before his membership of the PBPA had been ratified. This was a tactic that Graham Miles, for one, had employed in the past, in the hope of accruing enough paid work to then receive PBPA membership and thus be able to enter the World Championship.

Later in the year, Houlihan also appeared in the Castle Open tournament at Bernard Bennett's club in Southampton, an eight-man pro-am. He won 7-3 against Alf Hobbs and *Billiards and Snooker* reported that he and Rex Williams were 'the only professional winners' in the first round. While this somewhat low-key event – top prize £150 – was unfolding on the south coast of England, the year's second staging of the World Championship (confusingly regarded as the 1971 championship) was taking place in Australia.

Of the nine participants, only defending champion Reardon, former winners Spencer and Pulman and 1969 finalist Gary Owen made the lengthy and expensive trip from the UK. According to reports in April 1970, when it was initially announced that the tournament would be staged in Australia, Reardon and Pulman were offered free travel and accommodation by the organisers, while other participants from the UK were expected to meet their own expenses. Owen, keen to make the trip, immediately started looking for a sponsor and would enjoy the Australian experience so much that he emigrated there not long after the tournament's conclusion to take a job as resident professional in a Sydney snooker club. He would only appear in professional matches in the UK again on a handful of occasions.

PBPA head honcho Rex Williams had intended to make the trip down under, but was thwarted by a ruling from the newly renamed Billiards and Snooker Control Council (the BA&CC having thus become the B&SCC) that he must defend his world billiards crown in London against Leslie Driffield, rather than in Australia against Albert Johnson, a match he had planned to participate in after the conclusion of the snooker World Championship. The B&SCC's ruling would have far reaching consequences, precipitating yet another schism with the PBPA, which would ultimately lead to the players' association breaking free from the traditional governing body in October. Thus in December the PBPA renamed itself the WPBSA (World Professional Billiards and Snooker Association), with Williams installed as chairman, and promptly took over the running of professional snooker. 'It didn't go down too well with the Billiards and Snooker Control Council,' Williams explained. 'But we didn't think the amateur game should control the professional game.'

Against this turbulent political backdrop, Williams faced Houlihan in the semi-finals of the Castle Open tournament, edging out the Londoner – who received a seven-point start – 7-6 after an epic, seven-and-a-half-hour encounter. Houlihan displayed plenty of grit, rallying from 4-1 and 6-4 down to level matters at 6-6 before being denied in the decider. 'Pat's the best safety player I've ever played against,' Williams declared after the match. 'I expected him to attack a lot and perhaps leave me a few chances but his safety was the strongest part of his game.' The main reason Houlihan was relying more on his safety game was that eyesight issues had begun to affect his confidence with long potting, particularly in pressurised matchplay situations, or when tables were brightly lit. Not only was Houlihan's eyesight failing and fading, but the conjunctivitis he had picked up in prison was continuing to plague him.

By the new year Houlihan was definitely a fully-fledged professional association member. He ran advertisements announcing his availability for exhibitions in *World Snooker* and *Billiards and Snooker* magazines. The wording for the two ads was slightly different; in *World Snooker* it ran, 'Pat Houlihan – London's biggest Crowd-puller has turned pro and is available for EXHIBITION ENGAGEMENTS. Write: 43 Cornbury House, Evelyn Street, or phone: 01 858 8758, Deptford, London, SE8.' Meanwhile, in *Billiards and Snooker* the ad billed Houlihan as 'Seven times London Champion, 1965 English Amateur Champion'.

The March 1971 issue of *World Snooker* also featured Houlihan, both on its cover – in a dramatic and dynamic design alongside Welsh amateur billiards champion Roy Oriel and a young sensation named Alexander Gordon Higgins (of whom more will follow later) – as well as in a detailed preview of the 1971/72 Park Drive World Championship, which began that month. Houlihan took his place in a fascinating qualifying section which also included fellow former English Amateur champions Maurice Parkin, Geoffrey Thompson and Ron Gross, as well as Bernard Bennett, Graham Miles, John Dunning, and Alex Higgins.

Houlihan was drawn against Dunning, a tough Yorkshireman from Morley whose best performance at the English Amateur had been an appearance in the last four. 'A very experienced and determined match player,' was Clive Everton's assessment of Dunning in his tournament preview. '[He] can certainly be rated among the best players never to have won the amateur title.' Of Houlihan, Everton wrote, 'A fast player with a natural easy style, Houlihan suffered for many years from a tendency to attack too much but has now developed a game in which attack and defence are more evenly balanced. A veteran of many money matches both as an amateur and a professional Houlihan combines steadiness of nerve with wittiness of repartee.'

The Houlihan-Dunning match was played at the Brentham Club in Ealing, west London, and promoted by the tireless Gross, who played his qualifier against Higgins at the same venue, losing 15-6. It proved a nervy and drawn-out affair, with both men running in and out of form at various times; Dunning dominated early, winning the first session 5-2, and when he extended his lead to 9-5 overnight the match looked all but over, with the Yorkshireman requiring just two of the remaining seven frames to triumph. Back came Houlihan, however, as he whittled away the deficit to first 9-6, then 9-7 and 9-8. Dramatically, in frame 18, Houlihan notched a quickfire break of 63 to draw level at 9-9. In the words of *World Snooker* reporter Norman Haseldine this brilliant break brought 'the confident glint back into those devilish cockney eyes'. Houlihan now looked favourite to prevail but Dunning steeled himself to take frame 19 and a 10-9 lead. With a break of 39 and a clearance of 51, Houlihan once again levelled and the match headed into a decider. Devastatingly for Houlihan, however, it was Dunning who took the final frame courtesy of runs of 58 and 25.

It was not the World Championship debut Houlihan had hoped for. To add insult to injury, the 22-year-old Higgins went on to take the crown. With his breakneck pace and sensational potting, the Northern Irishman was a player very much in the Houlihan mould. The two men came from similarly humble backgrounds, however, that is where the comparisons between them ended, for – temperamentally as well as in personality – they were very different, diametric opposites even. Although both men grew up in tough working-class areas, Higgins was rarely disciplined by his parents, which bred in him a sense of entitlement and childish indulgence he would never succeed in shedding, whereas Houlihan's parents had scrupulously ensured he subsumed old-fashioned values of respect and politeness. As a consequence, Houlihan was a consummate sportsman, generous in defeat and modest in victory, with an impeccable sense of professional decorum. He extended this sense of respect and politeness towards match officials, his opponents and anyone else he met in the course of his snooker career. Even on the hustling scene he was regarded warmly as a man who paid his debts and didn't take liberties. Higgins, in contrast, had little if no respect for referees, those governing the game or pretty much anyone else for that matter.

There was certainly no love lost between the duo. 'He thought he was God's gift,' Houlihan later said of Higgins. 'He was a good player and all that, but Spencer beat him enough times. Reardon beat him enough times.' By 1971, in money match clashes, Higgins and Houlihan had met on several occasions, with Houlihan enjoying notable success due to clever tactics. 'Alex couldn't keep still in his chair,' Houlihan later explained. 'He was up and down, up and down. And that's how I used to beat him. I'd slow him down something terrible. Alex had the shots but he was … Put it this way – one time he fell out of a window and broke his leg, and he played in the tournament with a leg in a plaster.'

Houlihan and Higgins met for the first time in the professional ranks in a high-profile match promoted by Riley-Burwat and played on Thursday, 11 November 1971 at the B&SCC's new match hall in Haringey, north London. There were precious few professional snooker tournaments at this point and certainly no pro circuit as there is today. Such 'professional matches' were therefore much more keenly contested than modern-day exhibitions, with players often playing for decent money or sidestakes, as well as a share of the gate receipts. For Higgins, the match also had particular significance as it formed part of his preparation for his World Championship semi-final against Rex Williams, scheduled for the following month. With tickets priced at 60p, the event was a sell-out, indeed, according to *World Snooker* magazine the Haringey Hall was 'over-filled' with spectators.

Unfortunately, it did not prove quite as thrilling an encounter as might have been expected from a showdown between players who represented the philosophy of attacking snooker from two contrasting generations. There was only one break of over 50 in the match – a 53 made by Higgins – and both players seemed to have difficulty adjusting to the cloth and cushions on the brand-new match table. Although one observer claimed that Houlihan 'appeared out of touch', *World Snooker* asserted that he was 'by no means outclassed'. Indeed, after losing the first three frames, Houlihan struck back to trail 3-2 and then 4-3. In the eighth frame he had a great chance to level matters and take the match into a decider, but was 'unlucky to miss a green' with the remaining colours well set, enabling Higgins to 'sweep up' and win 5-3. 'Watching Higgins's style and potting ability,' noted referee Frank Little, 'I was very much reminded, in fact, of the way that Pat Houlihan played some eight or ten years ago.'

Higgins went on to beat Williams in the World Championship semi-finals in December and then Spencer in the final in February 1972 to become the first qualifier to win the championship and the then youngest champion to boot. One couldn't help but wonder how Houlihan would have fared had he been able to turn pro in his 20s. As it was, while Higgins celebrated his triumph, Houlihan was left twiddling his thumbs and reflecting whether he would ever again be able to regain the form of the past that Little had referred to.

What Houlihan really needed was more match practice, but unfortunately, although he was now a professional, there were very few pro tournaments. There was no calendar of events or qualifiers in which he could compete, and no world rankings he could climb to create better opportunities for himself. Having turned pro later than the likes of Reardon and Spencer, and lacking the connections of old-timers like Fred Davis and John Pulman, opportunities for Houlihan to prove himself were few and far between. In December and January a third series of the BBC TV's one-frame snooker showcase *Pot Black* was filmed, but Houlihan – a dangerous name with no formal manager or advisor to lobby for his inclusion – had zero chance of receiving an invite. Likewise with the Park Drive 2000, a lucrative four-man tournament held in the spring in which only Gary Owen, Rex Williams, John Spencer and John Pulman competed. The closed shop of the Joe Davis era had, for the time being, merely been replaced by another closed shop, albeit one with a slightly different cast of characters.

Despite his proven abilities and popularity, it was even hard for Houlihan to find exhibition engagements, with the heart of this side of the snooker industry being in the north of the country rather than London and the south. 'London was dead then,' Irish cueist Jackie Rea observed. 'It's a joke when a talented player like Pat Houlihan can't get bookings. He'd be turning work away if he lived in the north,

Drinking and pub culture were central to life in working-class Deptford. Houlihan's father William, nicknamed Happy, is pictured here (second right) in one of the many pubs that used to trade on Deptford High Street. (Patricia Houlihan)

Houlihan's sensational capture of the 1953/54 London amateur snooker title was marked with two photos on the front cover of *The Billiard Player*, the cue sports journal of record of the day. (Clive Everton/*The Billiard Player*)

A previously unpublished shot of Houlihan (right) with Clifford Wilson outside Burroughes and Watts, probably taken for use in *The Billiard Player*. A poster advertising the amateur snooker championship is in the background between the two men. (Seamus Phelan)

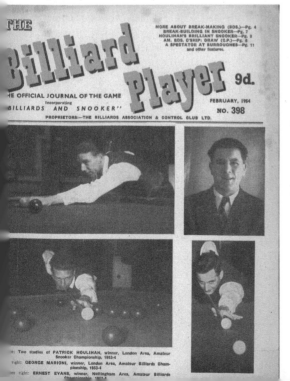

Houlihan receiving the London area snooker title for 1956/57, his third victory in the competition. Opponent Eric Stickler is on the right. (Clive Everton/*The Billiard Player*)

Houlihan (centre) flanked by other leading amateurs Clifford Wilson (left) and Geoffrey Thompson (right). The trio are pictured in the mid-1950s outside Burroughes and Watts' Soho Square headquarters, the spiritual home of amateur snooker for many years. (Clive Everton/*The Billiard Player*)

Houlihan (far right) next to his brother Terry in a photo of the Lewisham team who won the 1956/57 Temperance Billiards Hall Snooker League. (Clive Everton/*The Billiard Player*)

A very rare early colour photo of Houlihan, probably taken in the early 1960s. (Patricia Houlihan)

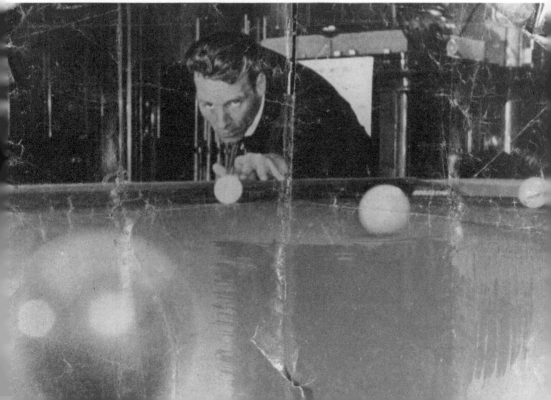

Houlihan socialising in his beloved Deptford with Siddy Randall (far left) and two other unidentified friends. (Patricia Houlihan)

Ray Reardon (left) alongside Houlihan (centre) after Patsy's classic 6-5 victory in the 1965 Southern Area Amateur Final at Burroughes and Watts. Houlihan had trailed 5-1 and is pictured here receiving the winning trophy and reward vouchers from the bookmaker Joe Coral (right). (Clive Everton/ *Billiards and Snooker*)

*(Left)* Houlihan advertises his availability for exhibitions in *Snooker Scene* magazine shortly after finally turning professional. (Clive Everton/*Snooker Scene*)(Right)

*(Right)* The Pot Black Snooker Centre in Vardens Road employed Houlihan as its resident professional – they clearly saw his presence as a selling point, as this advertisement in *Snooker Scene* from 1978 issue shows. (Clive Everton/*Snooker Scene*)

The 'Vardens Road gang'. From left to right: Houlihan, Tony Meo, Wally West, Noel Miller Cheevers, Jimmy White and Bob Harris. White called the Pot Black Club 'one of the greatest snooker clubs in the world'. (Patricia Houlihan)

Houlihan at the table in an unidentified club, probably in the 1970s. (Patricia Houlihan)

Three photos of Houlihan in the Lewisham Lucania snooker hall during the 1981/82 season, taken by Mary Rafferty for her sister Jean's seminal snooker book *The Cruel Game*. The last photo was not included in the book and is published here for the first time. (Jean Rafferty/Mary Rafferty)

Houlihan with wife Brenda (left), brother Terry (right) and Terry's wife Joan (second right). (Patricia Houlihan)

Houlihan and Jimmy White after their classic but frustratingly untelevised encounter at the 1989 British Open at the Assembly Rooms in Derby. White won 5-3 in a 'classic potting match' that only lasted 102 minutes, an average of less than 13 minutes per frame. (Clive Everton/*Pot Black*)

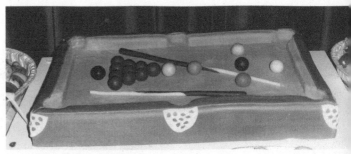

The snooker themed birthday cake Houlihan's family had made for his 60th birthday in 1989 at the Lord Hood pub. (Patricia Houlihan)

Houlihan in his beloved Osborne Arms with his mate of several decades Terry Dempsey (left). (Patricia Houlihan)

A publicity photo of Houlihan taken at an unknown location and date during his days on the pro tour. (Patricia Houlihan)

Houlihan with his only daughter Patsy Girl, here serving as maid of honour at a family wedding. (Patricia Houlihan)

Lancashire, Yorkshire and the north-east – they're the places where people really appreciate their snooker.' Although Houlihan struggled to find engagements across the spring and summer of 1972, he found some good form in money matches and practice, hitting a 137 at the Hatcham Liberal Club in April and two centuries and two 90s on a spectacular evening of play at the Redriff Transport Club in Bermondsey. Cheered by such form he spoke optimistically to *Snooker Scene*, declaring, 'I've still got the eagerness if I can get the games.'

It was to be a long wait before Houlihan's next match of significance, although when it eventually came it was within an exciting context. While the 1972 World Championship had been a peripatetic event spread over 11 months with matches taking place in a motley collection of venues, the 1973 staging was scheduled for one venue across 13 days from 16–28 April. The championship was sponsored by Park Drive, a tobacco brand owned by the Gallaher Group, who had also supported the previous season's tournament, as well as round-robin events the Park Drive 1000 and 2000. To ensure maximum profile and professionalism, the WPBSA had enlisted the support and organisational abilities of West Nally, a sports public relations group founded by BBC television commentator Peter West and Patrick Nally, an ambitious 23-year-old who had been working for an advertising agency when he met West. West Nally organised and promoted the tournament through a subsidiary they had set up named Snooker Promotions, who were also managing Higgins at the time.

The 1973 World Championship took place at Manchester's City Exhibition Hall, a large facility built in 1879 to house an indoor market but later converted into a space for exhibitions and events (today the hall has become the home of the Science and Industry Museum). Although not a perfect venue for matchplay snooker – the glass domed roof providing far too much light on a sunny day, and even cracking later in the tournament causing a 'rain stopped play' delay – the one-venue setup was a massive step forward, as was the fact the BBC were on board to provide televised coverage, albeit heavily truncated, of some of the later matches. Attendances at the tournament would prove to be hugely encouraging, with 25,000 attending over the 13-day stretch.

Houlihan was among the 16 unseeded players in round one, with the eight winners then scheduled to advance to round two where the eight seeds – champion Higgins, Fred Davis, John Pulman, Eddie Charlton, Gary Owen, Ray Reardon, John Spencer and Rex Williams – lay in wait. For these early games eight tables were placed in sections in the main arena, with tiered seating on four sides of the hall. Photographs of the tournament setup look terribly amateurish to modern eyes, with sheets haphazardly draped under the glass roof to keep out the sun, and the tiered temporary seating looking like something from a church hall social event, but at the time snooker had never seen anything so progressive. In a further indication of how much society, and snooker, has changed in the ensuing decades, the official programme for the tournament included an article by Clive Everton entitled 'Gentleman, you may smoke' which examined the connection between smoking and snooker, and explained how tobacco sponsorship had helped drive the sport's rising profile – no health warnings attached!

The round one draw paired Houlihan with Jackie Rea, a genial Northern Irishman whose long dominance of snooker in his homeland had been ended by Higgins, who beat him in round one of the 1972 World Championship and had deposed him as Irish professional champion the same year after a long reign that had begun in 1947. To help prepare for his match against Rea, Houlihan had warmed up with a 37-frame challenge encounter against his old friend and rival Ron Gross, played across six days from 12–17 February at the Albany Institute in Deptford. Houlihan won or drew every session, notching breaks including 60, 61, 63 and 68 as he ran out the 24-13 winner. 'I found it very difficult to keep Pat safe as he was potting the long balls very well and was very consistent all week,' Gross said afterwards.

Houlihan's game therefore seemed to be in fine fettle ahead of his clash with Rea over 17 frames on Monday, 16 April, although the preview in the official programme sounded a cautionary note, arguing that 'this championship will prove whether [Houlihan's] game has suffered from lack of competitive play in the professional game'. Rea had his own problems. After returning from an exhibition tour of

Zambia, the 52-year-old had stored his cue in a Manchester snooker club but when he went to collect it two days ahead of the Houlihan match it had been stolen. 'There's no replacement,' the disconsolate 'Clown Prince of Snooker' told the *Belfast Telegraph*. 'I had it for 34 years and to suffer such a blow a few hours before playing in this match is beyond words.'

According to *Snooker Scene*, Rea was so desperate to find his beloved cue that he spent much of the time in the final hours before the Houlihan match with the local police touring the residences of known criminals in an attempt to locate it. Rea witnessed several batches of stolen goods being recovered, including four cases of Durex condoms ('Obviously someone who goes in for a lot of safety play,' he quipped), but failed to locate the cue.

When the match began, Rea was forced to employ a replacement cue but Houlihan extended his luckless foe no mercy, winning the first two frames at a canter. Although Rea clawed his way back to 2-2, Houlihan then swept his way to seven frames in a row, notching breaks of 40 and 41 along the way, to secure a crushing 9-2 victory – easily the best performance and result of his pro career thus far. To his credit, Rea, whose cue had finally been returned to him shortly before the end of the match, gave his conqueror full credit. 'Pat played very well,' he admitted. 'I doubt whether I would have beaten him even if I had had my own cue. But if I had had it, I might have stopped him playing so well.' Houlihan's own assessment of the match was as honest and gracious as ever, 'When I won the first two frames, I felt I was going to win. Even when I lost the next two I still felt confident. Jack didn't have a very good run of the balls, but I was very pleased to win after having hardly any matches for such a long time.'

Suddenly Houlihan was attracting national press attention, including from a legend of the Fleet Street sports writing scene, Peter Batt, a hard-drinking journalist of the old school. Legendary sports scribe Norman Giller once observed of Batt, 'Everybody has a Peter Batt story.' One of the best? When Batt was a writer on the *Stratford Express* he was once reprimanded by his editor for repeated and unrepentant tardiness. After being shouted at, Batt protested that the reason – this time – for his lateness was that he had 'cut me old

John Thomas while with a bird last night', and by way of proof plonked his bandaged member on the editor's desk.

Batt left the *Stratford Express* not long afterwards after turning up for work paralytically drunk. Batt had been born in Stepney, east London, on 7 June 1933 and – like Houlihan – was a working-class lad of Irish extraction. After leaving school at 14 he worked as a labourer until a job as a copy taker gave him the opportunity to get a foot in the door of journalism. By 1973 Batt was a columnist with *The Sun*, relaunched as a tabloid in 1969 under the guidance of new owner Rupert Murdoch and steadily building in popularity and influence.

As Batt explained in a column headlined 'The Hooligan Meets Up with The Hurricane' on 18 April 1973, his and Houlihan's lives had intersected in years gone by. 'Like a good many Englishmen,' Batt wrote, 'I spent a considerable number of my formative years beneath the autumn tint of snooker table shades … My world then was populated by Cockney equivalents of Minnesota Fats and my own real-life hero was Patsy Houlihan alias The Hooligan.' Batt described Houlihan as the '[Alex] Higgins of the '50s … a stevedore by day and a genius of the green baize by night'.

'Between 1957 and 1967 he was unplayable at pool room level and had to roam the country looking for opponents,' Batt continued. 'In his heyday, Houlihan was barred from certain venues because he had too big a following of gamblers.' Some of these gamblers – many of them old mates from Deptford – still remained, Batt noted, and had backed Houlihan at odds of 250/1 to win the World Championship. Houlihan's supporters were certainly loyal to their man; Terry Dempsey recalled that when Houlihan once played in a pool tournament in a local pub a group of his fans turned up wearing T-shirts with the words 'Today Hooley, tomorrow the world!' emblazoned across them.

Speaking to Houlihan for his column, Batt elicited an interesting insight, namely that Patsy's eyesight issues had led him to invest in some glasses, but that he was not yet wearing them. 'It would take at least six months to get my eye in again with bins on,' Houlihan told Batt. 'I haven't got that sort of time now.' An entranced Batt was in the crowd for Houlihan's first-round match against Rea. 'Rea had lost his regular cue somewhere and was lost without it,' he wrote.

'Houlihan was slower, more methodical, more composed, body and cue welded together into one beautifully synchronised instrument.' The column concluded almost wistfully, as Batt reflected on snooker's rise in mainstream popularity, 'The promoters are convinced the game is entering one of the most sensational booms of all time,' he wrote. 'They assure me that there are snooker establishments sprouting up where it will be "a pleasure to take your wife and children". But I have a feeling that my son would have preferred the smoke-filled romantic world of Minnesota Fats and The Hooligan.'

The world Batt was referring to was a world that had almost passed into history already and, sadly, Houlihan was finding it hard to orientate himself within the new and increasingly sanitised snooker environment that was replacing it. Unfortunately, his performance in the last 16 against Higgins proved to be a major disappointment, although there was a significant mitigating factor at a crucial juncture of the match. Higgins was in dazzling form from the first frame of the opening afternoon session, which he won in just seven minutes courtesy of a rapid break of 52, made despite splitting his cue tip. Although Houlihan won the second frame 65-21, Higgins reeled off the next two to go into the interval 3-1 up. 'I won't be changing the tip during the interval,' Higgins declared, somewhat patronisingly. 'No disrespect to Patsy, but I only need to go half speed here.'

After the resumption of play, Higgins won the next three frames to move 6-1 ahead, but it was in the evening session when trouble struck. Houlihan arrived promptly, but Higgins was nowhere to be seen until 22 minutes after the scheduled start. According to Houlihan, the referee offered him the chance to claim the match on a forfeit but he refused, not wanting to win in such a manner. Nevertheless, by the time Higgins finally arrived, both the crowd and Houlihan were frustrated and fractious. Higgins attempted an explanation, which involved a double excuse of having to clean his dazzling white Oxford bags trousers which he had spilt beer on, as well as attending to his split cue tip, but his words were largely drowned out by boos from the crowd. In later years, Houlihan suggested he was so enraged by Higgins's late arrival that he had even taken a swipe at the Hurricane's head with his cue. 'I got the cue but I didn't hurt him or nothing,' he told Jonathan Rendall in 2002, although it is far from certain from Rendall's framing of the quotation if Houlihan was definitely referring to this match.

Higgins was chastised for his lateness by tournament director Bruce Donkin, and warned as to his future conduct, but no further sanction was made against him (today, arriving 22 minutes late for a match would have seen him docked three frames). Unfortunately, the incident seemed to have more of a negative effect on Houlihan than on Higgins. With typical bloody mindedness the Northern Irishman fed off the crowd's displeasure, turning their boos into cheers within five minutes of the restart by notching a break of 78. Thereafter Houlihan's form, in the words of *Snooker Scene*, 'rapidly dwindled to nothing', with Higgins taking every frame in the session to lead 14-1 overnight. Gracelessly, Higgins spent much of the match when he wasn't at the table in conversation with women in the crowd and made a point of ostentatiously, and unnecessarily, handing Houlihan the rest whenever he needed it, rather than allowing the referee to do so. The next day Houlihan had calmed down, and won two of the first three frames played, but it was merely a case of delaying the inevitable. Higgins duly won 16-3 to end Houlihan's World Championship hopes for another year.

Reflecting on the match a couple of years later, Houlihan admitted that Higgins's tardiness had left him 'seething', adding, 'I know I should have been more experienced than to let my feelings run away with me.' To suffer such a crushing defeat against a man whose unrepentant arrogance was the very antithesis of Houlihan's own gentlemanly demeanour was a bitter blow. It seemed to symbolise the unfortunate reality that the promised land of professional snooker was proving, for Houlihan, to be something of a wasteland.

So disenchanted did Houlihan become with life in professional snooker that he was soon giving serious thought to making a return to the amateurs. He laid bare his disaffection in a startlingly candid interview in the November 1975 issue of *The Q-World* headlined 'Catch-22 For Pat'. 'You can't lick the system,' a frustrated Houlihan sighed. 'I'm seriously considering packing it all in and being reinstated as an amateur.' Admitting that his career had gone wrong 'the minute

I was accepted into the professional association', Houlihan went on to eviscerate the organisation and power structure of professional snooker. 'It's unfair to people like me the way the pro game is being run,' he said. 'I haven't got the looks of a Mark Spitz, the grace of a Nureyev or the style of a Dean Martin, but by God I can play snooker. On second thoughts, I COULD play snooker. I've knocked my head against a stone wall for so long that I've lost interest.

'It's diabolical the way the professional game is being run. Unless Lady Luck shines on you, there's no way to break into the big time. The top eight or ten players have it all carved up between them. They get richer while the Ron Grosses, Maurice Parkins, Marcus Owens and myself slowly starve. It's not sour grapes, I'm just bitter that snooker has come such a long way since I first started, but the game is still run by the select few. Who are they trying to kid when they talk about the bad old days? As far as I'm concerned they're still with us. I think we've been left out in the cold. Just thrown the odd crumbs to fight for a place in the World Championships.'

Houlihan argued that a lack of opportunities had stymied his progress as a professional, illustrating his point by drawing a comparison between himself and John Spencer. 'When Spencer and I were amateurs I played him three times and won them all,' he said. 'I'm not saying I'd beat him now. He's obviously a great player now. But while he improved leaps and bounds during his early professional days with the many opportunities he had, my game has steadily gone worse through lack of match play.'

Steve Davis, reflecting on the issues that Houlihan and many other pros faced in the early to mid-1970s, admitted, 'There wasn't that much room for making money from the game then. The professional circuit was a different beast to what it is now. Even when I turned professional in 1978 you had to be accepted by the board which was made up of other players. You wonder what the mentality was in terms of allowing or not allowing new professionals. It felt like it was very cliquey, even in the '70s. One problem for anyone who turned or wanted to turn professional was that there wasn't really any money to be made from the game, so where was the benefit? That's why Terry Griffiths didn't try until he was a lot older and why a lot of the Welsh players never bothered to try. For a lot of people, it was just an amateur game. Unless you were a Fred Davis or John Pulman and had a holiday camp contract, there wasn't much going on.'

Houlihan also had other grounds on which to feel aggrieved. After reaching the last 16 of the 1973 World Championships he received an invitation to participate in the 1973 Norwich Union Open, a tournament partly televised by ITV. He beat John Virgo 4-3 in the opening round – winning on the final black – and was then beaten 4-0 by rising Canadian Cliff Thorburn in the last 16. Two last-16 performances from the tiny number of tournaments staged during 1973 was a decent result but Houlihan saw no benefit from it, and was still dumped back into the qualifying section for the 1974 World Championships. In contrast, Kingsley Kennerley, who hadn't entered the World Championship since 1951, and Canadian Bill Werbeniuk, who had never entered it before, were placed straight into the opening round, while the eight privileged and untouchable seeds – unchanged from the previous season – were placed automatically in the last 16.

There was little rhyme, reason or meritocracy at work and Houlihan's misery was made complete in the qualifiers at Belle Vue in Manchester when he ran into an in-form Jim Meadowcroft and was eliminated 8-5. 'Why should we give a start to these so-called top players?' Houlihan protested of the undemocratic tournament structure. 'They have to win four matches to become world champion, we have to win seven. I know there has to be seeds, but let them pit their skills against us right from the start. There would be a few eyes opened!'

The following season the World Championship was hosted in Australia, and Houlihan – in common with many other UK pros – could not afford to make the lengthy and expensive trip down under and therefore did not enter, declaring, 'If the championships are played in another country, then forget it.' Morale battered, he sat out the 1976 and 1977 World Championships too. 'You could say I'm opting out,' he had told *The Q-World* in 1975 and he appeared to be making good on this threat.

Chapter 13

# The Vardens Road gang

IRONICALLY ENOUGH, although Houlihan had grown disillusioned with pro snooker by the mid-1970s, his career as a money-match player was undergoing a renaissance. The increased interest in snooker as the decade progressed had created a boom environment on the club and backstreets circuit.

'There was so much money in the snooker halls [in the '70s],' Houlihan would later recall. 'The reason being all the barrow boys had taken it up. The money was unbelievable. It was £10 a game but that would be £200 today.' Houlihan's repertoire didn't only extend to conventional money matches, but also to various other cash-creating tricks and japes as well, some of which sailed a little close to the wind.

Joseph McIvor – who worked as a barrow boy in Lewisham market in the early 1970s – recalled one memorable incident involving Houlihan. 'Each day I'd get the teas in from the snooker hall above Burton's in the High Street,' McIvor said. 'On one occasion, there was a big discussion going on involving virtually everyone in there, about a trick shot "some cunt" did the evening before. I don't know if the shot was played in that hall or in the Green Man at the top of Blackheath Hill, but the discussion was really heated. It kind of divided opinions between it being really funny or the act of a flash bastard.

'The trick shot was this: two red balls were placed against the end cushion with a gap of a millimetre or so less between them. The aim was to put the two reds in each corner pocket with one shot. It's a very difficult shot – if the white hits one red before the other they go all

137

over the place, so the shot has to be very accurate and played with a lot of pace. But … with this shot there was a *third* ball, a white which sat between the reds but off the table. It was placed [on the rail] where the wood started and the baize ended. The player then took bets that he could get all three balls "in a pocket" with one shot.

'Money hit the table. Quite a bit too by all accounts. The bloke then placed the white ball in the "D" and took aim. He smashed the ball perfectly between the two reds, sending them flying into the corner pockets. And, while the cue ball was going up and down, he walked around the table to where the remaining white ball was and calmly rolled it with his finger into his waistcoat pocket. He then picked up the money and left the hall – very quickly! – to let everyone discuss what had happened. I'm 62 now and was only about 14 at the time. But that story stayed with me. I didn't actually witness the shot – I only witnessed the aftermath of a visit by Patsy Houlihan!'

In the best traditions of a south-east London ducker and diver (think Del Boy, but classier and much more dapper) Houlihan had other income streams too. Out of one of his local pubs in Deptford he ran his own makeshift bookmaking service. Once in a while, however, he came a cropper. 'One time in the pub he was taking bets and half a dozen people all backed the same winner and Patsy didn't have enough money to pay out,' Terry Dempsey recalled. 'At which point he made one of his famous statements – one which we never let him forget – namely, "The missus will be by in a minute, she'll give you your money! She'll give us a tap on the window first." Unfortunately, no tap came! From then on, any time Patsy didn't have any cash we'd always say to him, "What, we got to wait for the tap on the window?"'

Another time, Houlihan literally lost the coat off his back. 'One day Patsy and my father went into Burton's on a cold winter's day, got measured up and bought big Cromby overcoats,' Dempsey explained. 'They walked into the fucking snooker hall in these coats. Patsy lost all his money so they put the coats down and lost those too. They had to come home in the freezing cold without coats on their back. My father never forgave him for that!'

Houlihan also had a financial interest in a cafe at Crawley's scrap metal yard which his daughter Patsy Girl ran for a while. He even received daily payments from the landlord of the Windsor Castle pub for clearing out and lighting the fireplace each day. Furthermore, when he was on the move he was also something of a mobile jewellery salesman. 'Patsy often wore a big overcoat,' Roy Bacon recalled. 'Inside the coat were numerous pockets with watches and rings and all sorts of things like that which Patsy would try to sell to people if they showed any interest at all! I think I bought something for my wife from him once!'

Not all of Houlihan's antics were focused on making money. He was also an expert at keeping everyone entertained down the pub, particularly through his penchant for flashy coin tricks. 'He was a great person to be in the company of,' Dempsey said. 'He was an all-round talented man. He used to put seven of the old half-crown coins along his arm, flick them up in the air, catch six of them with one hand, and then hit the last one with his heel into his shirt pocket. In the pub he could play a tune on a beer glass – a proper tune I mean, it was amazing. He'd play a glass or tray along with someone on the piano or what have you in the pub. He could tap dance too. I remember him tap dancing on the tables in the pub.' A common sight in the pubs of Deptford was Terry Houlihan – who had a great voice – singing old standards while Patsy accompanied him by playing a tune on a glass or tray and the rest of the pub sung or clapped along.

With his skills on the baize, as well as his entertaining routine of tricks and anecdotes off it, Houlihan would soon become a hero and something of a mentor to a fast-rising duo of extravagant young south London snooker talents. Born in Tooting in 1959 and 1962 respectively, Tony Meo and Jimmy White were both pupils at the Ernest Bevin comprehensive school. By the time they were teenagers in the 1970s, however, they were more familiar with the inside of Tony Zanoncelli's snooker hall on Lynwood Road, Tooting – known to all and sundry as Zan's – than they were with the interior of a classroom. Both youngsters were precocious cueists and were soon being ferried around by a taxi driver known as 'Dodgy' Bob Davis to participate in money match escapades around the country.

It was Ron Gross who first told Houlihan about White, telling him that there was a kid from south London who often played at

Ron's club in Neasden and was 'a bit special'. Although Houlihan didn't realise it at the time, that young kid was White and White had already seen Houlihan play, having been dazzled when he made an appearance at Zan's around 1974 in a money match against Charlie Poole, another brilliant attacking talent. The stakes were a tenner a frame and Poole and Houlihan – with utter disregard for anything that even mildly resembled a safety shot – rattled through around 16 frames in just three hours, leaving the Zan's regulars agog with admiration.

White and Houlihan would soon be reunited due to the intervention of Noel Miller Cheevers, a Dublin property developer and a decent amateur cueist himself, who had even played Houlihan in the London area championship a couple of times back in the 1950s. In 1976 Cheevers opened a brand-new snooker club, the Pot Black, on Vardens Road, Battersea Rise and asked Houlihan to fulfil the role of 'resident professional'. The plush 24-table setup and Houlihan's presence soon helped attract a large slice of London's snooker talent to Vardens Road, White and Meo among them. It was, in the words of White, 'one of the greatest snooker clubs in the world'.

Meo also loved the Pot Black club. Although he quit snooker in 1997 and customarily refuses interview requests, he made an exception for this book, ringing the author one afternoon in reply to a letter sent to the business address of the watch and jewellery company he now runs. 'I've been approached to do all sorts of stuff about snooker in the 1980s or about myself, and I'm just not interested,' Meo told me. 'But you're doing something very good by writing about someone who was such a nice man, and that means more to me. It's nice that Patsy Houlihan's being remembered because he was a decent soul.'

Meo went on, 'I started playing snooker when I was about 15. I first met Patsy when I was about 16 at the Pot Black club. I was just a kid and he was lovely. Jimmy met him there too. We probably both met him at the same time – I'm just a couple of years older than Jimmy. We're talking a long time ago. Forty-five years. It's kind of scary. When I met him I thought Patsy must have been in his 50s but he was actually in his 40s. Everyone looks a lot older when you're a kid.'

Young Turks Meo and White naturally gravitated towards Houlihan's gnarled but charismatic gunslinger and ended up spending many an hour playing, chatting and laughing with him. There was a natural camaraderie between the trio, united as they were by their working-class roots, eye for a money-making opportunity and the flair-filled manner with which they attacked the snooker table. 'Dad grew up with nothing, just like Jimmy and Tony,' Patsy Girl once explained. 'They understood each other because of that. They knew what life was really like.'

It's a point Meo elaborated on. 'Patsy had grown up in and around tough environments,' he said. 'He had a reputation for being a hustler and all that – he was probably doing that well before Jimmy and I were even born. But when we were kids we played for money too. It was a way of making the game more interesting. If someone challenged you for money you'd play them because everyone needs money don't they? Patsy was brought up in a tough era and he was a hustler and all of that but people shouldn't look down on him for that. It was what it was and it was a living. Besides, in Houlihan's day, with Joe Davis and the others, snooker was a closed shop. It was very snobby. They wouldn't let Patsy in, they wouldn't let Marcus Owen in. So what was Patsy meant to do? The thing is, far from being a snob, people like Patsy were real. He didn't look down on us, even though we were just kids. We all came from working-class backgrounds, you see.'

As for White, he admitted, with a twinkle in his eye and a slight lump in his throat, that he 'loved being around Patsy all day'. 'The Whirlwind' also talked warmly of treasuring the stories Houlihan told him and the tricks he performed for him, whether with coins or snooker balls. Sometimes, White recalled, he 'ended up with bellyache' from laughing so much at Houlihan's jokes and antics. 'Patsy was great craic to go out with,' he added. 'We went out quite a few times. He was a good friend. I knew him very well.' White never saw Houlihan at the peak of his powers in the 1950s and '60s, but still rated him extremely highly. 'When I was 14 or 15 I'd be watching him in the snooker hall,' he said. 'And some days Patsy struggled because he'd been drinking the night before or gambling or whatever, but when it all connected and he started performing, he was like no one else on earth. There are certain people in this world, certain sports people, like Floyd Mayweather in boxing or Tiger Woods in golf, like Ronnie

O'Sullivan at times today, that when they hit their peak they just can't be beat. It's a sickener that there's no video footage of him in action, because Houlihan was like that too.'

White was adamant that had circumstances been different, Houlihan would have definitely won the World Championship. 'The story I heard is that Joe Davis wasn't having any of it when Patsy wanted to turn pro originally,' he said. 'If he had turned professional back then he would have won the World Championship for sure. Unfortunately, Patsy just missed out. He was caught in between two eras; his best days came in the amateurs in the '50s and '60s before snooker really became popular again in the late '70s and '80s. By that time he was 50 or 60. He just missed out. It's such a shame.'

Meo also rated Houlihan as a top-drawer talent. 'There's no doubt about it,' he asserted with conviction. 'If Patsy had been born in a different kind of era and had different guidance he would have made it right to the very top. He was just so natural on the table. He used to get down, take one look and then bang! He was so smooth, so fluent and the balls used to go in the pockets like rockets! And he could pot balls from anywhere. He was a really good player. Patsy could have beaten any of those people that were around when Joe Davis was playing.'

Like White, Meo recalled Houlihan's tricks and banter with the utmost affection. 'He used to hold five coins in his hand,' he recalled with a chuckle. 'He'd throw them up in the air and then catch them – one, two, three, four, five! – very quickly before they hit the floor. Amazing. You try doing that with just two coins! He had lots of those tricks, lots of stories and we would love it. It helped fuel our love of snooker.'

Another rising talent who frequented the Pot Black club in the 1970s was Steve Davis, the future six-time world champion. Although he didn't forge the personal connection and friendship with Houlihan that White and Meo did, Davis also recalled Patsy extremely fondly. 'There were two players in the London area that were the underground heroes on the amateur snooker scene before the game was ever well known or popular,' Davis explained. 'They were Patsy Houlihan and Marcus Owen. One was north of the river and one was south. I was already aware of Patsy Houlihan and his status as this folklore hero when I started to go to and practise at the new snooker club that was opened in Clapham. Patsy was there and he was a great character, a lovely guy.'

Davis would often practise at the Pot Black on a Tuesday and watch Houlihan in action. One week, they even played each other in a money match, as 'The Nugget' recalled, 'I remember playing 24 frames with him one day for 50p a frame when I was an up-and-comer and knocking on the doors of becoming a professional. I was a pretty decent player by then. Patsy knew who to stake big money against and who not to and I was pretty decent so that's why it was only 50p a frame! We had some real fun and the match ended up level, I think it was 12-all. There was great respect there.

'Because of the hustler image he had, people possibly thought Patsy was a bad boy in the Alex Higgins mould but he wasn't at all. He was a lovely guy. Very polite. A gentleman. Maybe a Robin Hood character in a way. You'd hear stories about him – about how to try and make money from the game he'd invent ways to try and gamble. He'd play people and he wouldn't be allowed to have the cue ball touch a cushion or whatever. People would think they would be able to beat him if he had that type of handicap but he was so skilful that he could still win.'

Davis also gave his assessment of Houlihan's style and skillset, 'He was fast and fluent. Ahead of his time in style. He wasn't a defensive player like Ron Gross, for example. I also got the feeling that he was professional standard in his mentality and outlook about how to play the game of snooker compared to run-of-the-mill amateurs of the time. Players like Jack Fitzmaurice and so on were very pedestrian in terms of their shot selection and their style of play. That's why Houlihan was effectively a forerunner to Alex Higgins in as much as he was an attacking player.

'He was very talented. I've seen clips of Joe Davis, Fred Davis and John Pulman play and he was in their league easily, I would have thought. I only ever really saw Patsy playing in practice so I don't know what his match temperament was like. [But beating Reardon and Spencer in 1965] shows you the quality he had. He was certainly a character. He had a good sense of humour and he was a good laugh.

I enjoyed my time around him. He played a good game and a game that was ahead of its time.'

Irishman Eugene Hughes was another talented cueist who encountered Houlihan at Vardens Road. 'I first went to England in 1977,' Hughes recalled. 'Patsy was the resident pro at the Pot Black. Tony Meo, Jimmy White and Steve Davis all played there in those days and we all looked up to Patsy. Every day you went into the club you'd hope for a game with Patsy. He was a great character and an absolute gentleman. He liked a pint and he liked a game of snooker. He was a legend around London. You'd hear stories about his days as an amateur. It was always said that Joe Davis wouldn't let him turn pro. Joe used to give amateurs a 14 start and Patsy would beat him by more than that. Most people think Patsy wasn't allowed to become pro because he was too good. People speak well of anyone who's passed away but in Patsy's case I could genuinely say I've never heard anyone say an ill word about him.'

Hughes also credited Houlihan as a snooker innovator. 'A lot of shots we play today, Patsy brought into the game,' he argued. 'He was an inventor of shots. And he'd pass on his knowledge to all and sundry. He was a fantastic potter and break builder and he was great under pressure. Alongside Jimmy and Ronnie he was the most naturally gifted player I ever saw, and remember I only knew him in his later years when he was past his peak, but still he was such a talent.'

Memories are hazy now, and dates impossible to pin down, but it seems Houlihan joined White and Meo for some of their money match escapades, sitting in the back of 'Dodgy' Bob Davis's taxi before the trio would stride into anonymous darkened snooker halls in dingy backstreets and triumph in matches which some locals probably still talk about in hushed and disbelieving tones. At other times, locals would pour into the Pot Black to try their hand on the baize. 'There was a used car lot nearby,' White remembered. 'All the car salesmen used to come in there to play and gamble. We used to give them mad starts, like 100 or something, and we'd still clean up. We used to play in the Pot Black until everybody got thirsty and then we'd pour out of there into The Invitation [a pub].'

Another memorable aspect of the Vardens Road days were the £500 challenge matches that the Pot Black would arrange against other clubs. 'Our line-up was incredible,' White said. 'Me and Tony Meo; Noel Miller Cheevers, who was a fantastic potter; Patsy Houlihan – one of the greatest players I've ever seen; Flash Bob [Harris] and Eugene Hughes. You couldn't have dreamt of a better side than that. We used to put notices in magazines challenging people to come and play us at the Pot Black … Contenders flocked from all over to try and win the £500 a match that was at stake but they never did. It was like walking into the lion's den. We never lost.'

As the 1970s drew to a close, the sun would finally set on the Vardens Road days. In 1979 White, not yet 17, became the then-youngest winner of the English Amateur Championship, beating Meo in the London section, and Dave Martin in the final. The world amateur title, which fate had prevented Houlihan competing for, was also snaffled by White in 1980 and then he turned professional. Meo had already joined the pro ranks a year earlier.

White, Meo and Houlihan would still see each other around the circuit in the coming years, and the bonds between them remained tight, but the Vardens Road days of carefree laughter, tricks and gambles with piles of cash on the snooker rail were soon nothing but a memory.

'We played and practised together for a few years before moving off to other places,' Meo recalled. 'Patsy always moved around. That's what he did. As for Jimmy and I, we were heading off into the pros. But I thoroughly enjoyed those few years I had with Patsy Houlihan. In fact, I enjoyed every minute of them. He was very special at what he did. And a real gent. He never had a cross word with anyone, ever. I can't really say any more than that. And I always speak it as it is.

'What can I say? We loved him.'

# Chapter 14

# Patsy's big day

TWO FACTORS galvanised a renewed enthusiasm within Patsy Houlihan for professional snooker after the low point of 1975. His enjoyment of his role as resident pro at the Pot Black club in Vardens Road was one, with the presence of Jimmy White and Tony Meo undoubtedly serving to reignite and reinvigorate his own passion for the game.

Another factor was his decision – after years of eyesight issues – to adopt contact lenses when playing. Hitherto, Houlihan had needed glasses, and even owned a pair, but had been nervous of using them. By 1976, however, he was finding that he could play increasingly effectively with contact lenses. The May issue of *Snooker Scene* observed that he had 'regained much of the form which made him such an exciting player a few years ago' since adopting contacts, pointing to his recent impressive 5-1 victory against Vic Harris at the Romford Lucania in a £50 challenge match, a contest in which Houlihan had, remarkably, made two centuries, an 86 and a 74. Not long after, Houlihan also scooped the £100 first prize in a pro-am at the newly renamed Southern Snooker Centre in Southend.

Pro-ams were one thing but making an impact on the professional circuit would be altogether more challenging, especially given the limited number of tournaments in existence and the difficulty in extracting invitations to them. Houlihan had appeared at number 23 on the 'order of merit' published after the 1975 world snooker championship in Australia – which he did not enter – the sport's first attempt at a structured, meritocratic rankings list. Calculated on the basis of players' performances in the three previous World Championships, Houlihan snuck in courtesy of his last-16 finish in 1973. However, after deciding to sit out the 1976 and 1977 championships, he did not appear in the first world rankings, published ahead of the 1976/77 season, or in those for 1977/78, both of which, like the order of merit, adopted the policy of using points accrued from the three previous World Championships.

The introduction of world rankings was an indication that interest in snooker was on the rise, with media interest picking up. In February 1977, the sport featured on the youth television programme *The London Weekend Show*, hosted by Janet Street-Porter, the first of many presenting gigs for a woman who was already well on her way to becoming one of the most recognisable media personalities in the country. Broadcast in the London area on 6 February, the episode 'Billiard Boom' examined the seemingly inexorable rise of snooker, and featured Houlihan as one of its guests, alongside writer Clive Everton and rising star Steve Davis. The section featuring Houlihan saw Street-Porter interview him about his hustling days. The transcript below represents the most extended interview Houlihan ever gave on camera:

Janet Street-Porter, 'In its less popular period after the war [snooker] gained something of a sinister reputation with people like the Kray twins running their hall in Mile End. To become a top-class player you had to spend months of full-time playing and as there wasn't much prize money around for amateurs, you had to find some other way of supporting yourself until you became a successful professional. And so hustlers arrived. One of London's best-known snooker characters at that time was Pat Houlihan, national amateur champion in 1965 and now a professional. Pat, how did you start playing?'

Patsy Houlihan, 'I first started at the age of 13. Started in them days playing for a sixpence, then a shilling. And then, I thought it was easy money, started to improve me play and then eventually was going all around the country, playing for hundreds eventually.'

JS-P, 'Yeah, I was going to say, what sort of stakes did you end up playing for?'

PH, 'Well, we had matches, you know, the best of so many frames, £300, £400, with of course a backer. I always had backers, like, I was well in demand in them days, there was so many people wanting to back me.'

JS-P, 'What does a backer do?'

PH, 'Well, they put the money down and whatever it is they give you a percentage of it. But I was fortunate I always got half of it, whatever it was I always got half, because I had so many people willing to put the money down. It was me living. I had me wife, I had to look after her and that was it – I had to get it.'

JS-P, 'So was it pretty tough?'

PH, 'Er, it was tough, but I had maybe luck or whatever it may be, but I always won.'

JS-P, 'If you were so good at snooker, how did you still manage to go round the country and find people to play you?'

PH, 'With snooker there's always someone out to try and beat you. I've played three brothers, two of 'em like you could beat 'em and the third one he might have been inferior to the other two, but he's still sacrificed his ten, 20 pounds with the hope of beating you so he can say to his brothers, "I beat him and you never." They sacrifice it, and it's even so today, all you hear of is money matches.'

JS-P, 'Did you develop tricks so that when you started playing people didn't think you were that great so they'd be tempted to bet on you?'

PH, 'Yeah, well it's your stance. You can stand different and people look at you and think he's a right mug or whatever the case may be.'

JS-P, 'Let's go over to the table and you can show me a few of these tricks for when I might need them … Pat, you were talking about stance and things like that where you can tell a good player from a bad player. Now what do you mean exactly? Are people who stand up very straight going to be bad or …?'

PH, 'Well, it doesn't mean they're actually going to be too bad, but it doesn't make them good. I mean, if you've got a chap who plays snooker and as he's going to the table, he's got his head right up like that, you can rest assured that he's not a good player. But if you get a chap who when he gets down to a ball, you can guarantee he's looking.

You can always tell. So you end up playing them and what you do is if you're playing a man who's, how can I put it, much worse than yourself, you play as much as you can to the way he's playing and then if it's need be that you've got to get down more, then you get down more.'

JS-P, 'So you're disguising your play?'

PH, 'You disguise your play. This is right. And then if you have got to bring it up, then you've got to bring it up, because pound notes tell stories.'

JS-P, 'How can you tell if someone's nervous?'

PH, 'You can always tell on those occasions, even playing in the championships, you can see like for a start, you can see the sleeve they start to shake and you see their hands moving and …'

JS-P, 'Those are the little signs you look for?'

PH, 'They're good signs. When you see this happen you know you've got 'em straightaway. You don't get many people, you know, especially where money's concerned. Anybody that's playing for money. You've got to be cool and don't let money interfere with your play. But if you see anybody that is shaking or their hands are moving, then you know you've got 'em. They can't possibly win.'

JS-P, 'How do you think the game's changed over the last ten years?'

PH, 'Er, well there's more hundred breaks being made today then there's ever been. I mean, years ago, they were scoring 20s and 30s and running safe but today they'll score 20 and they'll ping a red in out of the blue and go and make a hundred, whereas years ago they didn't look for 'em. You know there's still money to be earned. This is it. Young children are playing today, 14-year-olds making hundred breaks like myself when I was … this is it, it's something to play for, there's so much money at stake.'

JS-P, 'Is snooker going to become a younger game again?'

PH, 'I think it's improved. Snooker's improving all the time. You know, quite a lot of people, like I mean, my friend here Steve Davis, there's him, there's one, there's a few of 'em up and coming and they've got it in 'em, all it means is, let 'em prove it and bring it out.'

JS-P, 'Making things a bit tough for you …'

PH, 'This is it. Making it tougher, this is it, we might have to go to work!'

Encouraged by such media interest, as well as his form at the Pot Black and the general rise in snooker's popularity, Houlihan returned to the pro circuit, eagerly accepting an invitation to participate in the inaugural UK Championship in November 1977. The brainchild of Mike Watterson – a Derbyshire businessman and entrepreneur whose role in the rise of snooker in the late 1970s and early '80s cannot be overstated – the event was to be staged from 26 November to 3 December with sponsorship from ball manufacturer Super Crystalate. The venue was the Tower Circus in Blackpool, scene of Houlihan's great triumph against John Spencer 12 years earlier. Eight seeds were placed straight into the last 16, while 16 further pros were left to fight it out for the right to meet them.

Houlihan was drawn against Jim Meadowcroft, who had knocked him out of the 1974 World Championship in the qualifying round in what was still, unbelievably, Patsy's most recent major tournament match. Meadowcroft, an amiable and talented Lancastrian, would later find fame as an accomplished television commentator for both the BBC and ITV and had also been a World Championship quarter-finalist in 1976, knocking out Rex Williams along the way. He was a more than decent cueist and many thought he had the potential to become one of the top players in the world. Bearing in mind it was Houlihan's first major match in nearly four years he didn't play too badly, but Meadowcroft still beat him 5-1, Patsy having somehow contrived – for reasons lost to the mists of time – to have lost his contact lenses before the start.

It wasn't the romantic return to the Tower Circus that Houlihan might have dreamed of, but, undeterred, he entered the 1977/78 World Championship – his first entry since 1973/74. Much had changed in the intervening years. After an ill-advised sojourn to Australia in 1975 and a strange two-venue staging in 1976, the championship had, in 1977, finally found what would in time become its permanent and iconic home at the Crucible Theatre in Sheffield. Watterson had been key to this move, acting on the advice of his wife Carole who had watched a play at the Crucible and suggested to her husband that it was a perfect venue for snooker. Watterson brokered a deal whereby he rented the theatre for two weeks for £6,600, convincing the WPBSA to back the plan by guaranteeing them a certain financial return. With sponsorship from cigarette brand Embassy, expanded coverage of the final on the BBC, and a prize fund of £17,000 the tournament proved a rousing success, John Spencer defeating Cliff Thorburn in the final.

Expectation was therefore high ahead of the 1978 championship, which was returning to the Crucible with an increased prize fund of £24,000, the expanded exposure of a daily highlights programme on BBC2 and the honour of front page coverage in *Radio Times*, the BBC's television and radio listings magazine. If Houlihan was to reach Sheffield, though, he would first need to win two matches in the unforgiving confines of the Romiley Forum in Stockport. Watterson had manfully shouldered the financial burden of staging the qualifiers, despite the fact they would most likely – and indeed did – leave him out of pocket. Houlihan's preliminary round opponent was one of his old rivals from his amateur days, Chris Ross. Based in Woking, Ross had won the English Amateur Championship in 1976, but having turned pro he found himself suffering from a mystery illness – most likely psychosomatic in nature – that made him vomit several times a day and left him unable to pick up and use a pen, let alone a snooker cue, forcing him to give up playing for a while. Only when Ross adopted a new stance and an unusual cue grip was he able to resume snooker again, but his pro debut proved a disaster as he lost 11-0 to Cliff Thorburn in the qualifiers for the 1977 World Championship.

Houlihan was understandably installed as the pre-match favourite and had every reason to enter with confidence. But no one – probably not even Houlihan himself – expected his performance to be quite as sensational as it proved, as he swept to a 9-1 win, making 11 breaks of over 30 along the way, five of them north of 50, including dazzling runs of 79, 77 and 67. 'I haven't played as well as that since London Bridge was a lighthouse,' he quipped after the match, having shown form which, in the estimation of *Snooker Scene*, represented 'vintage stuff'.

'Poor Ross could do nothing to stop the avalanche of breaks,' the magazine added, remarking that Houlihan had put 'the clock back nearly 20 years to reproduce some of the form which made him one of the most exciting players of the early '60s'. *The Q-World* was equally impressed. 'Houlihan was in tremendous form,' purred Vince Laverty.

'On this showing [he] could turn the form books upside down! [This] victory was every bit as clinical as his 11-3 destruction of John Spencer in 1965. His potting and positional play were a delight to watch and such was his superiority that he needed only one opening to clinch a frame.'

Jack Fenton, assistant to Mike Watterson, was also staggered by the standard of Houlihan's play. 'That's the finest snooker I've seen for a long time,' he declared. 'It was like seeing the old Patsy again. He'll shake a few up if he keeps that sort of form up.'

Houlihan was now just one match from a place in the last 16 at the Crucible and a guaranteed £500 payday. The problem was that the fates had dictated that the man in his way was – yet again – Meadowcroft, who had dumped him out of his last two pro tournaments. Houlihan had his contact lenses back again though, as well as the confidence engendered in him by his slaughter of Ross, but all other signs – and the bookmakers' odds – pointed to a Meadowcroft victory. It was therefore no surprise when the first frame went according to expectation, the Lancastrian looking smooth, elegant and controlled as he took it 85-37. 'Victory [for Meadowcroft] seemed a foregone conclusion,' observed *The Q-World*. 'After all hadn't [he] cruised home against the Londoner in the UK Championships?'

Houlihan struck back in the second frame though with a break of 66 described by *Snooker Scene* as 'a classic', including as it did 'three cushioned balls on which he obtained perfect position'. Frame three was a sensation. Houlihan rattled off a 50 break, and then ran safe, but Meadowcroft's riposte, a superb long pot which kickstarted a break of 80, gave him a 2-1 lead. Frame four was also a high-quality affair. Houlihan was in first with a fine run of 43, only for a bad kick to stymie him. Meadowcroft – aided by a fluke – replied with 54, but it was Houlihan who swiped the remaining balls to take it 74-54 and draw level 2-2. Houlihan now had the bit between his teeth, winning the next three frames in rapid style, aided by excellent breaks of 62 and 37. Meadowcroft took the final frame of the session though, thanks to runs of 46 and 43, to narrow the deficit to 5-3.

The evening session was as tense and nervy as the first had been fluent and free-scoring. 'Houlihan showed signs of tension,' reported

*The Q-World*, 'but it was Meadowcroft who felt the pressure most.' The first four frames featured some attritional play, and were shared two apiece as Houlihan inched 7-5 ahead. Then, just as he needed it most, Houlihan summoned a brilliant break of 65 in frame 13, leaving him just one frame from victory. Meadowcroft clawed one back but Houlihan reached the winning post by taking frame 15 50-28 to secure a 9-6 victory. It had been a brilliant match, easily the most high-quality of the qualifiers, although 60-something veteran Fred Davis's nail-biting 9-8 win over John Virgo was arguably more dramatic.

'I would have been quite happy for this match to have been the final,' promoter Watterson admitted of the Houlihan-Meadowcroft match as he caught his breath afterwards. Meanwhile, a disgruntled Meadowcroft claimed it had been his 'worst display in the World Championship', a harsh assessment bearing in mind some of the brilliance he had shown in the early frames and given that – in the estimation of *Snooker Scene* – 'no more than half a dozen shots were missed [by either man during the entire match]'.

Houlihan was now Sheffield-bound and beginning to attract the sort of wider media attention he hadn't enjoyed since 1965. *The Guardian* ran a whole eight-paragraph piece on him by Clive Everton headlined 'The Hustler's return'. 'Among the 16 players who will compete in the Embassy World Professional Championship... is one who is not only unknown to the general public, but a man whom the snooker fraternity itself had put down as irretrievably past his best,' ran Everton's introduction. His description of Houlihan's early career was a classic of concision, 'A Cockney, Houlihan has spent most of his life in billiard halls up and down the country, leading the sort of life depicted in *The Hustler*, the American pool classic. In the 1950s and 1960s, when amateurism was rigidly defined, it was easier to pass through the eye of a needle than to penetrate the legit pro-circuit, so this was the only way he could earn even a precarious living with his cue.' Labelling Houlihan's play in the qualifiers a 'revelation' and his victory against Meadowcroft as 'a heartwarming win in a match whose quality would not have been inappropriate to the final', Everton concluded of Houlihan's chances in the tournament, 'If he can maintain his present inspiration ... he could have a few more surprises in store.'

Houlihan's joy at reaching Sheffield, however, and his natural optimism were tempered somewhat by the cold, harsh reality that he had drawn one of the toughest match players in the world, Cliff Thorburn, the sixth seed and runner-up to Spencer the previous year. Seemingly hewn from Canadian granite, Thorburn, like Houlihan, had grown up tough. His parents separated when he was 18 months old and when his mother subsequently abandoned him he spent two years in an orphanage at the centre of a custody battle before going to live with his father and grandmother. A talented pool and lacrosse player, Thorburn left school at 16 and was soon hustling at pool and snooker rooms across the tough Canadian money match circuit, working as a dishwasher and on a garbage truck to raise his stakes. By 1970 he was resident pro at a club in Toronto, and after playing a series of matches against visiting John Spencer in 1971, the Lancastrian encouraged him to give the UK circuit a try. A rock-solid tactician, Thorburn may not have had the natural flair of some of his rivals but he was one of the steeliest competitors the snooker world would ever produce, and his route from Canadian hustler to 1980 world champion remains one of the unlikeliest and most remarkable narratives in the sport's history.

Although they possessed sharply contrasting styles – Thorburn was a grinder and Houlihan a natural – the two men were full of respect for one another. Their mutually tough backgrounds probably had something to do with this, with both being working-class hustlers turned 'respectable' pros. This respect extended to a deep appreciation of each other's abilities; in later years, Houlihan would anoint Thorburn as the toughest opponent of his career. 'He was a hard man,' Patsy would intone admiringly.

Such respect and admiration were mutual. 'I really liked being around Patsy,' Thorburn told the author by telephone from Canada. 'Some of the people hanging around the game in the clubs back then you'd have to count your fingers after shaking their hand, but not Patsy. He was always a gentleman. I loved being around him and really enjoyed watching him play. He was a very renowned player. I didn't see tons of him but I loved seeing him play because, boy, was he a smooth player. He really had a way around the table. He knew he was good and looked it. He was also a very confident player. He was as smooth as they get. How could you be smoother than he was? He was one of those guys that made the pockets look really big. He was compact, you know and he got down on the cue so nicely.'

The Thorburn-Houlihan match – a best-of-25-frames encounter – was scheduled to be played across three sessions over the first two days of the tournament, Monday, 17 and Tuesday, 18 April, with highlights to be shown each evening on BBC2 at 10pm and 11.15pm respectively. From the first frame, Houlihan struggled under the bright lights set up by the BBC. 'With my contact lenses I found the television lights very strong,' he later admitted. 'I hardly potted a long ball.' Although Houlihan edged the first frame, Thorburn then won four in a row, accumulating breaks of 67 and 47, with Houlihan's best run being a 37. In the sixth frame, though, Houlihan found his form, notching a wondrous break of 83 made at speed and with grace. It could – indeed should – have been the tournament's first century, but with the colours on their spots Houlihan rushed and missed. He won the sixth frame as well though, before Thorburn took the last of the session. At just 5-3 down, however, Houlihan was still very much in the match.

The second session was a seesaw affair. Thorburn started confidently, winning the first two frames with breaks of 63 and 36 to lead 7-3, but Houlihan once again rallied, runs of 31 and 37 helping him cut the deficit to 7-5. Thorburn restored his three-frame advantage but Houlihan was undeterred, knocking in breaks of 48 and 43 in the 14th frame. Thorburn took the 15th frame but a brilliant Houlihan break of 79 saw the session shared, although Thorburn still led 9-7. Houlihan had thus far out-potted Thorburn, but the Canadian's fierce control of the tactical exchanges had proved crucial, and so it would prove again in the final session.

The key moment came in the 18th frame. With Thorburn 10-7 up, Houlihan led 64-47 with just green, brown, blue, pink and black left. With the brown out of commission on a side cushion, Houlihan unwisely elected to pot the green rather than go for a snooker. A misjudged shot on the brown then gave Thorburn the chance to clear the remaining colours and snatch the frame 69-67. A frustrated Houlihan now trailed 11-7 and although he smashed a 72 break in the next frame, Thorburn won the two frames he needed to reach the winning line 13-8, thus progressing to a quarter-final meeting with 'Steady' Eddie Charlton.

Reflecting on the match 43 years later, Thorburn admitted, 'I don't have a whole lot of memories of that match in 1978. The thing is I had a disastrous ending in that tournament when Eddie Charlton won the last five against me to win 13-12 and that overshadowed everything else for me. That's mostly what I remember now about 1978. But here's the deal: I had to be very careful against Patsy because if the balls were open he could get to you. When he got among the balls he would look like he was just at the practice table because he was that fluent. A very dangerous player.' Houlihan's own contemporary assessment of the match was short but characteristically accurate. 'I didn't do badly,' he shrugged of his two-day stay in Sheffield.

Sadly, Houlihan would never play at the Crucible again. It would be wonderful to report that those breaks of 83, 79 and 72 that he made against Thorburn are preserved for all time in some lovingly curated snooker archive, but they are not among the tapes of BBC footage that have survived the intervening decades, and they have never appeared on even the most shadowy corner of the internet. Indeed, the only footage that seemingly exists of Houlihan's match with Thorburn is a brief snippet of Patsy rising from a shot and walking away from the table with a look of disappointment etched across his face, which appears in a 1978 Granada TV documentary entitled *This England*.

'Boy, is it ever sad [that there's no footage of him],' is the assessment of Thorburn. 'But hopefully I've given you some words that will help people imagine what he was like.'

# Chapter 15

# Searching for the big break

DESPITE REACHING the Crucible in 1978, opportunities for Houlihan to build on his form the following season were few and far between. He had ended the season ranked 18th in the world, but this had little practical benefit. The world rankings were merely calculated on the basis of performance in the World Championships, and the only way to earn points was to reach the last 16 or further. More and more tournaments were appearing on the pro circuit, but they and the other staples of the tour were almost exclusively invitational events and carried no ranking points. Houlihan wasn't invited to them anyway – he was not among the ten players invited to the Masters at Wembley, the eight players invited to *Pot Black* or even the 16 entrants asked to participate in the Holsten Lager International. He remained on the outside looking in, hoping for the big breakthrough that might help him permanently breach the inner circle of professional snooker.

It did not come at the 1978 UK Championship, in which he lost 9-3 to Roy Andrewartha in the qualifying round of the only other tournament save the worlds that a lower-ranked pro was likely to receive an invitation to. Despite excellent tactical play against the Wallasey man, Houlihan's potting let him down and – concerningly – *Snooker Scene* observed, 'When Houlihan had chances to win frames a snatch tended to creep into this cue action.' There was also disappointment in qualifying for the 1979 World Championship. After beating John Barrie 9-5 in the first qualifying round, Houlihan fell 9-6 to the world number 14 and 1978 UK champion Doug Mountjoy in the last 32, thus denying him a place at the Crucible. At one stage Houlihan had led 4-2, notching breaks of 76 and 80 in frames one and three respectively as he began the match at a canter, but the Welshman rallied to win six on the trot and hit the front at 8-4. Houlihan, despite a valiant effort in winning the next two frames, simply couldn't catch him.

The following season was even more of a rollercoaster. Qualifying for the 1979 UK Championship began within two weeks of Houlihan celebrating his 50th birthday and he marked the occasion with a vintage performance against Jackie Rea, brushing aside the Irishman 9-3 and compiling his first century in a pro tournament in the process, a 103 in frame ten, as well as impressive runs of 64, 78 and 44. The victory secured a last-16 showdown against Alex Higgins, who hadn't won the World Championship since 1972 but remained the game's biggest commercial draw. The match was to take place in the well-appointed surrounds of the Guild Hall in Preston, the UK Championship having fast established itself as the second most important tournament on the snooker circuit.

Houlihan talked a good game ahead of the high-profile encounter. 'He's called the Hurricane, isn't he, because he can do a century break in four minutes?' he chuckled rhetorically, speaking to Alexander Clyde of the *London Evening Standard*. 'Well, I was doing them regularly in less than four minutes 25 years ago. Many people still think I'm faster.' Houlihan also spoke to Clyde about his struggles to establish himself on the pro circuit. 'It's all a bit of a closed shop,' he said. 'If you are lucky and your face happens to fit, you can be made and get into all the tournaments. Players like me, we only get two chances a year in match play, the World Championship and the UK. And we've got to beat fellows who are used to match play to survive. Look at the eight players who get into *Pot Black*. They can keep their form because they keep playing all the tournaments. There is nothing personal in this. I just feel that some players have been luckier than others.'

Reflecting on his 1950s and '60s amateur achievements and entry into the pro ranks in the early '70s, Houlihan added, 'I was working as a stevedore in those days, but when I saw Spencer and Reardon turning pro, I thought I'd give it a go as well. That was back in 1972 [sic.] and you could say I've had a few ups and downs since then, mostly downs!'

Clyde also quoted an anonymous 'leading official' on the subject of Houlihan, 'Pat was the Higgins of 15–20 years ago,' the official said. 'He should have been born about 20 years later. Mind you, he's still a very fine player but for some reason he has never had any sort of opportunity since he turned professional.'

Houlihan hoped the Higgins match would provide the big push forward he had been waiting for. 'I know this is my big chance against Alex,' he said, with characteristic optimism. 'If I could beat him I think I could make the breakthrough that I need and upset quite a few people.'

It wasn't to be. The ever unpredictable and inconsistent Higgins produced one of his better performances, running out a 9-3 victor. 'Higgins is simply magic!' ran *The Q-World*'s report, which also declared, 'There is no finer sight than Higgins charging around the table knocking balls in from everywhere ... Houlihan had no answer and just had to take it on the chin.'

There was some better news in the new year for Houlihan, though, as a newcomer to the snooker calendar arrived in the form of the British Gold Cup. In a welcome if unusually meritocratic manoeuvre, the tournament, which would eventually transmogrify into the British Open, featured a qualifying competition which opened the event to a wider range of pros than the usual exclusive enclave found at invitationals. With a 2-1 victory over Jim Meadowcroft and a 3-0 win against one of the great names from his amateur days, Welsh potter extraordinaire Cliff Wilson, Houlihan was among the qualifiers who headed to the Derby Assembly Rooms for the 24–28 February final stages.

The innovative – and not entirely satisfactory – tournament structure saw the final 16 divided into four groups of four, with each member of the group playing three frames against each of their rivals. The group winners (decided on total number of frames won) would then advance to the semi-finals. Houlihan's group saw him drawn against old rival Ray Reardon, but it did not prove a happy reunion as the Welshman was at his imperious best in winning 3-0, the same score by which Houlihan lost to Bill Werbeniuk, while Fred Davis edged him out 2-1.

Despite this setback, Houlihan had every reason to approach the 1980 World Championship qualifiers in good heart, having had more match play during the season than at any other time since turning professional. However, ahead of the qualifiers disaster struck, as he suffered a severe recurrence of the conjunctivitis that had, on and off, plagued him for years. Drawn to face Joe Johnson, a promising young pro from Bradford who six years later would become world champion in one of the biggest upsets in snooker history, Houlihan had no choice but to dispense with his contact lenses and play with no visual aids at all. Without contacts or glasses his eyesight was now so poor that he could barely sight long pots adequately, let alone take them on with any degree of confidence.

Playing largely on memory and instinct, his eyes increasingly red and sore, Houlihan produced perhaps the bravest performance of his career in the best-of-17 encounter. The first session was nip and tuck, Houlihan leading 2-0, 3-2 and 4-3 only for Johnson to peg him back each time. Then, at 6-5 up and the match looking like it might be going the distance, Houlihan conjured a magical break of 108 – the first century of the tournament that season, and the only one that would be made in the qualifiers. Given how restricted his sight was it was a stunning reminder of his remarkable, if now flickering, talents. Houlihan won the next frame too and, although Johnson pulled one more back to trail 8-6, Houlihan once again conjured a decisive break in frame 15, a run of 46 enabling him to triumph 9-6.

Despite these heroics there was sadly no fairy tale in the last 32. With a place in Sheffield so close that Houlihan could almost touch it, he was – with cruel irony – drawn against Tony Meo, his old mate from Vardens Road. Meo was now 20 and one of the newest and most talented pros on the circuit. Hopes that the two old friends might conjure a match for the ages were soon dead in the water; by the time the match began Houlihan's conjunctivitis was so severe that he could barely open his swollen, red eyes. Meo unsurprisingly steamrollered him, winning all seven frames in the first session. Somehow a near blind Houlihan put together the gutsiest break of 45 you could ever hope to see in the first frame after the interval to take it 78-50 and avoid the ignominy of being whitewashed, but it was Meo who advanced to the Crucible 9-1.

Meo's joy at reaching Sheffield for the first time in his nascent career was tempered by sadness for his old friend's woes. While the Anglo-Italian lad from south London had his whole career ahead of him, Houlihan – now past 50 and with his big pro break seemingly forever out of his grasp – looked all played out.

## Chapter 16

# The cruel game

PATSY HOULIHAN was always persistent and optimistic to a fault. Like fictional south London icon Derek 'Del Boy' Trotter from *Only Fools and Horses*, Houlihan always believed better times were just around the corner – he was under no illusions about becoming a millionaire, but 'this time next year, I'll be climbing the rankings' was very much his attitude.

As much as snooker had not always treated Houlihan well, he still loved the sport and couldn't conceive of life without it. Although he was no longer operating at anywhere near the peak of his powers throughout the 1980s, he was still playing snooker for money, he was still making ends meet, he was still entertaining everyone who encountered him and he was still searching for that big, life-changing victory.

The 1980/81 season was a quiet one for Houlihan. He lost 9-1 against Tony Meo in the UK Championship qualifiers and submitted his entry form for the World Championship too late to compete. However, he did pick up a couple of wins in his qualifying group for the Yamaha Organs Trophy, defeating Patsy Fagan and John Pulman 2-1 apiece.

Ironically it was Jimmy White, in his first tournament since turning pro, who denied Houlihan a place in the final stages of the tournament at the Derby Assembly Rooms, beating him 2-1. Houlihan won the opening frame but White clinched the decider courtesy of a dazzling 126.

During the 1981/82 season, writer Jean Rafferty followed the snooker circuit for a year, meeting Houlihan as well as many more of the game's most vivid characters. The seminal book she wrote about her experiences and impressions was entitled *The Cruel Game: The Inside Story of Snooker*. Published in 1983 and reissued on Kindle in 2021, it provides a brilliant insight not only into the game of snooker at a pivotal time in its history, but also into Houlihan's lifestyle and personality. Rafferty, in the foreword to the Kindle edition, put the book into context. '*The Cruel Game* was written at a time when the game was on the cusp,' she wrote. 'For years it had been a backstreet game, played in dark snooker halls where teenage boys dogged off school and unemployed men tried to gamble their way to a bit of extra pocket money. But with the advent of colour television it was moving into a different league. Big money sponsors were coming into the game – and entrepreneurs.'

For Rafferty, snooker was a 'crazy subterranean world where all sorts of eccentric characters were seething and teeming beneath the newly respectable veneer … it was a world in flux, one that was moving from the darkness into the light, that was full of chaotic characters playing a game that demands intense control'.

Rafferty devoted two chapters to Houlihan, the first subtitled 'An Honest-to-God Hustler' which described her meeting Houlihan in the Lucania snooker club above Burton's menswear store on Lewisham High Street. 'In the days before television made snooker a game people actually knew about,' she wrote, 'Pat was a hustler, a real live honest-to-God hustler who travelled all around the country pretending to be a worse player than he was and relieving people of the trouble of having to carry their money around with them.'

For Rafferty the changes to the Lucania, where Houlihan had now been playing for more than 30 years, served as a metaphor for the revolution sweeping through snooker. As Houlihan told Rafferty, 'This used to be such a dive. The chap that's bought it now is putting new cloths on all the tables. That floor was all wood boards and some was out. The place is really nice now.'

However, for all the cosmetic changes, Rafferty discerned that for Houlihan much of the charm and heart of snooker was being lost with the onset of the brave new commercial world. 'It used to be unbelievable,' Houlihan lamented nostalgically. 'It's much more comfortable here now, but in those days there was so many comedians up here you used to have a right laugh. People'd come and they didn't play but they could get a living just marking up. That was how much money there was in them days ... I was good in them days. I always produced it. I was playing more and more matches and that keeps you up all the time. These chaps today, I know for a fact that I could still be up there with them now if I could get the right opportunities.'

For Rafferty, Houlihan was the living embodiment of why snooker was 'the cruel game'. 'That life,' she wrote. 'The travelling, the betting, the money matches, the tatty clubs – was the only way Pat Houlihan knew then of making a living at what he did best. In the end though, he has been condemned to it for life. Today when snooker means big cars, big houses, big money for its top stars, Pat Houlihan is still playing money matches and a few exhibitions where he can get them ... Snooker like all competitive sports is cruel to those it leaves behind. Pat Houlihan, having been in the sport all his life, is now struggling to make a living from it, victim of our devotion to the media – if you haven't seen it on the telly it hasn't happened. People like Pat Houlihan exist only for the real snooker people.'

When Rafferty spoke to Houlihan he had enjoyed a decent start to the season in the lead-up to the Christmas of 1981, putting the disappointment of the previous season behind him. Ahead of a stern qualifying competition for the UK Championship, Houlihan had knocked in a 147 break at the Top Spot club in Balham, and had then won three qualifiers to reach the main stages of the tournament in Preston, beating Kingsley Kennerley 9-1, Scottish champion Ian Black 9-4 and perennial foe Jim Meadowcroft 9-4. Although he lost 9-5 to Graham Miles in Preston in the last 24 of the tournament proper, Houlihan was looking ahead with characteristic optimism to the Stockport-based qualifiers for the 1982 World Championship – albeit an optimism tempered by concern about how to pay for his travel and accommodation if he didn't win his first match.

'The top people are paid £1,250 for just walking in,' Houlihan pointed out. 'Something should be done about that. They could have taken a couple of thousand off the top prize and then given the preliminary round chaps their expenses. Last year we had to win five matches before we came across the top eight. It's better now, we've only got to win two or three matches more than them, but you're playing people like Willie Thorne and Jim Meadowcroft in the qualifying – you can beat them or they could beat you, it's very close. In the '70s I hardly got to play the top men at all.

'I don't fear them when I go there to Stockport. That was my strong point once. But I over-try now. Getting on the table once a year you do, because you know you'll only get one chance ... I've got to try and tell myself it ain't just this tournament once a year. I've got to try and take it in my stride. It was a lot easier mentally when I was younger. I was a Steve Davis in those days for coolness. I was very fast. I had the flair. I still have as a matter of fact.'

Ahead of his arrival in Stockport, Houlihan made a nostalgic and sentimental day trip to Blackpool with his old friend and sometime driver and backer Derek, a massive man nicknamed 'Block Of' (as in 'Block Of Flats' because he was so large) who had known Houlihan for years and worked as a driving instructor when he wasn't travelling with Houlihan. In between a stroll on the beach and a drink or two, Patsy reminisced about beating John Spencer at the Tower Circus 17 years earlier. Derek had been there with him that day when he put Spencer to the sword. 'Some match, that,' Derek told Rafferty with awe. Houlihan's assessment was that it was, 'The best experience I ever had in snooker. And not just because I won it. Up there in the Tower with 1,500 people in front of you.'

In contrast to 1965, there were about 30 spectators in attendance in Stockport for Houlihan's first World Championship qualifying round encounter against Australia's Ian Anderson. The Romiley Forum was a far cry from the Tower Circus, but no less dramatic, in its own low-key way. It proved an attritional battle; Houlihan led 5-3 at the interval with the majority of frames taking 30 to 40 minutes to complete. As Houlihan began the decisive evening session, Rafferty described him vividly, 'Chirpy and comical as he is off the table, on it he looks grim, hard, and his face has the adamantine planes of a Red Indian. Two bright spots of red burn on his cheekbones as he steps under the light.'

Houlihan was leading 6-4 when the 11th frame assumed an almost absurd level of scrappiness – the two players making a combined 88 approaches to the table while ceding 11 fouls between them. Anderson eventually took it on the black to narrow the deficit to 6-5 and had a great chance to draw level in the next frame, only to miss a crucial blue when just a few points behind. Using all his ringcraft and experience, Houlihan closed out the match 9-5, leaving Anderson, 12,000 miles from home in Sydney and his season in tatters, utterly disconsolate. 'It's a bloody long way to come for one day's snooker,' the Aussie told Rafferty bitterly. 'I could have been up on the Gold Coast and played a day's snooker there. And lain in the sunshine afterwards.'

Once again Houlihan was one match from Sheffield, but once again the promised land was just out of his grasp. Dave Martin, a promising pro from Chesterfield – who according to *The Q-World* gave 'every indication of being a bit special' – beat him 9-3 in the final qualifying round, leaving a devastated and morose Derek to ponder, in a line that eventually provided Rafferty with the title for her book, 'It's a cruel game, Pat. It's a cruel game.' Houlihan, in contrast, was as philosophical as ever. After the match in the bar, coaching guru Frank Callan observed that Patsy was taking the defeat well. 'I takes it well because I've had to get used to it,' Houlihan replied. He also talked with characteristic optimism of how he might give contact lenses another go, having lost his last pair after leaving them on the top of a taxi one night when he'd had a few drinks.

Later in the evening, Houlihan and Martin returned to the arena to play a few exhibition frames – a quaint tradition now long gone – and all of a sudden Patsy's form returned. Before anyone knew what was happening, he was banging in pots from all angles against a disorientated and somewhat puzzled Martin. Half close your eyes as he dashed around the table, and he might have been that young dashing teenager in the Lewisham Lucania all over again, back in the days when the cloths were poor, the balls heavy, there was no snooker on the telly and the game was somehow simpler; before things turned cruel.

Chapter 17

# Patsy hits the big screen

BY THE mid-1980s snooker was big business. '*Coronation Street*
with balls,' as promoter Barry Hearn called it, or '*Dallas* with balls'
depending on who he was speaking to. The sport had steadily risen
in profile and popularity throughout the 1970s, largely due to the
double whammy of increased television coverage and Alex Higgins's
penchant for garnering newspaper columns with his controversial
antics. However, it was Hearn's commercial and promotional chutzpah
and Steve Davis's domineering professionalism that transformed it
from a minor sport into a cultural phenomenon.

Snooker's new and central role in British life was soon reflected in
a trio of televisual and cinematic off-shoots – Les Blair's film *Number
One*, Alan Clarke's bizarre movie musical *Billy the Kid and the Green
Baize Vampire*, and Geoff McQueen's snooker-based television drama-
comedy *Give Us a Break*. Patsy Houlihan's appearance in the former
of these three unlikely products of snooker's boom years was one of
the most unusual detours of a career characterised by the unexpected.

*Number One* was originally intended, and commissioned, as
a television film. The pedigree of the creative team behind the
project – in the form of writer G.F. Newman and director Blair –
was formidable. Blair was a former contemporary of Mike Leigh at
both Salford Grammar School and the Midland Arts Centre, and
shared with him – initially at least – an improvisatory approach to
filmmaking. Blair's work was also characterised by a naturalistic
and unflinching examination of social issues. In Newman he found

a natural collaborator. A novelist as well as a screenwriter, it is no exaggeration to say that Newman revolutionised British television drama by challenging the traditionally deferential portrayal of British policing with his 1978 series *Law and Order*. Directed by Blair, *Law and Order* was so incendiary that it provoked discussion in parliament and a putative move by some Conservative MPs to have Newman prosecuted for sedition. Later, Newman and Blair would also examine institutional issues within the NHS in their 1983 series *The National Health*.

Writing in 2015, Newman explained that 'a constant theme' within his work is the 'quest to reveal some of the corruption that cripples our society'. Expanding on his point he explained, 'Whether it's from the police, businesspeople, lawyers, doctors, politicians, even undertakers! None of it is victimless crime. Crime is never victimless. Corruption at every level diminishes our society and robs us all. Will I change this? I very much doubt it, for as we lose sight of spiritual values so we become more materialistic, and with materialism comes corruption, inevitably.'

In some respects *Number One* is typical of Newman's tropes and thematic concerns, taking place as it does in a murky world in which corruption and exploitation are endemic, with most of the characters in the film crooked, exploited or on the take. As Alison Steadman's 'tart with a heart' character Doreen comments at one point, 'Nothing's straight anymore.'

However, Newman's original intention was not that the film would serve as a grand inquisition into sporting corruption; rather his vision was a comedic one. 'Yes, the theme in my work has always been to expose corruption,' he told the author. 'And there was certainly corruption in snooker and many players certainly went bent. But with *Number One* there wasn't any intention to have any sort of big exposé of snooker because, to be honest, corruption in snooker isn't that impactful on society as a whole, in the way that corrupt policemen or corrupt prison officers are, or corruption in the NHS or in the court systems is. My vision for the film was completely comedic.'

An admirer of Robert Rossen's classic 1961 pool picture *The Hustler* ('a great film with great actors'), Newman partly based *Number One* on his own experiences of the snooker hall scene growing up ('I spent quite a bit of time hanging around snooker halls in my late teens'). He had written about the hustling world before, in his 1972 novel *The Player and the Guest*, which – in his own words – told the story of 'a n'er do well who played snooker, latched on to people and made money off them'. *Number One* is a slight variation on the hustling trope, telling the story of 'Flash' Harry Gordon (Bob Geldolf), a petty Irish criminal and hustler based in south London and the scrapes he finds himself in. After initially resisting overtures to turn pro from a dodgy bookmaker Billy Evans (Mel Smith), Harry eventually relents, enjoying a meteoric rise and making his way to the World Championship final, winning on the black, rather than throwing the match as Evans had urged.

Possessing a brilliant cast – including Alfred Molina, Phil Daniels, Alison Steadman, Ray Winstone and Alun Armstrong – *Number One* nevertheless conspires to equal less than the sum of its parts. The biggest issue with the film is its uneven tone, in which serious scenes of gritty realism jar with scenes of comedic, Keystone Kops-style violence, including a brawl between Harry and opponent Brad Brookie during the climactic snooker match. Ultimately, the film can't decide whether it wants to be a serious examination of the murky underbelly of snooker, or a wise-cracking hero-to-zero sports romp, and ends up falling short on both fronts.

Newman was honest about its shortcomings. 'In retrospect I think Les directing it was a mistake,' he said. 'He brought his observational style to the film but most of the actors cast couldn't do comedy. It was meant to be very funny. When we had a read-through of the script with the crew and so on it took nearly all day because we were all laughing so much, but I don't think there were more than two laughs in the final film. There's a scene where the police are sawing off a shotgun – it should have been funny but it was played dead straight while the scenes near the end look like a different film altogether.'

Perhaps the major issue with the film though is the casting of a 32-year-old pre-Band Aid Bob Geldof in the lead role. 'In order to get financing we had to get some stars and so forth,' Newman remembered. 'Geldof was a known name and that impressed Gerald Ronson [who put up the money for the film].' Geldof later admitted the

169

salary he picked up for the film bailed him out of significant financial issues, but unfortunately he has little discernible acting ability and never makes Harry someone you want to root for. As portrayed by the almost somnolent Geldof, Harry is sleazy rather than charming and his petulance grating; a stronger actor would have succeeded in making Newman's dialogue zing. 'Dear old Bob was a lovely guy but he wouldn't take direction,' Newman recalled. 'He thought he knew best.'

Newman recalled an interesting story about the film's somewhat chaotic funding, 'Ronson, who ran a load of garages and had a ton of property, notionally financed and cash flowed it. On the first day of filming he brought his whole entourage down to watch. He said, "This is great!" I said to him, "Well, this is the only day's filming we're doing though, Gerald." He said, "What do you mean? You've got another six weeks." I replied, "Yeah, but we don't have any money." So he went away, spoke to one of his minions and came back with a bag full of cash and said, "Will that keep you going?" Well, it did!'

Later, Ronson would become notorious as a member of the 'Guinness Four', being sent to prison for his role in a share-trading fraud. As for Houlihan, he appeared in *Number One* as Pete Phelan, a hustler and snooker pro, as well as serving as a technical advisor for the project and snooker coach to Geldof. Houlihan landed the job thanks to the presence in the cast of Paul Moriarty, who he had known for years. Moriarty successfully segued into acting in the late 1970s, appearing under the name P.H. Moriarty in iconic Brit flicks such as *Scum* and *Quadrophenia*, as well as an episode of Newman and Blair's *Law and Order* in 1978, before his breakout role as Razors in John McKenzie's masterful *The Long Good Friday* in 1980. 'Paul was very generous in introducing Patsy to the film,' Newman remembered. 'Patsy got paid cash as an advisor.'

Moriarty himself recalled, 'Yeah, I got Patsy on to the film. I recommended him. I was first in the snooker hall aged about 11 and I used to like him, Patsy. I saw him play a lot – he was fantastic.'

Houlihan also secured an appearance in the film for Danny Adds, a young snooker player from Eltham whose father had hailed from Deptford. The winner of the British Under-16 snooker championship in 1978, Adds never really fulfilled his potential and didn't turn pro. Nevertheless, he was billed in the cast list as playing 'himself'. Houlihan appeared in two scenes in *Number One*. The first was within the first five minutes and was notable for containing some of the only surviving footage of Houlihan playing snooker, as the audience saw him briefly but smoothly sink a pink, rise almost immediately from the shot and then nonchalantly chalk his cue before pocketing the black (off screen) and winning some cash from Moriarty's Mike the Throat. Houlihan even had a few lines with Geldof and Moriarty, ordering a light ale (his own drink of choice, of course) and acting Geldof off the screen with his gruff charisma.

Later in the film, Houlihan popped up again as Phelan, sitting in his chair looking plausibly disgruntled while being beaten at the World Championship. Houlihan's role as a technical advisor on the film lends the project a bit of polish; the snooker sequences and shots all look convincing enough, even if they could and should have been filmed with a bit more imagination à la Martin Scorsese's *The Color of Money* (released a year after *Number One*). According to Newman, in the finished film, 'All the pots where the balls go into pockets were Patsy. Bob couldn't pot a ball unless it was through luck, not design. There's a lot of Patsy's hand and arm in the film.' Director Blair elaborated on this point. 'There was only one actor in the cast who looked like he could even play,' he recalled. 'As for Bob Geldof, he looked like he'd never even held a cue before.'

There was – it seems – some tension between Geldof and Houlihan on set. Trailing a second part of a Houlihan interview which was due to appear in the June 1986 edition of *Pot Gold* magazine, the May release alluded to an 'on-set row' between the two men which you could 'read all about ... only in *Pot Gold* magazine!' However, the magazine folded and the next issue never appeared. On the subject of Houlihan and Geldof's working relationship, Pauline McLeod of the *Daily Mirror*, who visited the set during filming, wrote, 'The film's technical adviser Patsy Houlihan was impressed with Bob's efforts – but didn't rate him highly.' McLeod quoted Houlihan as saying, 'Bob's not very good, but then he's only just started.' In response, a somewhat surly Geldof told McLeod, 'Of course I can play snooker. I play at least once a week with my mates, but it's a different ball game playing as a professional.' Speaking to the *Reading Evening Post* he varied his story a little, admitting, 'I'm hopeless at snooker. I play about twice a month with friends and it takes me about three hours to clear the table. I had a few lessons for the movie but all they did was to point out to me how bad I was.'

Newman's recollection pretty much coalesces with the above accounts, 'Patsy would show Bob the most delicate shots, but all Bob would want to do was smash the balls around the table and hope one went in, which of course they didn't. He certainly wouldn't take Patsy's direction. But Patsy kept his patience I have to say. Although he sometimes turned away and pulled a face as though to say, "What's this clown up to?" Patsy was there for all the snooker scenes and probably did get a bit frustrated with Mr Geldof at times.' Houlihan and Geldof's relationship may have been frosty but Patsy was popular with the crew. 'He was a fun guy to have around,' was Newman's recollection. 'He was a great player, a bit fly of course. He was one of the chaps and got on very well with the crew. They all wanted to play him. Some of them fancied their chances. I don't remember but I'm sure he took some money off them!'

In a bid to capitalise on Geldof's rise in profile after the Christmas 1984 success of the Band Aid single 'Do They Know It's Christmas?' which the Irishman masterminded in aid of the famine in Ethiopia, *Number One* was granted a gala premiere screening on Thursday, 18 April 1985 at the Classic Cinema, on Haymarket in central London, and a cinema release the following day which coincided with the middle of the world snooker championship. Reviews were mixed. 'Why did Bob Geldof of Boomtown Rats and Ethiopia famine fame have to tarnish his reputation?' bemoaned the *Westminster and Pimlico News*, dismissing the film as 'badly made, poorly scripted and revelling in four-letter words'. *The Guardian*, meanwhile, was critical of *Number One*'s 'maladroit slapstick' and the narrative's late 'dive into sentimentality'. The most vicious notice came from *Film Review* which declared, 'Geldof carries the film like a deadpan plank of MDF as he gets systematically acted off the screen by the supporting cast and most of the snooker cues for that matter.'

*Number One* was also poorly received among some members of the snooker community who attended a preview in Sheffield. Tony Knowles, who had been happily photographed with Geldof before the screening, fumed, 'What a load of bloody rubbish. It showed players smashing cues over tables and brawling. The film is absolute nonsense.' Doug Mountjoy concurred with Knowles, declaring, 'This film isn't about the real lads who play snooker. It's a pity the star is such a kid's hero at the moment.' Steve Davis was more measured, commenting, 'I think a lot of people might watch the film as pure entertainment – but they'll know it's not what happens in the real world.'

Geldof defended the film, claiming, 'TV has sanitised snooker. People are paid to take a fall in horse racing and boxing – so perhaps it does happen in snooker. Maybe the film has touched a tender spot.' Later, in his autobiography, Geldof would admit the film 'teetered between playing for laughs and trying to say something serious'. Box office reaction to *Number One* was disappointingly lukewarm – audiences clearly preferred the real-life drama of the unfolding 1985 World Championship, culminating in the iconic Davis-Taylor 'black-ball final', to a fictional portrayal.

As such, *Number One* rapidly disappeared from cinema screens, although it still lingers in the shadows, a strange footnote in the history of snooker, British cinema, Patsy Houlihan and the brilliant career of G.F. Newman.

Chapter 18

# You can't buy kindness

THE MID-1980s were barren years for Patsy Houlihan in the professional ranks. Across three seasons from 1982/83 until 1984/85 he failed to win many of the matches he participated in, aside from receiving a walkover against John Dunning in the 1982 UK Championship, when his opponent confused the date of the match and failed to appear. A similar walkover was granted in the 1985 Rothmans Grand Prix against Australia's Gordon Robinson, a player who failed to appear in any of his matches that season, including another forfeited encounter against Houlihan in the 1986 British Open.

During this period of poor results, there were some particularly heartbreaking defeats for Houlihan, most notably against young Northern Irishman Tommy Murphy in the first qualifying round of the 1983 World Championship. Houlihan displayed vintage form early on, notching two half centuries as he raced into a 5-0 lead. However, as the match wore on his conjunctivitis flared up, and – as they had done against Tony Meo in 1981 – his eyes became swollen and almost completely closed. From 7-1 down Murphy hauled his way back to 8-8. Demonstrating heart-wrenching bravery and determination, Houlihan edged the next frame 73-53 to take a 9-8 lead, but Murphy won the final two frames to edge through 10-9.

Houlihan did have some success in the 1984 Yamaha Open, beating John Hargreaves, Marcel Gauvreau and Rex Williams, but a 2-0 loss to future 'Slimmer of the Year' Les Dodd meant he failed to qualify for the televised phase at the Derby Assembly Rooms. In a lot of games across this period Houlihan was unlucky to lose. In the 1982 Professional Players Tournament, for example, he was drawn against Tony Knowles who was fresh from winning the season-opening Jameson International. Houlihan was 2-0, 3-1 and 4-2 up and, after Knowles forced a decider, Patsy led by ten points with one red left. Knowles needed two attempts to clear to the pink before falling over the line a 5-4 victor.

Neal Foulds, later to reach a high of number three in the world rankings, faced Houlihan during qualifying for the 1984 Lada Classic and recalled a particular quirk of his playing style in these, Patsy's later years. 'The match was played in an echoey squash court in Warrington,' Foulds told the author. 'Patsy was beyond his best at that point. What I remember about the match was that when he missed a shot he would shout, "No, not in!" before the ball was even close to the pocket.'

Having seen Houlihan play at the Pot Black club in Balham years earlier, Foulds was well aware of his class. 'He was a very gifted player,' he stated on the *Snooker Scene* podcast in 2022. 'He was almost the Ronnie O'Sullivan of his time. I know that sounds like a massive statement but it was certainly [the case] in so far as he had an incredible talent for the game. He was quick, fluent, he made big breaks and was a really beautiful player. Honestly, to watch him play was a complete joy, in the same way as when you watched someone like Ronnie now. He was a great guy as well, a real old school Londoner.'

Houlihan failed to enter the final two tournaments of the 1984/85 season, thus not participating in the most famous snooker tournament of all time, the 1985 World Championship. It wasn't until October 1985, when Houlihan beat Canadian Gerry Watson 9-4 in the first round of the UK Open in Southampton, that he was able to claim a first win in a long-form match for three-and-a-half years.

Despite these travails, Houlihan refused to lapse into bitterness and remained immensely popular among his fellow pros and other figures on and around the snooker tour. New professionals and young hopefuls were particularly grateful for his encouragement. In the early 1980s, Houlihan had a short spell as resident pro at the Driffield snooker club in East India Dock Road, Poplar, managed by an Australian named Wayne Wattie.

While working there, Houlihan made a huge impact on a teenager named Lee Prickman, then a promising junior. 'Wayne really took me under his wing, for which I'm still very grateful,' Prickman recalled. 'He paid Patsy a weekly fee to be resident pro. That's how I first met and got to know him. Patsy probably never practised as much as he should have done for his upcoming tournaments, because he was usually busy playing the local rogues and villains for a few quid. He'd give them silly starts per frame and he was an absolutely sensational player.

'I've been around some of the best players you can think of and I saw Patsy do things that I've never, ever seen any other players do and in very poor conditions too. If he was playing today in the type of conditions they have now he'd be frightening. I remember watching him make a break of either 135 or 138 on an old table with very thick cloth that was very slow – I've never seen anyone hit the ball like that and I've never seen that kind of skill and talent in anyone else. He was just jaw dropping.

'Patsy did things with a cue ball that I still don't see players do today. For example, he could hit the ball in a certain place on the cue ball where it wouldn't be orthodox to get the reaction that he would get. I'd say to him, "How are you doing that?" I guess it was all to do with his timing and delivery of the cue. He would hit the cue ball in the middle or just under the middle and get incredible top spin, and also do the opposite – hit it in the middle and get extreme back spin. I never worked it out! What he was doing was completely against how I'd been taught to play the game.'

Prickman also observed Houlihan's incredible facility for improvising ways to monetise his skills at snooker. 'Obviously Patsy couldn't play regular people at normal snooker because he was just too good. He was 70, 80 or even a hundred points better than anyone else in the club apart from me and another young player called Chris Pellegrini. So Patsy would develop or play other types of games. There was a game called "cricket" we used to play where somebody had to pot all the reds while the other player was trying to get as many points as they could off the colours. Another thing Patsy would do is play one-handed. When he couldn't place the cue against the cushion rather than a bridge hand, for example when the cue ball

176

was in the middle of the table, he would hold it like a javelin. It was phenomenal.'

Prickman recalled one particular occasion when Houlihan proved his sharp wit while playing one-handed. 'Patsy had given one of the rogues in the club a start. He was clearing the table one-handed and had got the colours up to brown, with pink and black on their spots. He then potted the blue. It was a great shot and he stunned the white. What he was doing potting the balls one handed, cue like a javelin, was already incredible. One of the guys who was watching said to him, "Why didn't you screw back?" Patsy just looked at him, deadpan, and said, "I didn't have the right chalk with me today." That was Patsy. He was the archetypal cheeky chappy Londoner. Very sharp-witted and sharp tongued. Nothing ever happened that he hadn't seen before. That line will stay with me forever. It was a cracking response.'

However, it was Houlihan's kindness that made the biggest impression on Prickman, 'He was at the club for quite a short time. It didn't last forever. He moved on after a year or so. The tables and the conditions really weren't doing him any favours. But I'll never forget him. He was very kind and very good to me. The things he showed me and taught me have stayed with me. He was nurturing, helpful and kind. I hold him in very good memory.'

Another cueist who recalls Houlihan with affection is Tony Drago. In 1985, the Maltese potter was a shy 20-year-old rookie pro. He still remembers Houlihan's kindness to him as he adjusted to life in the UK. 'I met Patsy quite a few times in the early days of my career,' recalled Drago, a fast player in the Houlihan mould who would later reach a high of number ten in the world rankings.

'When I first came to London, Patsy was still playing, although he was towards the end of his career. I saw him play a few times in practice and in tournaments. He was very fast and very exciting – and that's my kind of player so I really enjoyed watching him. We played the same sort of game Patsy and I, except he was probably even faster than me. He was a fantastic potter and he had great cue ball control. He was well past his prime – you can't be at your best when you're nearly in your 60s – I'm 56 now and nowhere near the player I was. But you could tell what a great player he'd been from the shots he played.

When you're that age you can't execute the shots like you can in your 30s or 40s but you could still tell what a great player he was.

'Patsy was also such a nice man. He would tap me on my shoulder and say, "Don't ever change how you play." He was a very friendly guy. He always spoke nicely to me. He'd say things like, "Don't give up, even if it doesn't go well." I'd come all the way from Malta. I was very shy and my English wasn't very good, so to find someone willing to tap me on the shoulder and give me good advice meant such a lot – you can't buy that with any money.'

Paul Collier, now a leading referee, was another recipient of Patsy's kindness. 'I never met Patsy but he sent me a letter, via World Snooker, many years ago,' Collier said. 'It must have been in about 2002 because I started full time [refereeing] in 2001. Of course today with social media anyone can contact you, but back then we would occasionally get a little bit of fan mail which would go to the [WPBSA] office in Bristol. Every few months you would get things forwarded on to you.

'So one day I got a letter out of the blue from Patsy which he had sent to Bristol. It basically said he liked what I did and he liked my presence around the table. He also liked the fact I was a bit different, because I was wearing a black shirt and no one had done that before. He told me to keep up the good work, telling me how much he liked my attitude to refereeing and that doing things "my way" was sticking two fingers up to the establishment.

'I didn't know Jimmy White that well at the time but I mentioned it to him. He told me how much he respected Patsy and how he was such a great character that you couldn't even explain how he was to people. Jimmy told me he passed on his thanks to Patsy from me but I never got the chance to properly follow it up because Patsy didn't include his address with the letter. For him to make the effort of writing me a letter and sending it to Bristol to try and reach me really impressed me. I wish I'd had a pint with him!'

Houlihan's old-school charisma was also admired by players from abroad, such as Jim Wych, one of the group of Canadian players who turned pro in the late 1970s. Wych saw Patsy as the embodiment of an age of snooker that was fast disappearing, but remained captivating. 'I remember Patsy well,' Wych, later an accomplished broadcaster, recalled. 'I was always hearing from other players about the proposition bets he would come up with on the snooker table. He was a tremendous gambler.

'The Canadian players who came over to the UK were used to those sort of goofy gambling games, because back home it was the only way to get anyone to put up any money. I remember Kirk [Stevens] and I coming over in 1975 as amateurs and we couldn't find anyone to play us for money so we played each other. I wasn't around London much after turning pro, we were based in Liverpool, and I think the gambling side of things was much more prevalent down in London.

'Patsy had quite the reputation based on his tremendous gambling prowess and the unique games he would come up with. He was a terrific exhibition player too, who had some unbelievable trick shots. If I was ever lucky enough to be around Patsy, he could capture any player's attention with the shots he would show us. He was a very cool guy to be around. He had a lot of stories. I was young and had just come over to the UK so he made quite an impression. He was the sort of guy you could sit and listen to for hours and hours – engaging at the highest level. Everybody had time for him.'

Bill King, who saw Houlihan play during his pomp and has never wavered from his view that he was the greatest snooker player of them all, also recalled how Houlihan encouraged him and his son Mark, who would later spend seven seasons in the world's top 16 and win the Northern Ireland Open in 2016. 'I took Mark down to Lewisham around 1986 when he was about 12 and he played Houlihan a few times,' King said. 'Houlihan said to me, "Leave him alone. Just let him pot balls. Don't complicate things. He's gonna be all right."'

King also recalled an occasion when he took a gaggle of promising young players to watch and meet Houlihan. 'I took Ronnie [O'Sullivan], Chris Brooks, God rest his soul he's dead, Chris Scanlon – all these young kids – over the water to watch Houlihan. They all called me a liar before when I explained the tricks Houlihan could do but then they stood there and saw the tricks he done for themselves. They couldn't believe what Houlihan did with those balls. He was unbelievable. I've never seen anyone control a white ball like Houlihan. None of them, not even today. And he was so happy-go-lucky, Patsy. I don't think he had a mean bone in his body. Cor, he was a great character.'

Snooker coach Frank Sandell, who has guided more than 2,000 youngsters in Worthing over the years, including Allison Fisher, probably the greatest female cueist of all time, saw Houlihan up close on several occasions at exhibitions he organised and was knocked out by him. 'The guy all the fans wanted for exhibitions in those days – it was around 1981 I suppose – was Jimmy White,' Sandell recalled. 'Eventually through Jimmy's management we got in touch with him and down he came to Worthing and who should come along as his back-up man, but Patsy Houlihan! They were both very good. Jimmy didn't really do a trick shot show or anything like that and he was quite shy dealing with an audience. He'd just pot the balls – that was it. So after they played each other Patsy came on, did some trick shots, talked to the kids and so on and I thought, "What a cracking bloke!"'

Houlihan so impressed Sandell that he called on his services again. 'Seven or eight months later I was doing an event for disabled children which was linked into the charity work of the then-Duchess of Norfolk. I invited Patsy. Down he came and it was an evening of great fun for 50 or 60 children and their mums and dads. Patsy was absolutely brilliant, particularly with the disabled kids – he was very sympathetic to them without being patronising. I remember thinking: he really is a lovely bloke. He went down very well indeed and the Duchess even wrote me a letter thanking me for the event. You heard all these stories about Patsy hustling and the East End of London and so on, but once you met him you realised he was just an absolutely lovely guy.'

Throughout the 1980s, Houlihan continued to practise and play snooker in and around Deptford, where he was a recognisable and much-loved figure. Among the clubs he frequented was Shades, on Deptford High Street, which is now owned by Lee Suleymanoglu. 'I started working in Shades in 1984 and in 1989 I was made general manager,' Suleymanoglu said. 'But I met Patsy originally at the old Lucania in Lewisham above Burton's. In those days snooker was all about playing for money. Nobody played for fun. You'd play snooker or "killer" or "21". I remember playing for 24 hours non-stop, literally.

That was the 1980s for you. I just watched Patsy play at first, and then eventually asked him about his background and that's when I found out the full story behind his life and career.

'A couple of years later he appeared at Shades and his crowd started coming along too. He'd come in daily for years and would usually practise on his own. I used to give him free time on the table. He didn't have to pay. He appreciated that. Because of him a lot of other people came to the club so he was good for business. He'd entertain everyone in the club and he had a big following. We used to open at about eight in the morning. We'd do breakfast, tea and so on and Patsy would be here all day until about two or three in the afternoon. He was such a character and very charismatic. He would tell jokes. Not everyone can tell a joke, but he was a bit of an actor, a showman I would say! And because he was very well-known everyone wanted to buy him a drink. He was a real personality. He was such a fun guy to be around.'

Like most others who saw Houlihan play, Suleymanoglu was a huge admirer, 'It was a shame he didn't get the recognition or money out of the game that he would have done if he was born 30 or 40 years later. What is it these days – half a million when you win the World Championship? I'm a decent player, I played semi-pro and I've made a 130 clearance, so I appreciate a good player and he was that all right. Patsy had a unique technique – he never used to feather the cue. There was none of that – he was straight down and bang! He hit the ball just like that! I've never seen anyone do that. He was the most natural player I've ever seen.'

Another Deptford local who harbours warm memories of Patsy is Jeff Murray. 'I remember going with Tiny and Ginger, who ran a flower stall in Lewisham, to watch Patsy play at Burroughes and Watts in Soho Square, and he entertained us with his wizardry,' Murray said. 'Patsy was a breath of fresh air. We'd be sitting in Lucania over Burton's and he'd walk in. No sooner had he set the table up and we'd be around watching in awe. He was the equivalent of Alex Higgins, Jimmy White and Ronnie O'Sullivan all rolled into one. He wasn't flash or anything like that, just a really down-to-earth, normal bloke. Us kids were in awe of him. Many a time we used to see him in his evening suit and tie, with his cue case down Deptford High Street, but he always had time to pass the time of day. A thorough gent.'

Others who grew up in Deptford in the 1980s and '90s recall how Houlihan would give them pointers on the pool table. 'I reckon all the kids at the Deptford Arms had at least one lesson from him,' said Leigh Hughes. 'I had loads of them! He taught all us kids to be brilliant pool players.' Perry Roberts had a similar tale to tell of his formative years in the Harp of Erin pub. 'Patsy was the nuts at snooker and when we fledglings were playing pool and boozing he taught us a thing or two about pool too!'

Houlihan had a particularly significant impact on the life of Frank Gumbrell, now a professional snooker coach who has worked in Oman, Qatar and Bahrain among other locales. 'My father knew Patsy way back in the '60s and '70s,' Gumbrell explained. 'My dad was a south Londoner, a car dealer. He had car pitches all over London. He and Patsy somehow got to know each other and became mates. My dad would drive him around when he was hustling and playing money matches. They lost contact at some point but I met Patsy years later through Jimmy White. I'd grown up in Battersea and used to play snooker in Clapham Common, Battersea Rise, Wandsworth Road – all those old clubs that have gone now, pretty much.

'I got some great coaching from Patsy. I even spent about two weeks living with him at his house around 1985 or '86. He was amazing. He was past his best by then but he could still play unbelievable snooker. His cue action was like a piston. He didn't seem to do very much – he didn't bring his cue back far – but he'd get so much reaction from the ball. He controlled the white ball like it was on a piece of string. It was incredible what he could do. He was just a genius. And so very fast around the table. And then there were his tricks; he could get a ball, spin it up in the air and get it to land on any spot. And he'd pull pieces of paper out of his jacket pocket – he always wore a jacket – and he would show me newspaper clippings of the matches he won against Reardon and against Spencer on.'

Gumbrell recalled in particular two memorable nights in Houlihan's company, 'One time Patsy entered me into a competition in a snooker club in Deptford and in the group stages I got the highest break – a 57 – and they kicked me out the tournament and gave me my entry fee back! They said, "Patsy, you've put a ringer in!" I was only young! I was gutted! There was another time I went to meet Patsy and I couldn't find him to start with. In the end I got him out of the pub, he didn't even have his cue with him and he'd had a few drinks. We went to the snooker club and he made a total clearance – about 120 or something – with a club cue. He completely cleared up!'

Above all else Gumbrell – like so many others – remembers Houlihan for his kindness. 'I've got such fond memories of being with him, him coaching me, being with me, staying with him. I'm so lucky to have had someone like that around me when I was so young. Very lucky. God bless him, he was a lovely guy. Very humble, very funny and down to earth. He was very special, Houlihan. He was more than a natural. I can't even find a word for him. He was in a different class. He meant a lot to me, his coaching and his help. It's lovely to remember him and talk about him. It brings a tear to my eye just thinking about him.'

# Chapter 19

# The Hollywood ending

AFTER THREE seasons with barely a win, it would have been understandable if Patsy Houlihan had called it a day as a snooker professional. But he was no quitter. And the 1985/86 campaign was undoubtedly a better season for him; he won four of his 11 matches (as well as three more by walkover) including reaching the last 32 of the English Professional Championship, where he lost 9-5 to his old rival John Spencer.

One amusing memory of Houlihan's campaign is provided by Steve Davis, who watched him play Australian Robbie Foldvari in the last 96 of the 1986 Mercantile Credit Classic.

'The tournament was being played at a venue in Warrington which isn't there any more called the Spectrum Arena,' Davis recalled. 'I turned up for my match which was in the evening and I was watching some of the afternoon matches. Patsy was a very free-flowing player, of course, but he had been drawn against Robbie Foldvari, a billiards player first and foremost, who was trying to make it as a snooker player. Foldvari was one of the slowest players you could ever see. He would just get brain freeze when he played – 40 seconds a shot was probably an underestimate. I remember watching Robbie walking around the table in his match against Patsy, studying every possible position and not being able to commit to a shot and it was driving Patsy mad! Anyway, as this was going on Patsy happened to look up and spot me in the crowd. Exasperated, he put his hand up to his head as though to say to me, "What am I doing here and what is this bloke doing to me?" That's one of my abiding memories of Patsy Houlihan.'

Houlihan beat Foldvari 5-4 and – come the end of the season – had been sufficiently encouraged by the form he had shown to make a big effort on the practice table ahead of the following campaign. Before the qualifiers for the season-opening ranking event, the BCE International Open, he practised solidly for a month and reaped the rewards, beating Dave Chalmers and Graham Cripsey 5-1 apiece in the qualifiers to earn a last-64 showdown with old mate Tony Meo. At the time Meo was ranked 11th in the world, while Houlihan was a full 80 places lower, but Patsy turned back the clock to pull off a major upset, edging Meo out 5-4. Houlihan notched the highest break of the match – a 78 – in frame two, and snatched the final frame with a nerveless clearance of 32 consisting of red, brown and all the colours. 'The last time I beat a leading player, London Bridge was a lighthouse,' he quipped, recycling a killer line from 1978.

As fate would have it, Houlihan's opponent in the last 32 was, like Meo, one of his best friends in the game, Eugene Hughes, who he had known since the glory days of the Pot Black club at Vardens Road. The duo had stayed in touch ever since, and Hughes admitted he always relished the time he spent in Houlihan's company. 'If I played in a tournament and Patsy wasn't there I'd miss him,' he told the author. 'I remember once in the 1980s I was playing Patsy in an exhibition down in Portsmouth. I picked him up from New Cross and on the way down I switched the radio off and just listened to his amazing stories for the whole journey.'

If he could beat Hughes, Houlihan would have reached the last 16 and the televised stages of the tournament. However, the Irishman was in some of the best form of his life; he repelled Houlihan 5-1, then whitewashed Bob Chaperon 5-0 and in the quarter-finals defeated the mighty Steve Davis 5-4. Unfortunately for Hughes, Neal Foulds denied him 9-8 in the semi-finals. An odd footnote to the match was that when Foulds and Hughes returned to their hotel rooms they discovered that they had both been burgled – although Hughes only lost £45, which was handsomely offset by his £10,500 cheque for reaching the last four.

As for Houlihan, his promising early season form didn't last and he failed to win any of his other seven matches that season, losing 10-4 to 'Giro' Jon Wright in the World Championship qualifiers, although his run in the International Open helped him rise from 91st in the world rankings to 64th. In the off-season, in a column for *Pot Black* magazine, Alexander Clyde, long-time snooker writer for the *London Evening Standard*, produced an elegiac piece focused on Houlihan's attempts to rediscover the lost form of his youth. Headlined 'Glimmer of hope for the old King', Clyde's piece began,

'The little man in the horn-rimmed glasses did not rate so much as a second glance as he picked his way through the Sunday afternoon throng on the concourse at Euston Station. He was heading for the bus stop and the final leg of his journey home from Preston to his modest flat in Deptford, south-east London. The only clue to his identity was a battered cue case under his arm, along with the suitcase containing the clothes he wore for the one match that ended his snooker dreams for another year. Pat Houlihan, professional snooker player, was on his way home.'

Clyde's description of Houlihan and the mythic aura that still surrounded him was pitch perfect, 'He's 57 with failing eyesight, though he courts no sympathy. But there are many snooker people who get misty-eyed at the mere mention of his name. "Patsy Houlihan? Now that was some player," they insist. "If he'd been born 15–30 years later he'd be a real star, a household name."'

Speaking to Clyde, Houlihan was honest in his assessment of some of his failings as he reflected on the financial cost of his exit in the first qualifying round of the World Championship. 'I've no excuse for the way I played against Jon Wright,' he admitted. 'It's down to my own stupidity, really. But I'm lazy, if you like. I asked myself a lot of new questions. I worked out what it had cost me. First-round losers don't get a penny, which I don't think is fair. The return fare was £32 and the hotel cost me £68. With the other bits and pieces, like meals and drinks, [losing] must have cost me £140 or £150. It's money I've thrown away, really. If you don't practise properly, you can't expect to get anything out of it.'

Houlihan's self-recriminatory mood did not last long, however. Soon, he was looking forward, maintaining his cheerful insistence that better times might be just around the corner. 'I'm just pleased I got that ranking point [from beating Meo in the International Open],' he asserted. 'The way I'm feeling now I'm ready to give it a go and make a bit of a comeback next season. I could still upset a lot of players, you know. A lot of pros know that.'

There was indeed another good result to celebrate in the 1987/88 season as Houlihan knocked the world number 15 Dean Reynolds out of the Rothmans Grand Prix in qualifying at the Redwood Lodge in Bristol in September to reach the last 32 and the tournament proper, held at the Hexagon Theatre in Reading, a two-table setup played under television lights. Houlihan faced Canada's Bob Chaperon on the opening Saturday of the tournament in a match that was seemingly filmed but not televised. Wearing swivel-lens spectacles, Patsy struggled under the bright lights, losing 5-0. Nevertheless, the result helped Houlihan inch five places up the world rankings at the end of the season to 59th, as well as secure a career-high seasonal prize money haul of £4,539. These isolated wins helped keep Houlihan ticking over during a period when, although the professional snooker world was expanding – there would be over 200 pros by 1990 – the money-match circuit was contracting. Snooker clubs had become more mainstream, more sanitised, and owners less tolerant of gambling and other such antics which existed on the margins of legality.

The contrast between modern snooker and how the game had been when Houlihan was growing up was made starkly apparent in an episode of *Danny Baker's Londoners* broadcast on 28 August 1987. A short-lived documentary in which Baker examined various facets of London life, the third and final episode (entitled 'Players') featured Houlihan, as well as one of the earliest media appearances of prodigious young snooker talent Ronnie O'Sullivan, then just 11 years old.

Baker, 'Snooker is the classic success story. It flopped in black and white, but with colour telly snooker bloomed and the big money came in. Before that – as Patsy Houlihan – an old-time snooker hustler recalls – you couldn't earn a living from prize money.'

Houlihan, 'When I went in the London Championships, I went in it nine times [sic.] and I won it seven. But all I got was a trophy and, as you know, you can't eat trophies. So we had to go and get our bit of money. In the clubs there was backers, like, who'd always back the top Johnny as they called them, the best player. If you thought you could beat them you'd go and play them, and that was my strong suit, playing for money.'

Baker, 'Young snooker players today don't have to hustle. Ronnie O'Sullivan has already won several thousand pounds from snooker tournaments at the age of 11.'

Later in the item, Baker stated that 'the sponsorship bonanza has completely changed the game of snooker since Patsy Houlihan first played', an apt summation of how the sport's boom years had come too late for Houlihan, whereas O'Sullivan – born in 1975 – was perfectly placed to cash in.

There was – however – one last day in the sun for Patsy. It came on 20 February 1989 in the £350,000 Anglian British Open at the Assembly Rooms in Derby. Having beaten Nick Terry 5-2, Houlihan snared a last-64 showdown with his old mate Jimmy White, now world ranked number two. Sadly, the televised section of the tournament hadn't begun, so the minor classic the two men conjured has – like the rest of Houlihan's career – not been recorded for posterity, although it lingers as a folk memory.

For the 102 minutes the best-of-nine match lasted, White and Houlihan succeeded in conjuring what the *Daily Telegraph* admiringly labelled a 'high-speed potting match'. It was almost as though the last decade hadn't happened and the pair were back at Vardens Road again, playing for laughs and cash. White got in first, snatching the first frame courtesy of a rapid 66 break, before Houlihan smashed a 51 to level at 1-1. Houlihan took the third frame too – 71-46 – to move 2-1 up. White edged a tight fourth 73-66 on a re-spotted black and then blasted a brilliant 101 break to move 3-2 ahead. Another quickfire frame went White's way 63-17 and he was just one from victory. But Houlihan wasn't finished, summoning some breathtaking pots he won the seventh frame at a canter – 73-35.

The symmetry of the two men's shared history dictated that really the match should go to a decider, but prosaic reality intervened. White, his cue tip red hot, almost cleared the table – notching a 99 that was utterly perfect in its imperfection to secure a 5-3 victory. 'Jimmy has youth on his side and produced something extra out there,' Houlihan admitted after the match admiringly.

As for White, he generously made sure he told everyone and anyone that would listen just how special Houlihan was and how much he meant to him. 'I first met Pat when I was just 12 years old, and from 14 I practised with him for weeks on end,' he enthused to the assembled media. 'He taught both Tony Meo and myself a tremendous amount about the game and I have the utmost respect for him as a player. I believe that in his prime he was in the same class as Ray Reardon and John Spencer. He was one of the great players of that time. He was the business.'

The story of the young gun beating his former mentor resonated in the press, with articles appearing in under headlines such as 'White more than a match for mentor' and 'White beats the man who taught him'. A wonderful post-match photo of White and Houlihan was also published in the April 1989 edition of *Pot Black* magazine, showing them both grinning broadly, with White pointing playfully at Houlihan as though to say 'He's the man!' It's a photo that White has a copy of today and treasures.

If Houlihan's life was a film it would end with the White match at the 1989 British Open. The final scene would see him in the bar with White after the match announcing his retirement, and being applauded by the press and his peers as the torch of free-flowing attacking snooker was permanently passed from one south London legend to another.

Real life doesn't work like that though.

For Houlihan it wasn't quite the end, but Hollywood had long ceased writing his scripts.

Chapter 20

# The silent goodbye

AS THE 1980s drew to a close, snooker was in an enviable position and had attained the status of a televisual and sociocultural phenomenon. The main fact which supports such a hypothesis is well-worn but worth repeating – namely that the Steve Davis-Dennis Taylor World Championship final of 1985, at its peak, was watched by 18.5 million people, despite being screened on 'secondary' channel BBC2 and finishing well past midnight. This phenomenal viewing figure was no one-off – millions tuned in each year to the latter stages of the tournament and the myriad other snooker competitions featured on the BBC and ITV. Such was the sport's dominance of the televisual landscape that it has been theorised that 1980s snooker king Steve Davis appeared on British television for more hours during the decade than anyone else.

By the dawn of the 1990s, the professional snooker circuit was booming and seemingly ever-expanding. There were over 200 professionals, and in 1989/90 ten tournaments that players could enter to earn points which would contribute towards their world rankings, as well as a plethora of invitational events, many of them highly lucrative. The first world champion of the '90s was Stephen Hendry, who would dominate the ensuing decade in the way that Davis bestrode the previous one. In the 1990 World Championship final Hendry beat Jimmy White 18-12 to lift the crown and supplant Alex Higgins as the sport's youngest world champion, securing a payday of £120,000 in the process – it wasn't as much as the winner of the men's singles championship at Wimbledon picked up, but it was a damn sight more than the average salary of a top-flight footballer in England, which at the time was 'just' £41,600, and a huge increase on the £400 Alex Higgins pocketed in 1972, or the £6,000 John Spencer trousered in 1977 when the championship first graced the Crucible.

True, some aspects of the closed shop mentality established all those years ago by Joe Davis and his peers remained – for example, if you reached the lofty stages of the top 16 in the world at the end of the season then you were granted guaranteed and protected entry into the latter stages of all ranking tournaments for the following campaign and spared the tortuous indignity of the qualification rounds. However, the broadly meritocratic structure that graced snooker now was a far cry from the unbreakable and selective cartel which ruled the sport in the 1950s, '60s and even the '70s and early '80s. Snooker had become the sort of commercially lucrative and accessible environment that was unthinkable and inconceivable when Houlihan first picked up a cue in the 1940s. The tragedy for Houlihan was that the sport had become a money-making juggernaut far too late for him to join the party in any meaningful sense.

When the 1990s began Houlihan had just turned 60, an occasion that his family marked with a large party at the Lord Hood pub in Deptford, complete with a snooker table birthday cake. Ever captivated by a love of the sport that bordered on addiction, Houlihan carried on toiling manfully in the pro ranks for the first three years of the decade. Indeed, it was a signal of the game's expansion that the 1989/90 season was the busiest of Houlihan's entire professional career – he played 20 matches in all during this campaign, winning half of them, and featured in 13 in 1990/91, winning five. By way of comparison, in the first ten years of his professional career Houlihan only had the opportunity to play 19 matches, such were the strictures and limitations of the circuit at that point. One of Houlihan's defeats in 1990/91 came in qualifying for the World Championship against future WPBSA chairman Jason Ferguson, then in his debut year on the circuit. 'I don't remember that game to be honest, but I do remember Patsy,' Ferguson told the author. 'In my amateur days I played him in his club in London. He was quite a character and a very fluent player.'

Although Houlihan now had more opportunities to play and more tournaments to participate in than ever, the grind of travelling to often obscure venues for qualifiers and finding anonymous hotels that didn't charge the earth gradually became burdensome. There were also far more pros to compete against. Ahead of the 1991/92 season – in which Houlihan won just two matches out of the nine he played – the WPBSA had, remarkably, opened up the sport to anyone and everyone who wanted to compete. As long as you paid a £500 enrolment fee and an annual subscription of £100 you could enter any ranking tournaments you wanted, at a further cost of around £100 per tournament. Some of the newcomers were chancers or snooker enthusiasts with money to burn, but many were formidable talents from a generation of youngsters for whom 3x2 or 6x4 snooker tables were *the* go-to gift and becoming a professional as aspirational an ambition as becoming a footballer is today. Of particular note in the 1992/93 season was the fact that Ronnie O'Sullivan, Mark Williams and John Higgins all turned pro; retrospectively labelled the 'Class of '92' this trio would later accumulate – by the time of writing – a staggering 14 world titles between them.

That pivotal season, the WPBSA were able to boast of a staggering 719 registered professionals. To cater for the vast number of qualifiers now needed to determine which players would participate in the latter stages of the nine main ranking tournaments it became necessary to run a marathon series of qualifying events across several months from June until September. The venue for these matches was the Norbreck Castle Hotel in Blackpool, which had previously hosted the Mercantile Credit Classic from 1987 until 1990. A vast 480-bedroom establishment on Queen's Promenade with a view of the crashing waves of the Irish Sea, the Norbreck resembled a traditional English castle as reimagined by an over-ideological Soviet architect of the 1960s. For the purposes of the summer 1992 qualifiers, the main hall of the hotel was configured to accommodate 22 snooker tables, each surrounded on three sides by grey temporary walls, with three rows of seating at one end of each partition for spectators. Viewed from above, the setup resembled some sort of bizarre snooker prison.

Houlihan in the centre of the action in a party at the Osborne Arms in the 1990s. (Patricia Houlihan)

Houlihan with his wife Brenda during an annual weekend family trip to Cliftonville, near Margate. (Patricia Houlihan)

Houlihan with Brenda (second right) and all his children (left to right) Danny Boy, Patsy Boy, Patsy Girl and Lee. (Patricia Houlihan)

Houlihan's London Transport photocard, issued with a Freedom Travel pass when he turned 60 in 1994. Patsy sold the Freedom Pass. (Patricia Houlihan)

London Transport

**PHOTOCARD**
For concessionary
Travel Permit
For conditions see over

Holder   M

Houlihan with Danny Adds (centre), the former British Under-16 snooker champion who appeared with him in the 1984 film *Number One*. (Patricia Houlihan)

Houlihan with Mick (second right), landlord of his beloved Osborne Arms in Deptford. (Patricia Houlihan)

Houlihan in his late sixties, a bottle of his favourite light ale in front of him. (Patricia Houlihan)

Andy Hall's atmospheric photos of
Houlihan for *Observer Sports Monthly*
taken on 11 April 2002 perfectly captured
the mystique and drama of his hustling
lifestyle in inner-city Deptford. (Andy Hall)

**Top, left:** Houlihan's beloved step-granddaughter Justine whose death aged 13 from leukaemia was a blow from which Houlihan never recovered. (Patricia Houlihan)

**Top, right:** Justine (left) with Houlihan's granddaughter Tara (right). (Patricia Houlihan)

**Right:** The order of service for Houlihan's 2006 funeral. This copy was signed and given to the author by Houlihan's daughter Patsy Girl and son Patsy Boy. (Patricia Houlihan/ Luke G. Williams)

To Luke Luv Patsy Girl

✝ PATSY BOY

**PATSY HOULIHAN**
1929 – 2006

**Loving**
Husband, Father, Grandfather
And
Great Grandfather

Across the summer and early autumn of 1992, qualifying results were, in the words of Clive Everton, 'churned out on an industrial scale'. More than 5,000 matches were played in total, with the number of rounds debutant pros had to negotiate to reach the final stages of tournaments totalling ten or 11. Morning sessions began at 9.30am – an unearthly hour for snooker players who were traditionally night owls and often drinkers too – with evening matches often finishing around midnight. Ten minutes before each session, those who were due to play, 44 of them at times, would gather in the practice area for registration with the WPBSA's tournament director Ann Yates and press officer Colin Randle. Robert Foxall, the world number 174, observed of this practice to *Snooker Scene*, 'When you all go into the arena it's a bit like the soldiers in Colditz after they've been marched back to their cells from the recreation area. Come September, it'll be the Great Escape for some.'

With many pros in Blackpool for weeks or months at a time, it was common practice for players to bunk three or four to a room at the Norbreck (special 'snooker rate' £30 a night for a double room) or in one of the many local bed and breakfasts. What with the sleep deprivation, the drinking, the practical jokes and the labyrinthine playing schedule, some players barely knew which qualifying tournament they were playing in from one day to the next. Unsurprisingly, amid this surreal and exacting environment, some players thrived, some struggled, and some fell apart at the seams. Ronnie O'Sullivan, to take one example, seemed to positively relish snooker's equivalent of the Dickensian treadmill, winning a remarkable 74 out of his 76 qualifiers, thus launching his pro career in a blaze of brilliance and publicity. In contrast, Alex Higgins, in his fifth season outside the hallowed top 16, had a run of decidedly mixed results, falling at the qualifying hurdles with dispiriting regularity. Then there was Jon Wright, a talented but wayward Londoner, who conceded his best-of-nine match against reigning female world champion Alison Fisher while level at 3-3 with Fisher still at the table on a break of 20. 'Giro' Jon was subsequently found guilty of 'conduct unbecoming a professional sportsman' by the WPBSA. Banned for the rest of the season, he never returned to the pro game again.

Alain Robidoux, a talented Canadian who turned professional in 1987, recalled of the Norbreck, 'The Norbreck was not my favourite place and I don't know a lot of players who liked to play there! It was windy and cold and most of the players felt like it was some kind of punishment to be there. But as far as I was concerned at that time, it was the beginning of my career and I didn't know any better! It was only after I qualified for a few nice venues that I realised the Norbreck was probably the worst venue on the calendar. If I had to say one good thing about that venue, I had a lot of good laughs there and met most of the players at the bar at the back. On top of that, I made my 147 there [in qualifying for the 1989 European Open against Jim Meadowcroft], so for me, it will always be a venue I remember!'

Houlihan went about his business at the Norbreck with his usual dignity, albeit cloaked in virtual anonymity. New players on the circuit who knew their snooker appreciated that he had once had a reputation, but to many others he was just another veteran from yesteryear who they were trying to sweep aside. Robidoux was one of those who met Houlihan and was impressed by him. 'Unfortunately, I didn't have a chance to watch Patsy play but from what I heard from many people he was a top-class player,' he said. 'One thing I can say is he was *so* good at spinning the cue ball and doing tricks – all kind of tricks that I couldn't do to be fair. He was always nice to everyone and I couldn't ever imagine anyone having any problems or arguments with him. He was just a very nice human being. Another reason I'll always remember the Norbreck is that it was the place I met Patsy and where we exchanged our finger-spinning skills. Some of the other players probably lost a few pounds on our trick shot routines!'

Competitively, however, as the 1992/93 season began at the Norbreck, Houlihan was nearing the end. He was now 62 and entered six tournaments, his world ranking of 153 ensuring he joined at the sixth qualifying round stage each time. He lost his first five, including a 5-2 defeat in a World Championship qualifier to Mark O'Sullivan, an Irishman who had little further impact on the tournament. With no prize money for sixth qualifying round exits and entry for each tournament costing £100, and the World Championship a pricey £250 plus VAT, Houlihan was soon staring at a loss of nearly £800 without even taking into account his accommodation and travel costs. The brave new snooker world was a meritocracy all right, but it didn't come cheap.

In the sixth qualifying round of the Dubai Duty Free Classic, Houlihan salvaged £100 prize money by beating Jamie Rous, a 20-year-old pro in just his second season on the tour, 5-2. It was the last victory Houlihan would secure as a professional. On 13 or 14 August, judging by contemporary newspaper clippings, he lost 5-1 in the seventh qualifying round to Andrew Cairns, a talented young pro from Blackpool who would never quite make the grade in eight seasons on the circuit.

As Houlihan slowly and deliberately packed away his cue at the end of the Cairns match it is unclear if he had already decided that his pro career was over. There was certainly no official announcement to this effect. Without fuss, Houlihan merely slipped quietly back to Deptford on the train after a light ale or two at the Mariners pub on Norbreck Road, where many a cueist celebrated or commiserated during those long summer days in Blackpool.

'The personal balance sheets of all but a few are sure to be showing red at the end of the summer, but for most this is their life and this is their dream,' reflected *Snooker Scene* in elegiac fashion of the Norbreck experience for many pros. 'Some clearly have the ability to convert their dreams into reality. Disillusion awaits many more but all can say that at least they were given a chance and at least they tried.'

Snooker was still Houlihan's life, but he had run out of outlandish dreams or fanciful ambitions. Official confirmation that he was no longer a professional snooker player came 11 months after his defeat against Cairns, in the July 1993 edition of *Snooker Scene* magazine which reported 76 'resignations' from the WPBSA, adding the disclaimer that this term 'also encompasses those who have had their membership terminated through failure to pay the £100 a year subscription'. The name of 'the veteran Pat Houlihan' was included on this list, with the magazine labelling him one of the departures from the tour who was 'of more than ordinary ability'. It wasn't an intentional slight by *Snooker Scene*, but Houlihan's career deserved a far more in-depth epitaph.

In retrospect there was cruel irony in the fact that snooker's modern 'natural' talent Ronnie O'Sullivan entered the professional stage during the very same season that Houlihan – the original 'natural' – left it. O'Sullivan would go on to enjoy a glittering and garlanded career, accumulating nearly £12m in prize money (at the time of writing) and national celebrity. Inarguably he is a great talent, but equally he and his peers – Mark Williams, John Higgins et al – were fortunate to be born in an era when their youthful talents were given a fair chance to develop and a prominent and lucrative stage on which to shine. In contrast, Houlihan – prevented from achieving the status of professionalism until well past his peak – had to toil for scraps in his 20 years on the tour, the big breakthrough forever within his sights, but always just out of his grasp.

Ever willing and never bitter, Houlihan's talent and ability to entertain deserved far more reward than he ever reaped, but that's the way life is sometimes.

As Steve Davis, who has forgotten more about snooker than most people ever know, mused, 'Sometimes people get lucky and sometimes they get unlucky … Patsy was unlucky.'

Chapter 21

# Jonny Rendall and the Deptford Aesthetic

AFTER HIS retirement from the professional snooker circuit in 1993, Patsy Houlihan did something he had never done before. He travelled abroad, taking a holiday with Brenda to Lanzarote. It was, in Houlihan's own low-key way, a celebration, a way of marking the end of a remarkable competitive snooker career that had lasted nearly 40 years. The couple had a wonderful time too, sending a joyful postcard home to Patsy Girl and her family telling them of the 'scorching weather' and 'beautiful accommodation'.

When Houlihan got home, Patsy Girl having met him at the airport, life continued much as it had always done in Deptford. Houlihan was no longer on the snooker tour, but not much else had really changed. He was still drinking, socialising and spending time with his family and friends. It was a quiet life but one he loved, for he was a part of Deptford as Deptford was a part of him.

There was less travel now, of course, and less worrying about whether he could cover his costs to get to this tournament or that tournament in whatever anonymous corner of England was next on the snooker calendar. But Houlihan still gambled, and he still played snooker or pool for money. As ever, he also found other ways to make a few extra quid. Like all pensioners living in London, he qualified for a 'freedom pass', which allowed him to travel *gratis* on bus, rail or tube in the capital. Houlihan walked pretty much everywhere though and had no need for it, so he sold it for a tidy sum.

Within the snooker world, where Houlihan was no longer a familiar presence, tales and knowledge of his exploits inevitably faded as the years marched inexorably on. The number of people within the snooker community, or the wider public, who knew of him, had met him or had seen him play, receded steadily as mortality exacted its grim but inevitable toll.

Indeed, had it not been for the interest, enthusiasm and kindness of Jimmy White and writer Jonathan Rendall, then the name of Patsy Houlihan might have evaporated from popular consciousness altogether, and faded to something akin to a distant dream.

White, of course, needs no introduction. He was a long-time Houlihan advocate, having been wowed by Patsy's skills from the moment of their first meeting in the mid-1970s. In 1998, Houlihan still occupied a prominent place in White's affections, as shown by the fact he paid Patsy the ultimate tribute, declaring in his rollicking rollercoaster of an autobiography, *Behind the White Ball*, that he rated Houlihan alongside Charlie Poole and Alex Higgins as the greatest players he had ever seen. White's typically romantic rationale for choosing this trio of talents rather than more obvious names such as Steve Davis or Stephen Hendry was predominantly aesthetic, '[They were] potters and entertainers,' he asserted. 'Safety shots were too boring for them.' This tribute, as well as White's longstanding public advocacy of Houlihan's skills, deeply touched Patsy, serving as a much-needed corrective to the careless slur that John Spencer had made about the 1965 English Amateur Championship Final in his 1973 book *Spencer on Snooker.*

White's love of Houlihan was doubtless borne of the fact that he saw in him a reflection of his own precocious brilliance. 'Patsy was such a natural player,' he told the author. 'He just put the cue down once, drew it back and hit the ball. There's a fella from Hong Kong called Marco Fu who's got the same sort of cue action that Patsy had but he takes about 20 seconds a shot, while Patsy took about four seconds. He was so fast it was unbelievable and an incredible snooker player, all-out attacking at all times.'

Houlihan reciprocated White's depth of feeling. 'Jimmy's always been a beautiful player,' he once declared.

Houlihan's daughter Patsy Girl elaborated on the connection between the two men, 'Dad always spoke so highly of Jimmy. I heard him talking about him so many times. And dad meant a lot to Jimmy too.' Famously, of course, White reached six World Championship finals, all of which Houlihan watched unfold on television, sharing in the pain of the six heartbreaking defeats suffered by a man whose attacking philosophies mirrored his own.

If Houlihan and White's special gift was to conjure breathtaking magic with snooker balls, then the writer Jonathan Rendall's metier was creating bittersweet beauty through words. 'Pound for pound, Jonny was the best writer I've ever worked with,' is the verdict of former *Observer Sports Monthly* editor Matt Tench, at the time of writing assistant sports editor of *The Times*. 'He was just extraordinary. There's plenty of people I think are great writers, but he was a one-off. There was nobody else like him. His talent was transcendent. He had the best writing style I've ever seen. He brought to life characters in a way that nobody else did or could.'

If ever there was a writer born to tell the story of Houlihan it was Rendall, whose loyalties lay very much with sporting mavericks, underdogs and talents who refused to compromise aesthetics for the banalities of 'winning'. 'Jonny was a real romantic,' declared Rendall's friend Kevin Mitchell, a respected sportswriter for *The Guardian*. 'I'm sure the mystery and mystique surrounding Houlihan is one of the reasons Jonny loved him. Houlihan was the sort of character who Jonny would have loved to be cheering on from stage left.' Rendall was a deceptively simple writer, with a genius for character, pathos and humour, but for all his brilliance, he was also a complex and sometimes infuriating man. Deadlines and the factual discipline required of a journalist did not come naturally to him.

'He was difficult to work with,' Tench admitted. 'A lot of people in sports journalism – particularly those at the higher end – would look at Jonny and say, "Fucking hell, I thought I was good but he's brilliant!" But at the same time they'd think to themselves, "Is everything he's writing true?" People had legitimate questions about that. Up to a point Jonny would just laugh it off. I think he saw writing more as an exercise in creating something wonderful than in staying true to the facts.'

Mitchell concurred with Tench's analysis. 'The problem – if you want to call it that because I certainly don't think Jonny saw it as a problem – was that he blended fantasy and fact and then expected you to sort out one from the other. That's an indulgence that very few publishers will put up with, if they even know it is happening. Jonny painted world pictures, you see. In that sense he was inspired by a lot of those American writers of the 1920s and '30s – Damon Runyon and A.J. Leibling and so on. They used to take diabolical liberties with the facts. They'd write whatever they wanted. There were no checks and balances.'

Rendall's masterpiece – the 1997 boxing book *This Bloody Mary Is the Last Thing I Own* – won acclaim from voices as varied and renowned as Tom Stoppard and Tom Wolfe and snaffled a prestigious Somerset Maugham Award into the bargain. Yet questions remain over the veracity of many of its passages: did Frank Bruno really 'attack' Rendall in Betty Boop's bar at the MGM Grand as he claimed in the book's unforgettable opening sentence? Did Jonny really track down the legendary Cuban boxer Kid Chocolate to an anonymous Havana apartment as he lay dying?

Given the overwhelming lyrical beauty of the book – as well as the impossibility of ever knowing how much of it is true – perhaps it doesn't really matter. Tench, however, makes an interesting point about Rendall's obfuscation of fact and fantasy. 'Jonny would so want some things to be true that he would say they were true, hoping that would make them true. Ken Jones, who Jonny and I worked with at *The Independent*, was a very kind and decent man but he would express doubts about how accurate Jonny was being. When people would bring these things to Jonny's attention he would say, "OK, I'm not going to do that anymore." But then he'd just carry on!'

Regardless of any doubts his journalistic colleagues and peers harboured about Rendall's reliability, it was widely expected that the Somerset Maugham award, and the acclaim *This Bloody Mary* received, would launch him to journalistic stardom. But it was not to be. Mainstream acclaim and material success would evade Rendall, as they would Houlihan. In Rendall's case, his career, and ultimately his life, were curtailed by myriad issues, predominantly emotional and psychological, as well as alcohol related. His true character and personality often existed beneath the misdirection of myths and anecdotes, the truth and veracity of which – like his writing – were often difficult, if not impossible, to verify.

'He seemed to have layers of different lives buried within him,' Mitchell explained. 'He could have been an actor. In fact, in one sense he *was* an actor because lots of aspects of his character were representations of whatever took his fancy. A lot of the charisma and mystique around him stems from the fact there are so many loose ends, myths and stories that surround him and his life.'

Born on 11 June 1964, the complexities of Rendall can be traced – for the most part – to his troubled and traumatic upbringing. His relationship with his adopted parents John and Jay Rendall was highly problematic, as detailed in his devastating memoir *Garden-Hopping*, in which he also recounts the tragicomic story of how he later tracked down and attempted to build a relationship with his birth mother. It's a brilliantly written book, but the emotional devastation it lays bare is almost too much to take. Tench – for one – admitted, 'I couldn't read the whole book. Couldn't face it. I read the excerpts in *The Observer*. They were very strong stuff, and went some way to explaining the demons Jonny faced.'

A psychoanalyst might theorise that Rendall's adoption as a child led to him spending the rest of his life engaged in an ultimately futile pursuit for a permanent feeling of self-worth or belonging. Yet for long periods he was highly functional and conventionally successful too. After graduating from Oxford University, he found his way into journalism. He began his career working under the legendary boxing scribe Srikumar Sen of *The Times*, later also working for the *Sunday Correspondent* and *Independent on Sunday*.

Tench recalled an early Rendall masterpiece that caught his attention, 'I still remember the first piece of Jonny's I ever read which was in the *Independent on Sunday* – it was about the boxer Jack "Kid" Berg. There aren't many pieces where you can remember exactly where you were when you first read them, but I can with that. It was just extraordinary writing and I think Jonny was only in his 20s then. It was so beautifully done. It was literature. From early on I thought: this guy's a genius.'

Rendall's fascination with boxing led to an unusual sideline advising the British featherweight boxer Colin McMillan, as pure a pugilistic talent as British boxing has ever produced. 'He struck up a friendship with Colin after interviewing him and then began advising him,' Mitchell explained. 'Jonny was full of crazy stories about going with Colin over to New York, meeting Don King and various other adventures they had. They were a curious combination. You had Howard Rainey, Colin's trainer, a gruff old geezer from the old school. Then there was Colin, this bright young kid from Barking, and last of all, Jonny, this amazing free spirit.'

McMillan still recalls Rendall fondly. 'He was a real character and a great storyteller,' he told the author. 'He had real belief in me and my ability. He was full of ideas. He was a romantic. I really loved the guy and will always be indebted to him.'

Although boxing was his main sporting passion, Rendall also maintained a fascination with snooker, borne out of his affinity with the gritty underbelly of human existence, as well as his overwhelming love for the talents of Jimmy White. The leap from boxing to snooker was not a large one, as Mitchell pointed out, 'The worlds of boxing and snooker do intersect. Both have a great variety of characters, some of them scallywag types. They're both regulated but also exist on the margins as well. Both sports have a lot of room for the sort of fun and invention and mavericks you don't always get in other sports.'

Ironically, prior to Jimmy White enlisting Rosemary Kingsland as ghostwriter and Hutchinson as publisher for his 1998 book *Behind the White Ball*, Rendall had attempted to close a deal with White to write a book together, a process which he detailed in a picaresque 1999 article for the *Independent on Sunday* headlined 'Jimmy White: Join the Cue'. Rendall's planned book, *Whirlwind*, never came to pass, but during the time he spent with White discussing the project one conversation the duo shared stayed with him.

'I asked White who was the best player ever to pick up a cue,' Rendall later wrote. 'Was it "Hurricane" Higgins, Hendry, Davis (Joe), Davies [sic.] (Steve), himself? "None of them," White replied rather absent-mindedly. "It's a fella you won't have heard of ... a fella named Patsy Hoolihan [sic.].'"

Intrigued, Rendall began to pursue the few threads of Houlihan's life and career that were in the public domain in an attempt to try and track him down and interview him. At this point the snooker world hadn't heard of or seen Houlihan for nearly ten years, and as far as most of them were concerned he had disappeared off the face of the earth. The mythic grandeur of the idea of a great lost snooker talent chimed perfectly with Rendall's romantic sensibilities. Convinced there was mileage in a feature on Houlihan, Rendall made a pitch to former colleague Tench, who was now editing the *Observer Sports Monthly*.

*OSM*, as it was popularly known, can – in retrospect – be seen as one of the last great products of the print era of sports journalism, before the internet and new media assumed domination. Launched in May 2000, the 64-page over-size magazine was included free with *The Observer* every month, and was a quality product which combined in-depth and sometimes refreshingly niche articles, with lavish photographic splashes.

Tench, who was the publication's launch editor, explained, 'John Mulhullond who was deputy editor and Roger Alton who was editor of *The Observer* cooked up the idea back in 1999. They wanted a monthly sports magazine that came with the paper. They asked me to do a dummy. It was quite a big investment. I'd just finished being the editor of *FourFourTwo* [football] magazine at the time so the timing was good. They focus-grouped the dummy issue I edited and it went very well. I thought, "This is too good to be true. They're not really going to want me to do this!" But they came back to me and said, "We're going to go for it and we want you to edit it."'

*OSM* was an immediate success, with *The Observer* receiving sales spikes on the weeks when it appeared. 'I loved editing *OSM* and I think a lot of people appreciated it,' Tench said. 'I always thought there was a gap for really great sports journalism and "big reads" and that's the gap we wanted to fill. Later we won various awards and someone said we were the British equivalent of *Sports Illustrated* which was amazing because when I first saw an issue of *Sports Illustrated* in the 1990s I thought I'd died and gone to heaven.'

Writers and photographers loved landing assignments with *OSM*. 'It was an amazing publication to work on,' recalled photographer Andy Hall, who would ultimately photograph Rendall's piece on Houlihan. 'It didn't only look at sport but the stories behind sport. For some features the connection to sport could be quite tenuous. I'd go all over the place taking photos for it and had the freedom to go back to the picture desk, give them ideas about stories that might work. I photographed bull running for *OSM* in southern India which was my idea. It wasn't just football, rugby and cricket. I think I must have covered just about every sport for them at one time or another. They also gave the images space to breathe – full pages or double pages. A six-page feature might have a nice double-page opener. And of course you'd always try and get a shot that might make it to the cover. It was a very wide-ranging publication. There's nothing like it now. It was one of a kind.'

Tench explained the process by which Rendall pitched the idea of an *OSM* feature on Houlihan. 'The Houlihan piece was probably written about ten years after I first knew Jonny, if not more,' he recalled. 'By then he was sort of desperate for money and his life was spinning out of control. But in the midst of it all he could still produce beautiful writing. He came up with the Houlihan idea and I thought, "I don't know about this. Am I really interested in 2,000 words on some bloke I've never heard of?" It sounded interesting but Jonny was also saying things like, "I don't know if I can actually get hold of him." It was a risk, but I thought to myself, "A Jonny classic might come out of this." So in the end I thought, "Go on, give Jonny a go. He'll make it work." And he did!'

Tench is spot on. Rendall's quest to find Houlihan, and the interview he subsequently conducted with him in a Deptford pub, formed the basis for an utterly brilliant piece of writing entitled 'The Great Unknown', which appeared in *OSM*'s May 2002 edition. Spread luxuriously over four pages, accompanied by Hall's brilliant black and white photography, Rendall's article was the most detailed examination of Houlihan's life and career since Jean Rafferty's *The Cruel Game* 20 years earlier.

The first quarter of the piece was devoted to Rendall's quest in finding Houlihan. 'Tracking down Patsy Hoolihan [the spelling used throughout the article] is no easy task,' he admitted in his fifth paragraph. 'All documented phone numbers for him were defunct. The sport's governing body, the WPBSA, didn't even know where he was. If Jimmy White knew, he wasn't saying. There was only one lead – the Deptford Arms in south London, where someone said Hoolihan had been known to "drink and hustle pool". But this had been years ago.'

Rendall duly picked up the scent of Houlihan in the Deptford Arms pub, where he meet a man named John Jock who admitted he knew Houlihan, but told Rendall, 'Patsy's a man who keeps himself to himself,' emphasising he would only facilitate a meeting between the two men after 'vetting' Rendall and ensuring 'you are who you say you are'. As Rendall observed wryly, 'Thankfully, the vetting procedure turned out to be cursory – it did occur to me that it was fortunate for Hoolihan that I was not a hitman – and John Jock gave me directions to another pub where I would recognise a man "from his glasses and swept-back hair."'

In this second unnamed pub, Rendall did indeed find Houlihan and after a short conversation and a few drinks Patsy agreed to a 'proper chat' the following week. At this second meeting, the two men talked about Patsy's hustling days and his connection to Deptford, as well as his love of Jimmy White and fractious relationship with Alex Higgins. They also played a few racks of pool together; ever the gentleman, Houlihan let Rendall win 'by missing a large number of balls on purpose'.

'The Great Unknown' is – in this writer's view – a small and almost perfect masterpiece. Rendall evokes Houlihan's character and personality beautifully, as well as the Deptford milieu surrounding him in vivid detail. Tench was certainly delighted with the results. 'I thought it was one of Jonny's best pieces,' he said. 'I read it again recently and, fuck me, it was good, in a way that most writing – never mind most sports writing – just isn't. I challenge anyone to read it and not think, "Wow, what a read!"'

Tench also pinpointed a particular facet of Rendall's genius. 'I'm not a great fan of people who bring themselves into their articles,' he said. 'It's a very fine balance to get it right. But the one exception to that was Jonny Rendall. He was unbelievable at bringing himself into a piece and not making the reader think, "Get yourself out!" In the Houlihan piece you like him, he's in there and you can't tell the story without him. The Houlihan article felt like literature to me. Like a novel, or a film noir or something. It was just magnificent the way Jonny set the scene in the pubs of south London and the way characters appear and disappear. And the wonderful use of names like John Jock. It's like a piece by Runyon. An absolutely beautiful piece of writing.'

On a journalistic level, of course, there are issues with the article – issues that are typical of Rendall's work. For starters, there are the errors, the most glaring of which is the misspelling throughout the entire piece of Houlihan's surname as 'Hoolihan'. It's an astonishingly amateurish slip on Rendall's part, and one which Tench admits 'really annoyed' him when he learned of it, dryly observing, 'I think we were entitled to presume that because he was writing about someone quite obscure to the mainstream that he was going to bring that person into his article correctly spelt.'

Clive Everton, reviewing the article in *Snooker Scene*, also pointed out that Rendall had misquoted him when speaking about an alleged behind-closed-doors match between Houlihan and Ray Reardon which Rendall claimed occurred when Reardon was world champion. Everton also drew attention to other factual and interpretive errors, such as Rendall's assertion that Joe Davis was responsible for selecting which snooker players appeared on the BBC TV programme *Pot Black*. Knowing what we do of Rendall, it is also impossible not to suspect there is significant embroidery at work in other places too – as Tench put it, 'Who knows whether John Jock was really there or not or if he even existed.'

In the final analysis, however, engaging in factual nitpicking or speculation largely misses the point of Rendall's work. The ineffable but magical combination of Hall's photography and Rendall's words – as well as Tench's daring in commissioning an article few sports editors would have taken a gamble on – succeeded in creating an impressionistic masterpiece of sports writing. It may not be journalism, but Rendall's writing was all about evoking feeling and atmosphere, and in 'The Great Unknown' he did that in spades.

As a gambler and card player, I like to think that's a metaphor Jonny Rendall would have approved of.

\* \* \*

Of the three men who met in that Deptford pub on the afternoon of Thursday, 11 April 2002, only photographer Andy Hall is still alive. These days he's a staff photographer for *The Guardian* and – funnily enough – lives less than three miles from where Patsy Houlihan was born, lived and died.

Hall's memories of his afternoon in the company of Rendall and Houlihan are warm and vivid. 'It was a good afternoon in the pub,' he smiles. 'I wanted to frame Houlihan as a cult hero. A working-class guy from Deptford who was a modern version of Paul Newman's Hustler. I also wanted to focus on the small details – his gnarled hands on the pool cue, for example. At the time most of the work I was doing was in colour but these had to be in black and white. There were a lot of monochrome colours anyway, his dark suit, a dingy pub. It also helped that Houlihan had a fag hanging from his mouth! I probably asked him to light up a few extra times so we got extra smoke for the shots. Of course, you could still smoke in the pubs back then!'

For nearly 20 years the majority of the shots that Hall took of Rendall and Houlihan were tucked away on contact sheets in Hall's personal archive, unseen by the wider public. 'I filed the contact sheets away very carefully because I was proud of them,' Hall told me, when I met him during the research for this book. It was a meeting that ended with us cutting a deal for ten of his images to appear in the pages of this book, the majority never before seen by the public. Hall seemed happy, touched even, that the photos he took so long ago were still capable of causing such interest and pleasure.

'Every now and then somebody comes looking for photos of something I did years ago that most people have forgotten,' he mused. 'Just like you did.'

\* \* \*

On Sunday, 5 May, when the *OSM* issue with Rendall's feature in it was published, Houlihan walked to his local newsagents in Deptford and bought himself a copy of *The Observer*. Usually he read the *London Evening Standard*, and took the *News of the World* on a Sunday, but this particular Sunday he made an exception. Later he would carefully cut out and keep his copy of the article. Houlihan wasn't a vain man, or one for making a fuss or a scene, but he liked to feel appreciated, and Rendall's interest and enthusiasm in his extraordinary and vivid life made him feel just that.

When Houlihan died in 2006, a copy of Rendall's article was among the collection of artefacts from his career that he had kept. The same copy survives to this day – residing in that treasured box alongside the other lovingly curated items Patsy Girl has kept safe for more than 16 years now and always will – there's the swivel-lens spectacles, the London transport photocard (sans 'freedom pass'), the yellowing newspaper cuttings from the 1950s and '60s, the watch with someone else's initials on and then there's Jonny Rendall's *OSM* masterpiece.

It's fitting really, because Rendall, in the way that only he could, pinpointed what was so special about Houlihan.

To Rendall, Houlihan was a romantic hero par excellence. 'Hoolihan,' he wrote, 'invented the romantic and selfless idea of the gunslinging fast player, the player of pure panache – romantic and selfless, because the selfish thing to do would be to play pragmatically like all the rest.'

Rendall's concluding paragraph also absolutely nailed the ethos of Patsy Houlihan. 'There is an aesthetic behind the way Hoolihan has lived – the Deptford Aesthetic, if you like,' he wrote. 'With a different background and talent, he might be called a bohemian. Just as he played fast, whatever the risks, he lived according to his own code, of manners, of pleasures, whatever the consequences to himself. The small routines of his Deptford world might seem banal to us, but they contain magic for him, because he knows what they mean. I left Hoolihan standing on the spot where, give or take a few yards across an alley, he will have been from birth to grave. It really is his Crucible. "Ta-ra," he said.'

It feels almost perverse to point it out when you're dealing with prose that borders on poetry, but that final line contains one final Rendall flourish that is plain wrong.

'That's not right,' Patsy Girl told me when we looked through the article together, a slight frown etching across her features. 'My dad never would have said "ta-ra", that's a northern thing. Maybe he would have said, "ta-da".'

## Chapter 22

# The final frames

SOMETIME AROUND 2004 Patsy Houlihan withdrew from life as he knew it and as he had always known it, becoming bed- and house-bound. There were no more nights at the Osborne or Deptford Arms, no more frames of snooker at Shades, no more tap dancing on the tables or playing the glass in the pub. Houlihan had always loved life and the constant hustle and bustle of south-east London life, and his sudden retreat into virtual reclusivity was borne of a broken heart. One day after her 13th birthday, Houlihan's beloved step-granddaughter Justine died tragically of leukaemia, an illness she battled three times in all. It was a devastating blow for her sister Sharon and brother Eray, but also the whole family. Although Patsy wasn't her grandfather by blood, the death hit him particularly hard.

According to his friend 'Legs', Houlihan also suffered a fall outside a pub just before he took to his bed. 'He was sat on a wall outside a pub one night and he fell backwards off the wall,' 'Legs' recalled. 'I dropped him back home and he never came out again.' Did the accident and Justine's death awaken in Houlihan some long-dormant anxiety or fear of his own mortality? Who knows, but in the end his last few years ended up playing out as a strange and sad echo of his brother Billy's interior existence. 'Remember, Billy stayed indoors for years,' John Butler pointed out. 'Patsy stayed indoors for those last years too. He gave up. He just gave up.'

It was Patsy's wife Brenda who devotedly looked after him through his final years. To those around him, Brenda included, these reclusive years were painful, heartbreaking even. Terry Mahoney, father of Patsy Girl's best friend Denise, was a frequent visitor, despite the fact he was suffering from cancer.

Terry Dempsey also called in on his old mate once or twice every week. 'I'd try to talk him into getting out of bed and coming out,' Dempsey recalled. 'I'd say, "Come on, Pats!" because he wasn't dying of anything. But he just wouldn't move. He had a bell he'd ring when he wanted something and Brenda would bring it to him. I'd say to him, "Look, Pats, you've been lying there for 12, 14 months, come on out!" I used to go down his house once, twice a week. Brenda was there looking after him and I used to try and convince him to get out of bed. But he wouldn't budge.'

Once, and once only, Patsy did venture out. But hopes of a grand night out – one last night of glory like in the good old days when Deptford was magical – were soon dashed. 'There was only one time we got him out of his deathbed,' Dempsey sadly recalled. 'It was his birthday. I said to him, "Look Pats, we've got a party for you down the Osborne. We've got cards, a cake and so on, come down, Pats." And he did. He got Patsy Girl to bring him down. He walked in, opened his birthday cards, took the fivers and tenners out of them and went home. Didn't stay for a drink or nothing. That was the only time.'

Jimmy White was devastated at the way that Houlihan passed his last few years. 'I was a bit angry about the situation he ended up in,' he said. 'A bit like Alex Higgins, it's like he gave up. There was nothing more his family or anyone could have done, but it was very sad.'

Eventually, Houlihan's body and broken spirit slipped into the afterlife. He died of heart failure on 8 November 2006, the day after his 77th birthday. The first person the devastated Patsy Girl rang after her dad's death was White. 'I can't explain it, but I knew Dad would have wanted me to ring him,' she said. 'Straightaway Jimmy said to make sure I told him as soon as I knew the funeral arrangements and sure enough he was there.'

The news of Houlihan's death filtered slowly into the media, making less of a splash than it should have. World Snooker's website was first to report it, with White paying a typically generous and heartfelt tribute, 'He was one of the greatest who ever played,' White said. 'He didn't fulfil his potential and it's hard to say why but he had such an influence on my game. If anyone has any footage of him playing I would like to buy it and show it, because the way he played was phenomenal.'

The *Snooker Scene* blog and magazine also paid tribute. Clive Everton – eternally the doyen of snooker scribes – penned a fine obituary in the December 2006 edition, writing that Houlihan was 'an old fashioned snooker hustler in the days when the professional game was moribund and private money matches were the only way to make a living with a cue'. Everton also added, 'Many shared Jimmy White's view that, in his prime, "he was one of the best players I've ever seen".'

Among the mainstream media, only *Daily Mail* columnist Ian Wooldridge initially picked up on the sad news, mentioning Houlihan in his column on 8 December under the headline 'Houlihan, last of the great hustlers'. Frustratingly, and painfully for Patsy's family, Wooldridge incorrectly claimed that Houlihan's conviction in 1966 had been for housebreaking. Patsy Girl sent a letter of complaint to the *Mail* but never received a response, let alone an apology. Wooldridge also wrote, in a somewhat strange final line, that 'Pat Houlihan died laughing aged 77'. It was an attempted stylistic flourish that merely betrayed the writer's ignorance of the sad circumstances surrounding Houlihan's final few years.

*The Guardian* eventually ran a short obituary of Houlihan by this writer in January 2007 in its 'Other Lives' section. It was a piece written in collaboration with Patsy Girl and Patsy Boy, who fact-checked it. A longer and more detailed appreciation that this writer penned also appeared in the February 2007 edition of *Snooker Scene*, including contributions and quotations from White and Eugene Hughes, among others.

By then, Houlihan's funeral had been and gone and the multitude of flowers that had surrounded his body and coffin on its final journey had withered, dried and died too. The funeral ceremony was held in Hither Green a couple of weeks after Patsy's death. Patsy Girl can still recall the 'untold flowers' that were there, and she still has the cards that were tucked into the many bouquets, one of which read, poignantly, 'This was one snooker you couldn't get out of Hooley.'

Another, from Houlihan's old Harp of Erin mate Harry Haward, read, 'There must be a big championship in heaven, so they sent for you. Play well, Patsy.' Patsy Girl's tribute to her father was typically heartfelt, 'My dad, my life and soul. I miss you so much, I don't know what I'm going to do without you.'

To Patsy Girl, Houlihan's death had been a particularly painful blow. Father and daughter had always had a close relationship. She had spent years drinking with him, singing with him, laughing with him and travelling to snooker tournaments with him. 'He was my soul mate, a wonderful dad,' she reflects today.

The order of service for the funeral provided Houlihan with an apt and eloquent epitaph. 'Never mind "he could have been the best",' it read. 'He may not of [sic.] had the money and fame, he certainly didn't get the recognition he deserved, but those in the know knew he was the best. His family and friends and everyone gathered here today know without a doubt, the world of snooker has lost a legend. His family however have lost a great deal more. Patsy Girl feels as if she has lost her soul mate. Deptford has lost one of its greatest characters. But he will never be forgotten by all those who knew him and loved him … God bless Patsy, sleep easy."

White was there at the funeral, as promised. 'I had all the time in the world for Patsy Houlihan,' he said, recalling the day as a 'great send-off'.

Patsy's friends concurred. 'When you get to our age you get so used to funerals,' shrugged Terry Dempsey 16 years after the event. 'But it was a lovely send-off, a beautiful day. And afterwards we gave him his just desserts in the pub like we do for everybody. We'll never forget him, that's for sure. He's still missed.' After the funeral, Houlihan's body was cremated at Lewisham Crematorium. In a nod to his Irish Catholic roots, mourners were handed a card asking them to pray for his soul. 'For the peace of my years in the long green grasses will yours and yours and yours,' read the accompanying prayer.

After collecting her dad's ashes, Patsy Girl wondered for years what to do with them. In the end she kept them close to her at home until her own mother Julia died in 2017. Then she buried them together. 'They're in my plot,' she explained. 'And I'm going to be with them there one day.'

Epilogue

# 'Enough stories for ten fucking books'

THE RED Lion pub in Shooter's Hill is about five miles from Deptford. It's what they call an old-fashioned boozer, the sort of place that used to exist on every London street corner in the days when you could smoke inside, everyone knew everybody else's name and going to the pub was as much a part of urban working-class existence as getting up in the morning and breathing.

There were dozens of friends and families who Patsy Houlihan used to know, drink and socialise with back then – old-school Deptford families like the Arnolds, Chapmans, Mahoneys, Frenches, Smiths, Norrises, Moodys, Dempseys, Butlers and Sultans. Many from these families have passed away or moved on from Deptford, but today I'm here to meet three who have survived and knew Patsy for the best part of 40 or 50 years.

'I'll give you enough stories for ten fucking books, although you might not be able to print all of them,' Terry Dempsey told me on the phone when we were arranging to meet, and he doesn't disappoint.

An imposing but good-humoured man with a deep, infectious laugh, Terry takes a gulp of lager from behind his shaded spectacles before telling me, 'The first time I met Patsy was when I was with my father in the early '60s in the Noah's Ark, one of the locals in Deptford. We used to go over to Lewisham snooker hall to watch him play snooker and hustle.'

Another of Patsy's old friends, John Butler, goes next, tapping me on the arm with his hand to emphasise certain points. 'I knew Patsy for even longer than Terry because I'm older. I first met him in the '50s in Deptford where we were all born. What can I say about Patsy? He was a likeable tyke. A likeable rogue. That's what he was. That's true isn't it? He liked a gamble and he liked a drink, but he didn't like buying them.' The table dissolves into laughter.

'They call me "Legs",' says the final member of the trio, from beneath a flat cap, his voice as deep as I can imagine a human voice can possibly be. 'I first met Patsy around 1972. I used to hang about with his son Danny. I was fascinated with the game of snooker. Patsy was a magnificent player. I used to pick balls out of the pockets for him and he'd give me a pound or whatever. If we played, he'd give me a 50 start. I was a 50-break kid at the time, a decent player, and Patsy would only be able to pot the yellow. You know, red, yellow, red, yellow and so on. But all I'd end up doing was walking around the table and picking the balls out. He was fascinating to watch. For years I followed him and I hung about with his son for about four or five years too. We'd go over to Tooting and so on. We'd see him play with Jimmy White and Tony Meo. Don't ever think he was Mother Teresa, because he wasn't. Like John said, he was a loveable rogue.'

It's clear that Patsy's old mates loved him to bits, despite his constant money-making schemes and hustles, some of which they wound up on the wrong end of. Hustling and looking for ways to make a few pound notes 'was how Patsy was', as Terry puts it. 'It was part of his nature.' As such, Patsy would invariably keep his true motives, form and intentions hidden behind his poker face – not even letting on to his friends what he was plotting. It was all part of the hustle.

Terry gives an example. 'One night I picked Patsy up from his house,' he recalls. 'I was taking him to Greenwich. There used to be a snooker club where the Up the Creek comedy club now is. The week before Patsy played this guy called Chris Carpenter. They had a match, best of seven, and Carpenter had beaten him. This was the return. I said to Pats as we drove over, "You got any chance of beating this Chris Carpenter, Pats?" He said, "Tel, not an earthly. I couldn't beat him if I had two cues in my hand." I didn't take any notice until I got to the club and went up to the bar to get a drink. As I was stood there I overheard Patsy talking to his daughter. He said to her, "Have you got your rent money on you?" She said, "Yes, Dad." Patsy told her, "Put it on me. I'm a certainty."

'After I heard that I went to the back room and put a monkey on the Hoo. Of course, Patsy murdered Carpenter 4-0. So I came out from the backroom with a big handful of cash. Patsy raised an eyebrow and looked at me and I said to him, "You're not getting a tanner of it. In fact, I'm leaving you here to get a fucking cab home because I heard you telling your daughter to put her rent money on you when you told me you hadn't a prayer."' Terry laughs, deeply and with his whole body.

'That's gospel truth, that story,' John chimes in. 'Patsy had no scruples whatsoever when it came to money. He had to have a drink and he had to have a bet. And he'd bet on anything. Horses, cards, dogs. One night I saw him in the Swan. *Pot Black* was on the television. A guy there wanted to back someone, not knowing the match had already been played. Patsy knew what the result was and took his money off him. True story.'

It's clear from the reminiscences of Terry, John and Legs that the Deptford of yesteryear was a place they loved. And it was characters like Patsy who made it the place it was. When Patsy was around there was always something happening, a hustle or a money-making scheme in the works, from when he had his breakfast of bacon and tomatoes in the cafe in the morning to when he was in the pub at night, the drinks and banter flowing.

'It was a hard life, but it was a magical life,' Terry says. 'You could be standing in the pub and someone would walk in and say, "Look what I've got here." Now you can sit in the pub all day and no one comes in with nothing. Patsy made a lot of things happen. If there was nothing going on in the pub he'd get the balls off the pool table and start a game of bowls on the carpet. He'd put the white as the jack, someone would have the yellows and someone would have the reds and we'd play bowls in the pub. He was such a character. Who was that actor in *Yankee Doodle Dandy*? James Cagney. That's what Hooley was like. He was very smartly dressed and, like Cagney, there was something in the way he moved – he was always on his toes. Light on his feet.'

The anecdotes and memories keep coming as the lagers are refilled. 'One night we came out of the Spanish Galleon in Greenwich,' John says, deadpan as ever. 'At the time I was driving a convertible. We came out half-drunk to go to another pub, me, Patsy and Terry. Patsy said to me, "Let me drive it, John." I said, "Go on then, give it a drive." Now Patsy never had a driving licence. Never. So as we came around the one-way system and past a zebra crossing I spotted there was a copper by the road so I yelled out, "Here mate, got a driver with no licence here!" Patsy had to jump out the car and do a runner!'

Terry leans in with a smile. 'Patsy had a joke he used to tell. "I was standing there in the pub Tel," he'd say. "And this bloke came up to me and said, "Give us a light, Pats."

'And I said, "No, I can't give you a light."

'And he said, "Why won't you give me a light?"

'And I said, "Because if I give you a light you'll want to be my friend and I don't want you to be my friend. Because if you're my friend I'll have to buy you a light ale and you'll have to buy me a light ale, all because of that light."

'The bloke looked at me and said, "But Patsy, all I want is a light."

'And I said, "No because after you've had that light you'll want to stand here and talk to me all night and then we'll go home together and you'll want to buy fish and chips and we'll have nowhere to eat them – and all because of that light. Then you'll want to come round my house and eat those fish and chips round my house when you know that I've got a lovely daughter and you'll want to sleep with my daughter. And all because of that light."

'And he said, "No, I won't, Pats, I won't sleep with your daughter."

'And I said, "Yeah, and I won't give you a fucking light neither."'

The table erupts in laughter. 'I've never heard that one, Tel,' Legs says.

When the laughter finally subsides, the tone becomes more reflective. 'Patsy was a proper all-round talent,' Terry says. 'A character. If I could pay £50,000 to have him back I would. We loved him.'

'You'd always see him on Deptford High Street,' John adds. 'He walked everywhere and I'd love to see him walk in here now. He still wouldn't buy me a drink, but I'd love to see him.'

A slightly uneasy silence hovers over the table, each of us – for a moment – lost in our private thoughts.

Terry finally breaks it. 'I'll tell you one last story. I came into the Osborne Arms one day and Patsy said to me, "How much you got on you, Tel?"

'And I said, "Not a lot, Pats."

'He sighed and went, "I'm fucking skint. I've only got a tanner."

'As that happened the guv'nor in the pub – bloke called Mick – accidentally dropped 50 quid on the floor behind the bar. I turned and whispered to him, "Pats, there's a bullseye down there on the floor!"

'Patsy looked at me and said, "Fucking hell, Tel. How we gonna get that 50?" A second later he said, "Go round the other side of the bar, Tel."

'Out of Mick's sight, he pulled out a blank betting slip, wrote some horse's name on it and "£50 to win", and shouted over to me, "'Ere Tel, put this bet on for me." He threw the slip at me and it landed right by the 50 quid.

'Then he looked at Mick and – calm as you like – said, "Here Mick, could you pick up my 50 quid and betting slip, please mate?"

'*Instantly* he thought of that,' Terry concludes with admiration and a rueful shake of the head. 'I couldn't think of any way to get that 50 quid, but he thought of it *instantly*.'

Terry takes a deep pull of his lager and exhales. 'That was Patsy for you. A character. A character we all loved. He was what he was, but we loved him. We'll never forget him, that's for sure. He's missed, but he had a full life. I loved him to death.'

'How long ago did he die now?' John asks.

'Nearly 16 years,' I reply.

John shakes his head slowly before quickly draining his glass. 'Sixteen years ... Where's that time gone?'

\* \* \*

The world that Patsy Houlihan once inhabited and the places that meant so much to him have gradually but inevitably receded, eroded or changed beyond recognition. Parts of Deptford's architectural past survive, but other sections of this unique area of south-east London have become wracked with irretrievable decay or subsumed by the onward march of progress and redevelopment.

Of course, some of the places that provided the backdrop to Houlihan's life and times were gone in his own lifetime. In 1969 the Surrey Docks, where he once 'bomped on' and hauled timber and sugar, were forced into closure after changes in world trade patterns, primarily brought about by the decline and break-up of the British Empire, as well as the docks' inability to handle the massive increase in size of container ships. Filled in by Southwark Council in the 1970s and sold on to developers, Surrey Docks would eventually become Surrey Quays – a maze of soulless red-brick developments topped off by a Tesco superstore and shopping centre that once looked hi-tech but now looks irretrievably tired.

Most of the pubs that Houlihan frequented in Deptford have also gone. The Osborne Arms closed in 2010 and the Deptford Arms is now a Paddy Power bookmakers. Barely any of the old-fashioned boozers on the high street have survived. Locals used to say that if you went in the Centurion pub at the top of Deptford High Street and had a teaspoonful of beer, then kept doubling what you drank at every pub along the road, you'd be drunk by the time you reached the Noah's Ark at the bottom. But not anymore.

Snooker itself – a folk sport that offered predominantly unofficial earning opportunities when Houlihan first picked up a cue – has now completed its transmogrification from a pastime associated with back-street disreputability to a glittering and lucrative, internationally televised sporting spectacle. Thanks to the modern miracles of satellite television and internet streaming, professional snooker is now beamed to hundreds of millions of fans around the world, while the modern multimillion-pound tour boasts players from China, Belgium, Ukraine, Iran, Brazil and many more nations besides.

In its British heartlands, however, participation in snooker is in slow decline. Snooker halls have faced blow after blow in recent years – from the tobacco ban in pubs and other licensed premises in 2007 to the Covid-19 pandemic, to the massive boom in housing development which has persuaded many landlords to cash in their property chips rather than rely on the variable and comparatively paltry rental income a snooker hall can generate. Working men's clubs – once a snooker bedrock – have also largely disappeared. Even pool tables are seldom sighted in pubs these days, where once they were commonplace.

The Deptford Temperance Billiard Hall – where Houlihan first picked up a cue and carried on playing for decades, including when it was rebranded as a Lucania hall and then a Riley's snooker club – finally closed for good in the late 1980s. Eventually it was redeveloped into a modern residential and retail building. The building which once housed the Lewisham Temperance Hall, in which Houlihan also honed his skills, is still standing and is now Grade II-listed due to its 'clever plan, eclectic detailing, good compositional qualities and … strong presence in the streetscape'. However, its days as a cue sports venue are long gone.

Shades on Deptford High Street is still there though, and business is good, helped by the fact it's the only snooker hall for miles around. Lee Suleymanoglu, who worked in the club when Patsy first started playing there, now owns it. 'At one point, when he got unwell, Patsy stopped coming in,' Suleymanoglu said. 'Deptford had started to change by then and the club changed too. We had the slow gentrification of the area taking place. The white working class started to leave. Some 20,000 Vietnamese were housed here by Lewisham Council around 1986. A big percentage of our customers here now are Vietnamese. A lot of people think they're Chinese but they're not.

'In 1994 I bought the lease when New World Snooker Clubs, the previous owners, went bankrupt. I didn't have the funds but knew people who did and they bought the freehold and leased it to me. Then in 2008 they came to me and asked if I wanted to buy the freehold, so I went to the bank and bang – I bought the whole place. Because I don't have to pay rent I wasn't so badly affected by the pandemic. We're OK here because there isn't much competition. Our nearest competitor is in Catford. I don't need to advertise or anything. People find us if they want to play because there aren't that many places anymore. I've got eight tables, Catford's got ten. What's that – 18 tables available for about two million people? There used to be snooker clubs everywhere, but not anymore.'

Many of the people Houlihan loved, drank with and played snooker with have also fallen prey to the cruel inevitabilities of time. The cueists he duelled with in his amateur pomp in the 1950s and '60s are nearly all gone now. Potting wizard Cliff Wilson made an unlikely comeback in the late 1970s, winning the world amateur title in 1978 and having some success on the pro tour, even reaching number 16 in the world rankings in 1988/89, but the genial and charismatic Welshman died in 1994 aged 60. John Spencer passed in 2006 after long periods of various illnesses, stomach cancer doing for him in the end. The Owen brothers, Marcus and Gary, died in 1987 and 1995 respectively.

Of the great generation of players who lit up the amateur scene of the 1950s and '60s, just Ray Reardon – stubborn and irrepressible as ever – is still standing, now past his 90th birthday and living in comfort and contentment in the south-west of England and still playing snooker so regularly that he reportedly notched a 94 break at the age of 89. The whereabouts of many of Houlihan's other amateur rivals – the likes of Doug Melchior, Eric Stickler and other names that even snooker aficionados would struggle to recognise – is unknown, lost somewhere amid the fog of history. The overwhelming likelihood is that most of them are dead.

The fate of Jonathan Rendall – the man who helped resurrect Houlihan's name with his magisterial feature article for *Observer Sports Monthly* in 2002 – provides one of the saddest codas of all to the Houlihan story.

After the publication of his book *Garden Hopping* in 2006, Rendall drifted away from journalism and cut himself off from many of his old friends and contacts. A planned biography of Mike Tyson never quite came to fruition. He moved to Ipswich and his life appeared to come apart at the seams. Around 2012, his friend and former colleague Kevin Mitchell received a phone call from Rendall. 'I hadn't heard from him in forever,' Mitchell recalled. 'He was so out of touch with what was going on in the business that he thought that Roger Alton was still editor of *The Observer*. A lot of what he was saying didn't really make much sense. Then he disappeared again and went and lived in the country. I think in a small village somewhere. He was alone and it was really sad. He was drinking too much and he wasn't physically well.'

Boxer Colin McMillan stayed in touch with the troubled writer after the end of their professional relationship. 'I went down to see him in Ipswich,' McMillan said. 'I could tell he wasn't in a great place. He wasn't the Jonathan of old.'

On 23 January 2013, police found Rendall's body at his home in St George's Street, Ipswich. He had been dead for several days. 'He was only 50-odd when he died,' Mitchell said with sadness. 'That's way too young for someone who had so much to offer. But that's the way it was with Jonny.'

McMillan had called Rendall a few weeks before his death and never heard back from him. 'I'd left him a message and he didn't come back to me. That wasn't like him. Then I heard the news that he had passed away. It was really sad.'

As well as through Rendall's work, it is through the testimonies of those who knew Patsy Houlihan in his later days on the pro tour that his legend lives on.

The words of Steve Davis, Tony Meo and Jimmy White recounted earlier in this book make it clear the esteem in which they all held Houlihan. Davis doesn't play now, not even on the seniors tour, but he remains a vital and respected voice on the BBC's television coverage of the sport, while he has also developed a fascinating sideline as a DJ and musician. As for Meo, he gave up snooker completely after leaving the pro ranks in 1997 and now trades watches and jewellery. Only Jimmy White, of this trio, still plays professionally, despite now having passed his 60th birthday. If Jimmy is still on the tour in 2025 then he will have matched the age at which Houlihan was still playing competitive snooker.

Despite diminishing returns from his pro matches, White retains his class and artistry, as well as a particularly Houlihan-esque faith and optimism that tomorrow will be a better day, and that his natural talent may still be crowned with ultimate glory of a World Championship triumph. 'I don't feel 60 at all,' White insisted in May 2022. 'More like 25.'

Above all else, White is always happy to share his memories of Houlihan, whether for this book or within private conversations.

For example, Lee Prickman, who knew Patsy in the early 1980s and now lives and coaches in Gibraltar, recalled, 'When Jimmy played in Gibraltar a few years ago we got talking about Patsy. I think Jimmy had seen something I wrote on Twitter about Patsy so when he was over we had a beer for an hour or so and we chatted about Patsy. We shared old stories about him and our interactions with him.'

To Prickman, as he was to many others, Houlihan 'really was an unsung hero of the sport'. Indeed, he goes even further, as many others do too, when assessing Houlihan's place in the pantheon of snooker greatness. 'Perhaps we can't include the likes of Ronnie [O'Sullivan] and [Stephen] Hendry in this assessment, or perhaps we can – but when people like Jimmy say that Patsy was the best player they ever saw there's certainly a decent argument for it. For him to do what he did back then on very poor quality tables was simply astonishing.'

The absence of any extended video footage of Houlihan in action makes forming an objective opinion impossible, of course, which is why the testimonies and memories of those that did see him in action are so important. A memory, of course, is something that has been lost, something that is gone forever, but it's also – paradoxically – something we still have. And so it is, when we read descriptions of Houlihan by those who knew him and loved him we can imagine what he was like with his elegant, compact cue action, his granite visage, his immaculately parted hair and that indescribable magic in his cue tip. He's there in the depths of our subconscious, a fuzzy figure, but there nevertheless.

The Houlihan family have suffered more than their fair share of slings and arrows since their beloved Patsy passed away. Houlihan's sons Patsy Boy and Danny died in 2009 and 2019 respectively. Wife Brenda, who nursed him in his final years, didn't last long after Patsy's death either.

But his daughter Patsy Girl is still with us, and so is his son Lee. Patsy Girl guards and protects her dad's memory and legacy with care and love, keeping the old photos, clippings and those two remaining trophies safe and secure. And then there are the grandkids: Nathalie, Tara, Nicky, Dan Dan, Hayley and Josh. Patsy Girl also has four grandchildren herself now: Ellie, Georgie Boy, Cerise and Riley Rose. They never knew their great-grandad, but a part of him lives on through them.

In September 2022 I completed my final draft of this book and printed it off. It was a big print job – over 200 pages. I carefully placed the pages in a folder and took them round to Patsy Girl's flat in Deptford, a few hundred yards from where her dad lived from cradle to grave.

Lee was there too. It was the first time I'd met him. Lee had one final killer Patsy Houlihan story to add to the book, about his dad and his great mate Jimmy White. 'I remember dad telling me about one night he was out with Jimmy.' Lee told me, drawing on a cigarette, his eyes glittering with the memory. 'They were in a car after going out somewhere or other, and suddenly this huge house opened up in front of them, out of the darkness. Dad ended up staying there for three nights.

'"Whose house was it, Dad?" I asked him.

'"Some bloke called Ronnie Wood," he said.

'"I said, bloody hell dad! Ronnie Wood, you know who that is?"

'Dad shook his head. I said, "*Ronnie Wood*! He's from the *Rolling Stones*!"

'Dad shook his head again and said, "Who are they?"

'"I sighed, "You know the Rolling Stones – Mick Jagger!"

'"Oh," Dad replied. "I know Mick Jagger … He weren't there though."'

Among the stories and the laughter as we sat, smoked, drank tea and read parts of the book, we got a bit emotional too.

When we had finished reading, Patsy Girl showed me her beloved dad's final legacy: his snooker cue.

Patsy had a few to be honest, but this is the one that has survived. He hustled with it, he made some of his 2,000 centuries – or maybe 3,000 centuries – with it and above all he *dreamed* with it.

For a while the cue was missing, but miraculously it's come home to Patsy Girl now. Like the other ephemera from her dad's life, she keeps it safe and she always will.

She got it out to show me though.

Truth be told, it made me feel a bit sad to see it and handle it. It looked naked and lonely without Patsy Houlihan holding it. They say a snooker player's cue is part of them don't they? Like an arm or a leg.

It made me think, holding that cue. We lose so much as we grow older, so the things that remain, that we don't lose, we cling to, reminders of the people we once knew, the lives we once lived and the world we once lived in.

Along with the old photos, the clippings, the memories and this book, that cue is all that's left of Patsy Houlihan now.

But maybe that means he's still with us, in a funny sort of way.

As happy endings go, it's not much. But it's something, isn't it?

It might even be enough to keep us all going.

# Acknowledgements

ABOVE EVERYONE else, I must thank Patsy Girl, for having faith in me to write this book and for supporting the project from beginning to end, as well as for her kindness many years ago in first meeting me to speak about her dad.

Patsy Girl, I vowed I would do justice to your dad's story and I hope I haven't disappointed you.

Patsy Boy did not live to see this book written, but it is also for him and every other member of the Houlihan family, alive and dead, as well as for all of Patsy's friends and the people of Deptford.

I owe a huge debt to the brilliant Paul Zanon, who kindly introduced me to Pitch Publishing, as well as to everyone at Pitch, primarily Jane Camillin for her efficiency and hard work, Duncan for his brilliant cover design and Graham for his work on the images.

A massive thank you to everyone who gave up their time so willingly and freely to speak to me about Patsy – in person or by telephone – as well as those who shared their memories of him via various social media channels and email. A full list of all interviewees appears in the sources section.

This book would not have been possible without the incredible kindness and support of snooker fans across the world. All of the following wonderful people helped me – someone they had never met – for no reason other than the fact that they love snooker and have incredibly kind and helpful hearts: Dean Howell, Seamus Phelan, Marco Staiano, Gareth McGinley, Chris Bland and James Bielby. Thank you from the bottom of my heart for the information, articles, suggestions and support.

The professional snooker writing and broadcasting community were also very helpful and encouraging to me, especially Dave Hendon, Nick Metcalfe and Phil Haigh. I must also extend a huge thank you to the greatest snooker journalist of them all – the incomparable and magisterial Clive Everton, for his permission to reproduce material from *The Billiard Player*, *Billiards and Snooker*, *Pot Black* and *Snooker Scene* magazines, a kindness which I will never forget and can never adequately repay. Clive's recent retirement from editing *Snooker Scene* after over 50 years has left a void that will never and can never be filled within the snooker universe.

Jean Rafferty was also extremely helpful and kindly gave me permission to reprint photos taken by her sister Mary for her brilliant book *The Cruel Game*.

My great friend Russ Anber has been a constant source of support while writing this book, as well as an invaluable resource in setting up interviews for me with his snooker contacts in Canada. The next book, Russ, will be your one – I promise! Thank you for your friendship, brother.

Others who helped me and deserve thanks include Nick Teale, Stephen Slater, Mark King, Gordon Newman, Lucy Archer and Don McRae. There are many others whose names, sadly, I do not have the time and space to include.

My family, friends and colleagues have always supported me and I thank them all, principally my wife and children, as well as my mother and sister and my late father, who bequeathed to me his mighty love of sport.

I only ever briefly corresponded with – and sadly never met – the late, great Jonathan Rendall, but I owe him a heavy debt.

This book is written in memory of Patsy Houlihan, but also in tribute to Jonathan too. Like Patsy, he was a wondrous talent who is much missed.

Finally, a heartfelt thank you to Patsy's great friend and my own sporting hero, Jimmy White. It was Jimmy who inspired my love of snooker as a small child and set me on this journey in the first place. They say you should never meet or speak to your heroes, but in the case of Jimmy the saying could not be more untrue.

Without Jimmy's kindness in writing the foreword to this book and encouraging the project, *The Natural* would never have been written.

**Luke G. Williams, October 2022**

# Appendix

## Patrick 'Patsy' Houlihan –
## career results and honours

### *Section A: amateur career 1953–1969*

Tracing and verifying amateur snooker results from the 1950s and '60s is a difficult task; what follows is not a complete set of results, merely as much information about Houlihan's amateur matches that I have thus far been able to trace. If you have knowledge of any further match or tournament results please email lgw007@yahoo.com.

**1952/53**
**Billiards Association and Control Council (BA&CC) National Breaks Competition award for highest certified amateur break of 1952**
122 at Lewisham Temperance Hall (either 11 or 14 November 1952)

**British Legion (Metropolitan Area) Billiards Team Shield, Burroughes Hall, London**
Final: Lee Green (Houlihan, Ted Ricks, Arthur Denchfield) beat Harrow 600-509

**1953/54**
**London Area Amateur Snooker Championship, Burroughes Hall, London**
Round 1: beat J. Hall 3-0 (16 December 1953)
Round 2: beat Ronald Hoare 3-2
Round 3: beat Sidney Hyams 3-1
Quarter-finals: beat A. Armstrong 3-1
Semi-finals: beat C. Barnett 3-0

Final: beat Jim Chapman 5-0 (8-1 including dead frames, 14 January 1954)
*First London Area snooker title*

**British Legion County Snooker Team Championship**
Final: Lee Green (team including Houlihan) beat Bromley 2-0 (25 January 1954)

**English Amateur Snooker Championship,
Burroughes Hall, London**
Round 1: beat Alfred Hobbs 5-0 (10 March 1954)
Round 2: beat James Heaton 5-4 (17 March 1954)
Quarter-finals: lost to Norman Buck 5-4 (24 March 1954)

**British Legion (Metropolitan Area) Billiards Team Shield,
Burroughes Hall, London**
Final: Lee Green (Arthur Denchfield, Houlihan, Herbert Watling) beat Muswell Hill 600-515 (April 1954)

**Finsbury Park Conservative Club Snooker Tournament**
Round 1: lost to Ron Gross 3-1

**British Legion (Metropolitan Area) Snooker Team Shield,
Burroughes Hall, London**
Final: Lee Green (Houlihan, Herbert Watling) beat Muswell Hill 2-0 (April 1954)

**1954/55**
**Invitation Snooker Tournament, Burroughes Hall, London (3–14 October 1954)**
This tournament was played on a league basis. Houlihan's results were as follows:
Beat Ron Gross 3-2
Beat Tom Gordon 3-2
Beat George Humphries 4-1
Beat Cliff Wilson 3-2
Lost to Norman Buck 3-2

## Final standings:

| | Won | Lost | Frames for | Against | Frame average |
|---|---|---|---|---|---|
| 1. Wilson | 4 | 1 | 17 | 8 | +2.1 |
| 2. Houlihan | 4 | 1 | 15 | 10 | +1.5 |
| 3. Buck | 4 | 1 | 14 | 11 | +1.2 |
| 4. Gross | 2 | 3 | 15 | 10 | +1.5 |
| 5. Gordon | 1 | 4 | 8 | 17 | -2.1 |
| 6. Humphries | 0 | 5 | 6 | 19 | -3.1 |

**London Area Snooker Championship, Burroughes Hall, London**
Round 1: lost to Douglas Melchior 3-1 (29 November 1954)

**Finsbury Park Conservative Club Snooker Tournament**
Round 1: lost to F. Jessup walk-over (29 March 1955)

**Central Croydon L&R Club snooker tournament**
Round 1: beat Derek Heming 3-2 (25 April 1955)
Quarter-finals: lost to Wally Smith 3-2 (9 May 1955)

**British Legion (Metropolitan Area) Individual Snooker Cup**
Winner (date of final and opponent unknown)
*First British Legion title*

**1955/56**
**London Area Snooker Championship, Burroughes Hall, London**
Round 1: bye
Round 2: beat R.C. Witt 3-0
Round 3: beat A. H. Hunter 3-0 (28 November 1955)
Quarter-finals: beat A.S. Foster 3-0
Semi-finals: beat Douglas Melchior 4-1
Final: beat Eric Stickler 5-1 (6 December 1955)
*Second London Area title*

**English Amateur Snooker Championship, Burroughes Hall, London**
Round 1: beat Dennis Hushley 5-2 (28 February 1956)
Round 2: beat Alan Barnett 5-4 (7 March 1956)
Quarter-finals: beat Jack Seffers 5-2 (14 March 1956)
Semi-finals: lost to Ray Reardon 6-4 (17 March 1956)

**British Legion (Metropolitan Area) Billiards Team Shield**
Final: Lee Green won (opponents and scores unknown)

**British Legion (Metropolitan Area) Individual Snooker Cup**
Final: beat J. Hazzard (score unknown, 25 April 1956)
*Second successive British Legion title*

## 1956/57
**London Area Snooker Championship, Burroughes Hall, London**
Round 1: Bye
Round 2: beat P. Garnett 3-1 (17 November 1956)
Round 3: beat Ernest Ball 3-0
Quarter-final: beat S. Hall 3-1 (30 November 1956)
Semi-final: beat Stanley Walklett 4-1 (3 December 1956)
Final: beat Eric Stickler 5-3 (5 December 1956)
*Third London Area title*

**English Amateur Snooker Championship,**
**Burroughes Hall, London**
Round 1: beat Alfred Burdett 5-3 (7 March 1957)
Round 2: beat Jack Fitzmaurice 5-3 (15 March 1957)
Quarter-finals: lost to Ron Gross 5-2 (21 March 1957)

**Temperance Billiard Hall Inter-Hall Snooker League**
Lewisham champions of the ten-team league (P. Miles (captain),
D. Skuse, D. Lewis, W. Small (manager), J. Hills, Terry Houlihan,
Patsy Houlihan)
Lewisham's record: Played 18, won 13, lost 3, drawn 2, points 205
Highest break prize: Patsy Houlihan (100)

**Lewisham vs The Rest challenge match**
Lewisham beat The Rest 12-6 (Houlihan beat Ron Gross 2-0)

**British Legion County Team Snooker Cup**
Final: Lee Green (Houlihan and Herbert Watling) beat Bromley
(score and date unknown)

**British Legion County Individual Snooker Cup**
Final: beat James Barr (score and date unknown)

**British Legion (Metropolitan Area) Individual Snooker Cup**
Winner (date of final and opponent unknown)
*Third successive British Legion title*

**Finsbury Park Conservative Club Snooker Tournament**
Round 1: lost to Douglas Melchior 3-2

**1957/58**
Did not enter London Area or English Amateur
Snooker Championship

**Temperance Billiard Hall Inter-Hall Snooker League**
Lewisham champions of the nine-team league (W. Small
(hall manager), Patsy Houlihan (captain), D. Lewis, D. Skuse,
P. Jennings, G. Furner)
Lewisham's record: Played 16, won 13, lost 0, drawn 3, points 215

**Challenge match (22 April 1958):**
Houlihan drew with Horace Lindrum 1-1

**Finsbury Park Conservative Club Snooker Tournament**
Round 1: lost to Sid Hyams 3-2

**British Legion (Metropolitan Area) Individual Snooker Cup**
Final: beat J. Chong (score and date unknown, trophy awarded
16 August 1958)
*Fourth successive British Legion title*

**1958/59**
**London Amateur Snooker Championship**
Round 1: beat Alex Hyams 3-1 (17 November 1958)
Round 2: beat T. Wright 3-0 (26 November 1958)
Quarter-finals: beat Noel Miller Cheevers 3-2 (1 December 1958)
Semi-finals: beat Ron Millard 4-1 (3 December 1958)
Final: beat George Gibson 5-3 (4 December 1958)
*Fourth London Area title*

**English Amateur Snooker Championship**
Round 1: Beat Ken Newsham 5-0 (3 March 1959)
Round 2: lost to Alan Barnett 5-4 (13 March 1959)

**British Legion (Metropolitan Area) Individual Snooker Cup**
Final: beat T.G. Wright 4-0
*Fifth successive British Legion title*

**Finsbury Park Conservative Club Snooker Tournament**
Round 1: beat Ken Price 3-2

Quarter-finals: lost to Ron Gross 3-2
*Houlihan's break of 74 in frame one vs Gross set a new tournament record*
*for highest break and won him the high break prize*

## 1959/60
### London Amateur Snooker Championship
Round 1: beat Noel Miller Cheevers 3-0
Round 2: beat Jack C. Warboys by walkover
Quarter-finals: beat Geoff Foulds 4-1 (6 January 1960)
Semi-final: lost to Mark Wildman 4-3 (8 January 1960)

### Temperance Billiard Hall Inter-Hall Snooker League challenge match
The Rest (including Houlihan) beat Streatham (champions) 11-9

### Finsbury Park Conservative Club Snooker Tournament
Round 1: beat Tom Gordon 3-2
Quarter-finals: beat Peter Marshall 3-2
Semi-finals: beat George Gibson 3-1
Final: beat Ron Gross 4-1
*First Finsbury Park title*

## 1960/61
### London Amateur Snooker Championship
Round 1: lost to Ken Price 3-0 (21 November 1960)

### Finsbury Park Conservative Club Snooker Tournament
Round 1: beat Sid Hyams 3-0
Round 2: lost to Mark Wildman 3-2

## 1961/62
Did not enter London Area or English Amateur
Snooker Championship

### Finsbury Park Conservative Club Snooker Tournament
Round 1: beat Peter Marshall by walkover
Round 2: beat Mark Wildman 3-1
Semi-finals: beat Douglas Melchior 3-1
Final: beat Geoffrey Thompson 4-2 (24 May 1962)
*Second Finsbury Park title*

## 1962/63
### Temperance Billiard Hall London Area Knock-out Snooker Championship
Final: Lewisham beat Wood Green 15-10 (Houlihan, playing for Lewisham, beat C. Gibson 4-1)

### London Amateur Snooker Championship, Burroughes Hall
Round 1: beat Michael Lieberman 3-0 (22 October 1962)
Round 2: beat C.F. Key 3-0 (29 October 1962)
Round 3: beat L.A. Poole 4-0
Quarter-finals: beat Ron Millard 4-1
Semi-finals: beat George Marioni 4-1
Final: beat George Humphries 6-3
*Fifth London Area title*

### Combined London-Home Counties Amateur Championship, Burroughes Hall
Round 1: beat Christopher Marks 3-1
Quarter-finals: beat Geoff Thompson 3-0
Semi-final: beat Bill Smith (Romford) 4-0
Final: Lost to Mark Wildman 6-1 (2 December 1962)

### English Amateur Snooker Championship: Southern section
Round 1: beat A. Powell 4-1 (12 February 1963)
Round 2: beat Ronald Foxley 4-3 (16 February 1963)
Quarter-finals: lost to Geoffrey Thompson 4-1 (19 February 1963)

### Muswell Hill Green Man Snooker Tournament
Round 1: beat Alex Hyams 4-2
Quarter-finals: beat George Gibson
Semi-finals: lost to Ron Gross
*Houlihan won the tournament's highest break prize with 81*

## 1963/64
### London Amateur Snooker Championship
Round 1: beat Ron Millard 4-0
Round 2: beat A.M. Gantert 4-0
Round 3: beat George Marioni 4-1 (25 November 1963)
Quarter-finals: beat Ken Price 4-1
Semi-final: beat Anthony Hodge (Streatham) 4-3
Final: beat Mark Wildman 4-3
*Sixth London Area title*

**English Amateur Snooker Championship:**
**Southern section:**
Round 1: beat Albert Ford 4-3 (20 February 1964)
Round 2: lost to George Humphries 4-3 (2 March 1964)

**Finsbury Park Conservative Club challenge match**
Lost to Gary Owen 4-3 (30 April 1964)

**Forest Gate Eagle and Child Hotel Tournament**
Lost to Marcus Own 4-1 (21 May 1964)
Beat Norman Buck 4-2 (28 May 1964)
*Other tournament results unknown*

**Muswell Hill Green Man Snooker Tournament**
Quarter-finals: beat Ron Gross 4-3
Semi-final: beat Ken Price (score unknown)
Final: beat Mark Wildman 4-3 (17 July 1964)

**1964/65**
**London Amateur Snooker Championship, Burroughes Hall**
Round 1: Bye
Round 2: beat W.H. Bedworth 4-0
Round 3: beat George Marioni 4-0 (18 November 1964)
Quarter-finals: beat R. Pacitti 4-2
Semi-finals: beat Geoff Thompson 4-3
Final: beat George Humphries 4-0
*Seventh London Area title*

**English Amateur Snooker Championship:**
**Southern section, Burroughes Hall**
Round 1: beat Stan Bate 4-3 (21 January 1965)
Round 2: beat John Bawden 4-0 (28 January 1965)
Quarter-final: beat Gary Owen 4-2 (1 February 1965)
Semi-final: beat John Price 5-3 (3 February 1965)
Final: beat Ray Reardon 6-5 (5 February 1965)

**English Amateur Championship Final (Blackpool Tower Circus,**
**18-19 March 1965)**
Beat John Spencer (Northern area champion) 11-3

**ITV Trophy, National Liberal Club**
Beat John Spencer 4-2 (5 December 1964)

Beat Mario Berni 4-0 (13 February 1965)
Final: beat Eric Stickler 4-1 (3 April 1965)

**Finsbury Park Conservative Club Snooker Tournament**
Round 1: beat Harry K. Welch 3-1
Quarter-finals: beat K. Lewis 3-1
Semi-finals: beat Chris Ross 3-0
Final: lost to Ron Gross 4-1

**Harmon Cup, Hollymount Snooker Club, Hendon**
Harrow lost to North London 7-5 (Houlihan, playing for Harrow,
beat J. Broughton 2-0) (4 June 1965)

**In recognition of his achievements throughout this season,
Houlihan was named the BA&CC Snooker Player of the Year.**

**1965/66**
**Fundraising challenge match, Finsbury Park
Conservative Club, London**
Houlihan vs Ray Edmonds (14 October 1965, to raise funds
for Houlihan and Gary Owen to travel to the World Amateur
championship in Pakistan)

**English Amateur Snooker Championship:
Southern section, Burroughes Hall**
Round 1: beat Anthony Hodge 4-2 (25 February 1966)
Round 2: lost to John Shepherd 4-0 (4 March 1966)

**Televised challenge match, Deptford**
Houlihan vs George Humphries, score and result unknown (played 9
February, televised 12 February 1966, ITV *World of Sport*)

**Televised challenge match**
Lost to Gary Owen 3-2 (26 March 1966, ITV *World of Sport*)

**1966/67**
**Challenge match to mark the opening of the Highway Snooker
Club, Rye Lane, Peckham**
Beat Fred Davis 5-0 (Houlihan received 14-point start, 3
September 1966)

**Fundraising challenge match, Yardley Wood Social Club, Birmingham**
Lost to Gary Owen 4-3 (13 September 1966, to raise funds for Owen and John Spencer to travel to the World Amateur championship in Pakistan)

**Coventry Works Snooker League Invitational Tournament, Alfred Herbert Social Club**
Houlihan was eliminated in the group stage on aggregate score over three frames. Houlihan was in group one, alongside Ray Edmonds, Gary Owen and Ray Reardon – Owen and Edmonds qualified for the semi-finals, Houlihan lost his single frames against Owen and Edmonds, but beat Reardon (3–8 October 1966)

**English Amateur Snooker Championship:
Southern section, Burroughes Hall, London**
Round 1: beat Ronald Foxley 4-2
Round 2: beat Graham Miles 4-1 (11 March 1967)
Quarter-finals: lost to Roger Coates 4-2 (14 March 1967)

**1967/68
National C.I.U. Billiards Team Championship**
Quarter-finals: Belvedere WMC (Houlihan, Bill Smith, John Hisee) beat Portsmouth Radical 693-685
Semi-finals: Belvedere WMC beat Lime Tree Park 638-557 (13 January 1968)
Final: Blaydon and District Club beat Belvedere WMC 954-595 (February 1968, Houlihan beat Brian Simpson 380-343)

**English Amateur Snooker Championship:
Southern section, Snooker Centre, Great Windmill Street**
Round 1: Lost to Harold 'Dickie' Laws 4-2 (10 March 1968)

**Player's No. 6 National Snooker Team Championship
Kent area:**
Final: Belvedere WMC (Houlihan, Bill Smith, John Hisee) lost to Herne Bay 3-2

**1968/69
London and Home Counties Billiards Championship**
Round 1: lost to Durant 491-436

**Watney's National Snooker Pairs Championship**
**Kent and Sussex Area Championship**
Final: Houlihan and Bill Smith (Belvedere WMC) beat W. Dew and
R. Hawkes (Brighton Labour) 3-0
**National Championship:**
Round 3: Houlihan and Bill Smith (Belvedere WMC) beat Frank
Draper and Ricky Pritchard 3-0 (15 January 1969)
Round 4: Houlihan and Bill Smith (Belvedere WMC) beat
John Ford and Bob Berryman (Central Club Abertillery) 3-0
(2 March 1969)
Quarter-finals: Houlihan and Bill Smith (Belvedere WMC) lost to
Doug Mountjoy and Norman Jaynes (Risca Colliery) by walkover
(after Bill Smith fell ill and later died)

**Player's No. 6 National Snooker Team Championship**
**Kent area**
Final: Belvedere WMC (Houlihan, Bill Smith, John Hisee) beat
Herne Bay Constitutional Club 6-0 (2 February 1969)

**National C.I.U. Billiards Team Championship**
Semi-final: Belvedere WMC (Houlihan, Bill Smith, Harry Welch)
lost to Mountain Ash 790-740 (February 1969, Barras Green
WMC, Coventry)

**English Amateur Snooker Championship:**
**Southern section**
Round 1: beat Bill Smith 2-0 (Smith retired after falling unwell)
Round 2: beat A. White 4-0
Semi-finals: beat Frank Gibbons 6-2 (30 March 1969)
Final: lost to Jonathan Barron 6-3 (Billiard and Snooker Centre,
London, 5 April 1969)

**Amateur international match, Afan Lido, Port Talbot**
England (Houlihan, Ray Edmonds, Jonathan Barron, Sidney Hood,
Geoff Thompson, Chris Ross) beat Wales 10-8 (7 June 1969)

## *Section B: professional career 1969–1993*

Houlihan's application to join the PBPA and turn professional in May 1969 was rejected. He appears to have turned professional sometime in 1970, although it is unclear when his membership of the PBPA began.

**1969/70**
**Chester & District League Professional Snooker Tournament**
Semi-finals: lost to John Spencer 5-2 (13 July 1970)

**1970/71**
**Castle Open Tournament, Southampton**
Quarter-finals: beat Alf Hobbs 7-3
Semi-finals: lost to Rex Williams 7-6 (Houlihan received seven-point start per frame)

**1971/72**
**World Professional Snooker Championship**
First qualifying round: lost to John Dunning 11-10 (March 1971)

**Challenge match**
Lost to Alex Higgins 5-3 (Match Hall, Haringey, 11 November 1971)

**Castle Open Tournament, Southampton**
Round 1: lost to Tony White 4-1

**1972/73**
**Castle Open Tournament, Southampton**
Round 1: lost to Geoff Thompson 4-2

**Challenge match**
Beat Ron Gross 24-13 (12–17 February 1973, Albany Institute, Deptford)

**Park Drive World Professional Snooker Championship, Manchester**
First round: beat Jackie Rea 9-2 (16 April 1973)
Second round: lost to Alex Higgins 16-3 (17–18 April 1973)

## 1973/74
**Norwich Union Open, Piccadilly Hotel, London**
Round 1: beat John Virgo 4-3 (25 November 1973)
Round 2: lost to Cliff Thorburn 4-0 (26 November 1973)

**Park Drive World Professional Snooker
Championship, Manchester**
First qualifying round: lost to Jim Meadowcroft 8-5

## 1974/75
**Challenge match, New Eltham Social Club**
Lost to Graham Miles 6-3

**Challenge match, Ron Gross Snooker Centre, Neasden**
Lost to Marcus Owen 4-1

## 1975/76
**Pro-Am, Victoria Billiards Club, Southend-on-Sea**
Semi-finals: lost 3-2 to Vic Harris (Houlihan conceded 14 start)

**Challenge match, Romford Lucania**
Beat Vic Harris 5-1

**Pro-Am Southern Snooker Centre, Southend**
Semi-finals: beat John Cresswell 3-0
Final: beat Jim Levett 3-2 (Houlihan conceded 14 start throughout
the tournament)

## 1976/77
**John Courage Open, Enfield Billiards and Snooker Club**
Round 1: beat R. Brown 4-2 (Houlihan conceded 14 start)
Round 2: beat Henry West 4-2 (Houlihan conceded 14 start)
Quarter-finals: beat Richard Birt 4-3 (Houlihan conceded 14 start)
Semi-finals: beat Mike Darrington 4-0 (Houlihan conceded 7 start)
Final: lost to Roy Connor 5-0 (Houlihan conceded 14 start)

**Pot Black Snooker Centre £500 Challenge Match**
Pot Black, Battersea (Jimmy White, Tony Meo, Patsy Houlihan,
Wally West, Bob Harris, Noel Miller Cheevers) vs Romford Lucania
(Geoff Foulds, Vic Harris, Steve Davis, Mike Darrington, Russell
Jarmak, Roger Brown) (result unknown, played over two legs, with
the second leg in Romford on 25 June 1977)

## 1977/78
**Super Crystalate UK Championship, Tower Circus, Blackpool**
Round 1: lost to Jim Meadowcroft 5-1 (November 1977)

**Embassy World Professional Snooker Championship**
Qualifying round 1: beat Chris Ross 9-1 (Romiley Forum, Stockport)
Round 1: beat Jim Meadowcroft 9-6 (Romiley Forum, Stockport)
Round 2: lost to Cliff Thorburn 13-8 (Crucible Theatre, Sheffield, 17–18 April 1978)

## 1978/79
**Coral UK Championship**
Qualifying section: lost to Roy Andrewartha 9-3 (Romford Lucania, September 1978)

**Embassy World Professional Snooker Championship**
Qualifying round: beat John Barrie 9-5
Round 1: lost to Doug Mountjoy 9-6

## 1979/80
**Coral UK Championship, Guild Hall Preston**
Round 1: beat Jackie Rea 9-3 (20 November 1979)
Round 2: lost to Alex Higgins 9-3 (23 November 1979)

**British Gold Cup**
Qualifying group:
Beat Cliff Wilson 3-0 (January 1980)
Beat Jim Meadowcroft 2-1 (January 1980)
Group stage (Assembly Rooms, Derby):
Lost to Bill Werbeniuk 3-0 (January 1980)
Lost to Ray Reardon 3-0 (February 1980)
Lost to Fred Davis 2-1 (February 1980)

**Embassy World Professional Snooker Championship**
Qualifying round 1: beat Joe Johnson 9-6 (April 1980)
Qualifying round 2: lost to Tony Meo 9-1 (April 1980)

## 1980/81
**Coral UK Championship, Guild Hall, Preston**
Round 1: lost to Tony Meo 9-1

**Yamaha Organs Trophy**
Qualifying group:
Lost to Jimmy White 2-1
Beat John Pulman 2-1
Beat Patsy Fagan 2-1 (January 1981)

**John Courage English Professional Championship, Haden Hill Leisure Centre, Birmingham**
Round 2: lost to John Spencer 9-1 (March 1981)

**1981/82**
**Jameson International**
Qualifying round 1: beat John Barrie by walkover (August 1981)
Qualifying round 2: lost to Doug French 5-3 (August 1981)

**Coral UK Championship**
Qualifying group 5: beat Kingsley Kennerley 9-1
Qualifying group 5: beat Ian Black 9-4
Qualifying group 5: beat Jim Meadowcroft 9-4
Round 1: lost to Graham Miles 9-5

**Embassy World Professional Snooker Championship**
Qualifying round 1: beat Ian Anderson 9-5 (25 April 1982)
Qualifying round 2: lost to Dave Martin 9-3

**1982/83**
**Jameson International**
Qualifying round 1: lost to Eddie McLaughlin 5-2

**Pro Players Tournament**
Qualifying round 1: lost to Tony Knowles 5-4

**Hofmeister World Doubles**
*Houlihan was partnered by Bernard Bennett*
Pre-qualifying: beat Eddie Sinclair and Ian Black 6-2
Qualifying round 1: lost to Dean Reynolds and Mike Watterson 6-3
(1–3 November 1982)

**Coral UK Championship**
Qualifying round 2: beat John Dunning by walkover
Round 1: lost to Doug Mountjoy 9-3 (21 November 1982)

**Embassy World Professional Snooker Championship**
Qualifying round 1: lost to Tommy Murphy 10-9 (28 March 1983)

**1983/84**
**Jameson International**
Qualifying round 1: lost to George Scott 5-0 (September 1983)

**Pro Players Tournament**
Qualifying round 1: lost to Dessie Sheehan 5-2 (September 1983)

**Coral UK Championship**
Qualifying round 1: lost to Vic Harris 9-6 (November 1983)

**Lada Classic**
Qualifying round 1: lost to Neal Foulds 5-3 (November 1983)

**Hofmeister World Doubles**
*Houlihan was partnered by Bernard Bennett*
Pre-qualifying: beat Matt Gibson and Murdo MacLeod 5-2
Qualifying round 1: lost to Jack Fitzmaurice and Vic Harris 5-4

**Yamaha International Masters**
Pre-qualifying group:
Beat Marcel Gauvreau 2-0
Beat John Hargreaves 2-0
Lost to Matt Gibson 2-0
Qualifying group:
Beat Rex Williams 2-0
Lost to Les Dodd 2-0

**Embassy World Professional Snooker Championship**
Qualifying round 1: lost to Ian Williamson 10-5

**1984/85**
**Jameson International**
Qualifying round 1: lost to John Hargreaves 5-2

**Rothmans Grand Prix**
Qualifying round 2: lost to Clive Everton 5-3

**Tolly Cobbold English Professional Championships**
Qualifying round 1: lost to Tony Jones 9-1

**Coral UK Open**
Qualifying round 1: lost to Tony Chappel 9-3

**Mercantile Credit Classic**
Qualifying round 2: lost to Robby Foldvari 5-1

**1985/86**
**Goya Matchroom Trophy**
Qualifying round 1: lost to Jim Bear 2-5

**Rothmans Grand Prix**
Qualifying round 1: beat Gordon Robinson by walkover

**Rothmans Grand Prix**
Qualifying round 2: lost to Tony Jones 5-4

**Coral UK Open**
Qualifying round 1: beat Gerry Watson 9-4
Qualifying round 2: lost to Steve Newbury 9-3

**Mercantile Credit Classic**
Qualifying round 1: beat Bernard Bennett 5-0
Qualifying round 2: beat Robby Foldvari 5-4
Qualifying round 3: lost to Dean Reynolds 5-1

**Tolly Cobbold English Professional Championship**
Qualifying round 1: beat John Hargreaves 9-5
Qualifying round 2: beat John Dunning by walkover
Round 1: lost to John Spencer 9-5

**Dulux British Open**
Qualifying round 1: beat Gordon Robinson by walkover

**Dulux British Open**
Qualifying round 2: lost to Steve Longworth 5-3

**Embassy World Professional Snooker Championship**
Qualifying round 1: lost to Dessie Sheehan 10-7

**1986/87**
**BCE International**
Qualifying round 1: beat Dave Chalmers 5-1
Qualifying round 2: beat Graham Cripsey 5-1
Qualifying round 3: beat Tony Meo 5-4 (11 September 1986)
Round 1: lost to Eugene Hughes 5-1

**Hofmeister World Doubles**
*Houlihan was partnered by Bernard Bennett*
Round 1: beat John Bear and Derek Mienie 5-0
Round 2: lost to Tony Drago and Ken Owers 5-2 (12–16 October 1986)

**Rothmans Grand Prix**
Qualifying round 1: lost to Robbie Grace 5-1

**Tennents UK Open**
Qualifying round 1: lost to Robbie Grace 9-6

**Dulux British Open**
Qualifying round 1: lost to Nigel Gilbert 5-4

**Mercantile Credit Classic**
Qualifying round 1: lost to Ken Owers 5-1

**Tolly Ales English Professional Championship**
Qualifying round 1: lost to Ken Owers by walkover

**Embassy World Professional Snooker Championship**
Qualifying round 1: lost to Jon Wright 10-4

**1987/88**
**Fidelity International**
Qualifying round 2: lost to Dave Gilbert 5-3

**Rothmans Grand Prix**
Qualifying round 2: beat Derek Heaton 5-0
Qualifying round 3: beat Dean Reynolds 5-4 (23 September 1987)
Round 1: lost to Bob Chaperon 5-0 (Hexagon Theatre, Reading, 17 October 1987)

**Tennents UK Open**
Qualifying round 2: lost to Graham Miles 9-3

**MIM Britannia British Open**
Qualifying round 2: lost to Jim Bear 5-0

**Mercantile Credit Classic**
Qualifying round 1: lost to Steve James 5-2

**English Professional Championship**
Qualifying round 2: lost to Robert Marshall 6-4

**Embassy World Professional Snooker Championship**
Qualifying round 3: beat Dave Gilbert by walkover
Qualifying round 4: lost to Graham Cripsey 10-4

**1988/89**
**Fidelity International**
Qualifying round 2: lost to Alain Robidoux 5-2

**Rothmans Grand Prix**
Qualifying round 2: lost to John Rea 5-1
Qualifying round 3: lost to Eddie Charlton 5-3

**Tennents UK Open**
Qualifying round 2: lost to Colin Roscoe 9-8

**Mercantile Credit Classic**
Qualifying round 2: lost to Mike Darrington 4-5

**BCE Canadian Masters**
Qualifying round 2: lost to Martin Smith 2-5

**ICI European Open**
Qualifying round 2: lost to Eddie Sinclair 5-1

**Anglian British Open**
Qualifying round 2: beat Nick Terry 5-2
Qualifying round 3: lost to Jimmy White 5-3 (20 February 1989)

**English Professional Championship**
Qualifying round 3: beat Jack Fitzmaurice 5-4
Round 1: lost to Mike Hallett 5-2

**Embassy World Professional Snooker Championship**
Qualifying round 3: lost to John Rea 10-5

**1989/90**
**BCE International**
Qualifying round 1: beat Jackie Rea 5-4
Qualifying round 2: beat Ray Edmonds 5-2
Qualifying round 3: lost to Wayne Jones 5-2

**Rothmans Grand Prix**
Qualifying round 1: beat Mike Watterson 5-4
Qualifying round 2: lost to Tony Jones 5-0

**Hong Kong Open**
Qualifying round 1: beat Tony Kearney 5-1
Qualifying round 2: beat John Campbell 5-3
Qualifying round 3: lost to Tony Meo 5-0

**555 Asian Open**
Qualifying round 1: lost to Andrew Cairns 5-0

**Dubai Classic**
Qualifying round 1: beat Barry Pinches 5-1
Qualifying round 2: lost to Darren Morgan 5-2

**Stormseal UK Open**
Qualifying round 1: beat Markham Wildman 6-3
Qualifying round 2: lost to Ian Graham 6-0

**Mercantile Credit Classic**
Qualifying round 1: beat Robbie Grace 5-2
Qualifying round 2: lost to Tony Chappel 5-0

**Pearl Assurance British Open**
Qualifying round 1: lost to Tony Kearney 5-2

**ICI European Open**
Qualifying round 1: lost to Duncan Campbell 5-4

**Embassy World Professional Snooker Championship**
Qualifying round 2: beat Derek Mienie 10-5
Qualifying round 3: beat Jack McLaughlin 10-5
Qualifying round 4: lost to Tony Wilson 10-6

## 1990/91
### Rothmans Grand Prix
Qualifying round 1: lost to Tony Wilson 5-3

### 555 Asian Open
Qualifying round 1: lost to Anthony Harris 5-1

### Dubai Classic
Qualifying round 1: beat Jon Wright 5-2
Qualifying round 2: lost to Jack McLaughlin 5-3

### Stormseal UK Open
Qualifying round 1: beat Jon Wright 6-1
Qualifying round 2: lost to Tony Chappel 6-3

### Mercantile Credit Classic
Qualifying round 2: beat Jason Whittaker 5-3
Qualifying round 3: beat David Taylor 5-2
Qualifying round 4: lost to Barry West 5-0

### Pearl Assurance British Open
Qualifying round 2: beat Dessie Sheehan 5-3
Qualifying round 3: lost to Robert Marshall 1-5

### Tulip European Open
Qualifying round 1: lost to Steve Campbell 5-2

### Embassy World Professional Snooker Championship
Qualifying round 2: lost to Jason Ferguson 10-4

## 1991/92
### Rothmans Grand Prix
Qualifying round 5: lost to Sergio Beggiato 5-2

### Dubai Classic
Qualifying round 5: beat Chris Brooks 5-2
Qualifying round 6: lost to Mario Morra 5-1

### Thai Sky Asian Open
Qualifying round 5: beat Darren Hackeson 5-3
Qualifying round 6: lost to David Taylor 5-1

**Mercantile Credit Classic**
Qualifying round 5: lost to Mark Davis 5-3

**Pearl Assurance British Open**
Qualifying round 5: lost to Leigh Robinson 5-3

**European Open**
Qualifying round 5: lost to Dave Harold 5-3

**UK Open**
Qualifying round 5: lost to Alan Trigg 6-4

**1992/93**
**Royal Liver Assurance UK Championship**
Qualifying round 6: lost to Paul S. Davison 5-2

**Rothmans Grand Prix**
Qualifying round 6: lost to Jason Wallace 5-4

**Nescafe Asian Open**
Qualifying round 6: lost to John Giles 5-0

**Regal Welsh Open**
Qualifying round 6: lost to Mike Stocks by walkover

**Embassy World Professional Snooker Championship**
Qualifying round 6: lost to Mark O'Sullivan 5-2

**Dubai Duty Free Classic**
Qualifying round 6: beat Jamie Rous 5-2
Qualifying round 7: lost to Andrew Cairns 5-1 (August 1992)

# Bibliography and sources

**Conversations, interviews and correspondence:**
John Archer, Les Blair, John Butler, Roy Bacon, David Carter, Paul Collier, David Cook, Malcolm Dale, Steve Davis, Terry Dempsey, Tony Drago, Clive Everton, Jason Ferguson, Neal Foulds, William Garrett, Mike Goodchild, Frank Gumbrell, Andy Hall, Lee Houlihan, Patricia Houlihan, Patrick Houlihan Sr, Patrick Houlihan Jr, Eugene Hughes, Lee Hughes, Bill King, 'Legs', Terry McCarthy, Joseph McIvor, Colin McMillan, Tony Meo, Kevin Mitchell, Paul Moriarty, Jeff Murray, G. F. Newman, Harry Pearson, Charlie Poole, Lee Prickman, Jean Rafferty, Perry Roberts, Alain Robidoux, Frank Sandell, Lee Suleymanoglu, Matt Tench, Cliff Thorburn, Rex Williams, Jimmy White, Jim Wych

**Books:**
Batt, P., *Batt Out Of Hell: The Life and Wild Times of the Guvnor of Fleet Street* (Headline Books, 2000)
Coulter, J., *Around Lewisham and Deptford: Britain in Old Photographs* (The History Press, 2005)
Davis, J., *The Breaks Came My Way* (W.H. Allen/ Virgin Books, 1976)
Everton, C., *Black Farce and Cue Ball Wizards: The Inside Story of the Snooker World* (Mainstream, 2007)
Everton, C., *The History of Snooker and Billiards* (Partridge Press, 1986)
Everton, C., *Simply the Best: A biography of Ronnie O'Sullivan* (Pitch Publishing, 2018)

Geldof, B., with Vallely, P., *Is That It?* (Sidgwick & Jackson, 1986)

Higgins, A., and Patmore, A., *Hurricane Higgins' Snooker Scrapbook* (Souvenir Press, 1981)

Rafferty, J., *The Cruel Game: The Inside Story of Snooker* (Elm Tree Books, 1983)

Reardon, R., and Buxton, P., *Ray Reardon* (David & Charles, 1982)

Rendall, J., *Garden Hopping* (Canongate, 2006)

Rendall, J., *This Bloody Mary Is The Last Thing I Own* (Faber & Faber, 1997)

Rendall, J., *Twelve Grand* (Yellow Jersey Press, 1999)

Smith, T. (ed), *Benson and Hedges Snooker Year Book (6th edition)* (Michael Joseph, 1989)

Spencer, J., *Spencer on Snooker* (Littlehampton Book Services, 1973)

Tevis, W., *The Hustler* (Weidenfeld & Nicolson, 2015 edition)

Thorburn, C., and Everton, C., *Playing for Keeps* (Partridge Press, 1987)

Virgo, J. with Wight, D., *John Virgo: Say Goodnight, JV – My Autobiography* (John Blake, 2017)

White, J. and Kingsland, R., *Behind the White Ball* (Hutchinson, 1998)

White, J. with Brereton, C., *Second Wind – My Autobiography* (Trinity Mirror Sport Media, 2014)

White, J. and Poole, C., *Jimmy White's Snooker Masterclass* (Queen Anne Press, 1988)

Williams, L., and Gadsby, P., *Masters of the Baize: Cue Legends, Bad Boys and Forgotten Men in Search of Snooker's Ultimate Prize* (Mainstream, 2005)

**Magazines:**
*The Billiard Player*
*Cue World*
*Observer Sports Monthly*
*Pot Black*
*Pot Gold*
*The Q-World*
*Snooker Scene*

*World Snooker*
*World Snooker Championship official programme*

**Newspapers:**
*Aberdeen Press and Journal*
*Belfast Telegraph*
*Birmingham Daily Gazette*
*Birmingham Daily News*
*Birmingham Daily Post*
*Birmingham Evening Mail and Despatch Sports Argu*s
*Birmingham Sports Argus*
*Bradford Observer*
*Cheshire Observer*
*Coventry Evening Telegraph*
*Coventry Standard*
*Croydon Times*
*Daily Herald*
*Daily Mail*
*Daily Mirror*
*Daily News*
*Daily Telegraph*
*Dundee Courier*
*Grimsby Evening Telegraph*
*The Guardian*
*Harrow Observer and Gazette*
*Herne Bay Express*
*Huddersfield Chronicle*
*Irish Independent*
*Kent & Sussex Courier*
*Lancashire Evening Post*
*Leicester Evening Mail*
*Liverpool Echo*
*London Evening Standard*
*Manchester Evening News*
*Marylebone Mercury*
*Neath Guardian*
*Newcastle Evening Chronicle*

*Newcastle Journal*
*Northants Evening Telegraph*
*Nottingham Evening Post*
*Nottingham Journal*
*Portsmouth Evening News*
*Port Talbot Guardian*
*Reading Evening Post*
*Runcorn Daily News*
*South Wales Gazette*
*Sporting Globe*
*Sports Argus*
*The Sun*
*Sunday Mirror*
*Sydenham, Forest Hill and Penge Gazette*
*Sydney Morning Herald*
*The Times*
*Torbay Express and South Devon Echo*
*Weekly Dispatch*
*Western Mail*
*Westminster & Pimlico News*
*Yorkshire Post and Leeds Intelligencer*

**Television:**
*Danny Baker's Londoners*, London Weekend Television,
   28 August 1987
*The London Weekend Show*, London Weekend Television,
   6 February 1977
*This England*, Granada TV, 1978

**Websites:**
www.britishnewspaperarchive.co.uk
www.cuesnviews.co.uk
www.cuetracker.net
www.snookerscene.blogspot.com
www.worldsnooker.com